Praise for *After You Vote*

"*After You Vote* is an invaluable resour̶ nge. This smart, accessible guide arms you ̶ake our political systems work for you—a̶nd the tools you need to fight for the causes you care about. Keep this book close as you take on the world!"

—**Emily Koh, director of strategic initiatives, TIME'S UP**

"*After You Vote* is a tremendous, well-timed, and highly accessible resource with proven and practical tools for women who are looking to use their minutes wisely to make the greatest impact, and it couldn't have come at a more critical time: women's political participation is more important now than ever."

—**Erin Loos Cutraro, CEO and founder, She Should Run**

"Courtney Emerson's new book, *After You Vote*, is a critical call to action empowering all women with the skills and resources to make an impact. Now, more than ever, we need women harnessing their full collective power to build a more inclusive and diverse political landscape."

—**Kathy Hochul, 77th Lt. Governor of New York and former Member of Congress**

"I know so many women who want to be more politically active but who hesitate, feeling lost or disillusioned with the current state of things. But, as *After You Vote* makes clear, the reality is that it's never been more important to get involved and fight for the causes you support. Let this brilliant book help you get started!"

—**Giovanna Gray Lockhart, founder, NYWC**

After You
VOTE

After You VOTE

A Woman's Guide to Making an Impact
from Town Hall to Capitol Hill

COURTNEY EMERSON

BenBella Books, Inc.
Dallas, TX

BenBella Books, Inc.
10440 N. Central Expressway
Suite 800
Dallas, TX 75231
www.benbellabooks.com
Send feedback to feedback@benbellabooks.com.

BenBella is a federally registered trademark.

Printed in the United States of America
10 9 8 7 6 5 4 3 2 1

Library of Congress Control Number: 2020036501
ISBN 9781950665396 (trade paper)
ISBN 9781950665594 (ebook)

Editing by Leah Wilson
Copyediting by Scott Calamar
Cover design by Sarah Avinger
Cover illustration by Sarah Avinger (floating ballots and town hall) and
    © Shutterstock / bsd (ballot box) and Tako design (Capitol Hill)
Author photo by Rose Lindley
Proofreading by Michael Fedison and Marissa Wold Uhrina
Indexing by Debra Bowman
Text design and composition by Jessika Rieck
Printed by Lake Book Manufacturing

Distributed to the trade by Two Rivers Distribution, an Ingram brand
www.tworiversdistribution.com

Special discounts for bulk sales are available.
Please contact bulkorders@benbellabooks.com.

CONTENTS

INTRODUCTION

WE ALL HAVE ISSUES

Listen: When it comes to politics, we all have issues—the things that make us furious, devastated, or wildly happy; the stuff that makes us call our best friend or our sister or mom to complain or celebrate. Your issues might be as small as that annoying pothole in the road that's been there since you moved into the neighborhood three years ago, or as big as worrying about not being able to afford your rent or your birth control, or why it's 100 degrees in New York City in October, or the threat of gun violence at your school.

And while these issues are deeply personal, they are also inextricably linked to politics; policies implemented at all levels of government have direct influence on our lives, our choices, and the realities in our communities, in ways both obvious and obscure. Not to mention, we increasingly make personal decisions *based* on our politics. Even when it comes to our romantic partners! OkCupid, the dating site and app, found that the number of women who said that similar political views are "more important in a partner than great sex" doubled between 2016 and 2018.[1] Or consider that, in 2016, Pew reported that 40 percent of both Democrats and Republicans view members of the opposing party as more closed-minded and dishonest than other Americans.[2]

So, while you certainly care about lots of issues, maybe you haven't wanted to jump into the political fray because it all feels overwhelming, or too contentious, or because you suspect that these issues are not always simple enough to be summed up in a 180-character tweet. Maybe you suspect that these issues are complicated and thorny. And you're right—most issues are. Maybe you're hesitant to get more involved because you don't feel you're an expert and, even if you wanted to, you don't have time to develop the expertise you believe is required of a bona fide advocate. Or maybe it seems like the problems are so big that you feel paralyzed—or that our political system is broken, and you don't know which tools and tactics will actually help you fix those issues or create real change.

But what if I told you that you already know more than you think? Political knowledge is not just about statistics, though it often feels that way. It's also about your experiences (the same personal experiences that get you fired up to begin with): what you see and feel around you every day, the joys and injustices you see in your communities.

And what if I told you political engagement is just like everything else that you're juggling (and kicking ass at) as a woman in the twenty-first century? Being an effective advocate for your issues requires research, planning, and prioritization. You can do that. It requires effective relationship building, intellectual humility, and the ability to listen as much as you speak. You can do that, too. It requires passion and persistence. Check, check, check. Many of the skills you need—to get that pothole fixed, to engage on issues of reproductive health or global warming or whatever issue you care about—you likely already have or can build. You've used many of these skills in your personal life, in school, and at work. Advocating for your issues just means learning how to take those skills and translate them into effective political participation (which means knowing how the system works and what tactics can help make a real difference). You just need to brush up on the basics and get focused. Because whether we realize it or not, we're already prioritizing, day to day, hour to hour, minute to minute. We're making choices about what's important, what we should focus on, and what is valuable. Productive advocacy also means making your engagement feel sustainable and meaningful (even fun!). Being an effective, engaged citizen is bigger than one president or one administration or election cycle.

Maybe you've been telling yourself that you just don't "do" politics. But as my friend, former All In Together (AIT) colleague and Obama White House staffer Simone Leiro, likes to say: "You may not 'do' politics . . . but politics will do you." Your lack of participation doesn't protect or prevent you from being impacted by politics—it just means you don't get a say in *how* you're impacted. Others who do participate, who do engage, who do advocate for their own interests will decide that for you.

My own first foray into politics (you'll see in a moment that I'm using the term "politics" loosely) wasn't super promising. It was 1999. I was in the eighth grade, and I was nominated by my classmates as a candidate for middle school student president. Looking back now, this was a genius (also, evil) strategy on the school's part—I never would have thrown my own proverbial hat in the ring. But, having been selected along with three of my classmates by our peers, I found myself unexpectedly contemplating middle school government leadership. My surprise quickly gave way to horror, however, when I found out that running required giving a campaign speech in front of the entire school.

Some context: At age 13, I was *painfully* shy. I spent most of middle school hiding behind my blunt-cut bangs. A quiet, anxious bookworm (my parents literally had to confiscate my books to get me to play outside . . . where I had hidden more books, just in case), I was the kid that parents and teachers liked to hang out with but whose nerdiness other kids worried could be contagious. I was uncoordinated and awkward, and it didn't help that I towered over most of the kids in my class at five foot eight. I had a few close friends, but I spent a lot of time on my own—and, throughout my eighth-grade presidential candidacy, a *lot* of time worried that my nomination was part of an elaborate hoax (à la Rachael Leigh Cook's nomination for prom queen in *She's All That*).

Inevitably, the day of the campaign speeches came. Shaking, I got up in front of the school and did the unthinkable: I performed a magic trick. In front of 200 middle school students. The details are fuzzy a couple decades later, but I remember that the trick involved pulling a red silk scarf from an ill-fitting fake plastic thumb. Long story short: It did not go well. But I still remember the point I was trying to make. I wanted my classmates to know that, unlike the trick I had performed, I would be the real deal. I wouldn't pull any punches. I would be transparent, hardworking, and committed to them. Whatever my performance cost me in my (already limited) social capital, it was, at the very least, an earnest and heartfelt appeal.

It was not, however, a winning one. The boy who won the election threw free candy at the crowd for the duration of his speech. I wish this didn't say as much about real-world politics as it does but, well, here we are.

Not the most auspicious beginning, nor one that ignited a passion for politics. In fact, as of seven years ago, despite graduating from college with a degree in political science (mostly studying governments *outside* of the US), I had virtually no background in politics at all. I would describe my political participation up to that point as "the bare minimum"—registered to vote and (mostly) voting in presidential elections but engaging in no other meaningful way. This was despite having grown up in New Hampshire, where politics is essentially a state sport, given its first-in-the-country presidential primary status (although I did once drag my mom to a rally for Barack Obama at a local air force base in early 2008; standing a hundred feet away from the man who would become our future president is something I'll never forget).

My family wasn't very politically engaged when I was growing up, nor were my friends. As a harp-playing (yes, really) Division I athlete in college, I already had a lot on my plate. Civic engagement wasn't a major part of my life. It wasn't a habit I'd developed, or a muscle I'd built. That doesn't mean I wasn't trying to improve my community for the better: I've always worked at mission-driven companies and nonprofits; I've always volunteered and donated to charities. Honestly, I always thought that was enough.

I was wrong.

In 2014, 15 years after my failed eighth-grade campaign, I was living in New York City and working at the Center for Talent Innovation (CTI), a think tank that conducts research on the systemic bias and barriers women, people of color, and LGBTQIA+ employees often experience in the workplace. The decision to do this work was, for me, a deeply personal one. My mom was a civil engineer early in her career, working as the only female engineer in an Indiana steel mine in the 1970s and dealing with bias left and right—from the male engineers who harassed her to the female secretaries who deliberately placed her requests at the very bottom of their work piles. Ultimately, she ended up leaving not only the job but engineering altogether. And while the world has changed since then, it hasn't changed enough (something made all too clear with the #MeToo movement and the important work of groups like Time's Up). So when my younger sister announced that it was her dream to become an engineer as well, the possibility that my brilliant, driven sister would face similar barriers as my mother was unacceptable.

At CTI, I was incredibly motivated by the work we did to create more inclusive, diverse company cultures and felt I was, in my small way, making a difference. I traveled around the world—Bangkok, London, Singapore, Munich—facilitating workshops and focus groups for global companies and developing strategies and initiatives to help organizations change the face of leadership for the better (in other words, make leadership less white, less male).

When *Lean In* was published, Sheryl Sandberg articulated much of what we were seeing in CTI's research; in fact, CTI's research was even cited in *Lean In*'s chapter on mentorship and sponsorship. Sandberg's work was a catalyst for the next generation to take ownership and action to advance women into positions of leadership in the private sector. And while we saw a renewed energy and uptick in interest regarding the topic of women's leadership in the US, it struck me that there was less attention being paid to gender gaps in political engagement and advocacy.

This conversational vacuum got me thinking: How did this renewed interest in women's leadership translate when it came to women's political participation? Beyond voting, I wasn't contributing to politics in any meaningful way. Nor were my sisters or many of my girlfriends. I didn't even know where to start. I also figured that I—someone who cared about lots of issues and kept up with the news—was likely not alone. So, like any good bookworm, I started digging into the research to better understand the landscape of women's engagement in American politics. Spoiler alert: It's not good. Overall, women are underengaged in nearly every political activity outside of voting—from speaking about politics, to lobbying representatives, to donating to political campaigns.

So in 2014, I started a nonprofit called the All In Together Campaign (AIT) to offer American women the tools they need to have influence on the issues they care about—whatever those issues might be. I cofounded AIT in partnership with two *amazing* women, Lauren Leader and Edda Collins Coleman. As chief operating officer, I developed and led our civic advocacy workshops for women across the country. These programs took me from conference rooms in Silicon Valley to suburban church basements, to the offices of senators on Capitol Hill, to Gracie Mansion in New York City—all with the goal of ensuring women have the information and inspiration they need to fully participate in political life.

When we launched the AIT workshops and community programs, we weren't sure how they would be received. But here's what we heard:

- "I feel like this workshop allowed me to forgive myself for not knowing it all and not being able to focus on every issue under the sun. I feel less paralyzed and more able to be effective. This is the most empowered and motivated I've felt in months!"

- "I think many women have no idea how to get involved and it's easier than most think."

- "This was one of the most powerful, inspiring, and impactful mornings I have spent in a long time."

Again and again, women told us that our programs were exactly what they had been looking for, especially in the aftermath of the 2016 election, which left many with more questions than answers about how our political system works for us (and also how it *doesn't* work). Today, tens of thousands of women from all over the country have participated in AIT civic education workshops and community programs. But while we haven't been able to reach everyone—at least not yet!—I've taken to heart the message from past participants about just how important civic education and advocacy tools are for women. It's why I decided to write this book, which includes the tools and resources I couldn't find for myself (certainly not all in one place!) when I realized I wanted and needed to do more.

But this book isn't about me; it's about you, and how you can help enact the changes you want to see in your community. I'll be your tour guide, sharing the resources and statistics that will be most helpful to you as you start your journey toward political advocacy. But I won't be your only guide; since founding AIT, I've met amazing women across the country who are inspiring their communities, using political engagement and advocacy as levers to lead change. Throughout the book, you'll hear from these **Advocates in Action**; I hope their personal stories, incredible leadership, and tactical advice will inspire you, too. These are women doing the tough work of improving their communities and our democracy all over the country.

Here's an overview of where we're headed:

- In **Part I**, we'll discuss the gender gaps in political engagement in American politics today. One of the biggest barriers to women participating politically is feeling that we don't "know enough," which we'll address by breaking down the civics basics. Think *Schoolhouse Rock* but with a much-needed upgrade (if you haven't watched it recently, literally every character in the "I'm Just a Bill" video is a dude—even the bill). We'll discuss how the government is structured at all levels (when was the last time you took a look at what your state senator was up to?) and what that means for your advocacy.

- **Part II** is all about getting clear on your personal political platform—homing in on the issues that are most important to you by articulating your expertise, your passion, and the timeliness of the issue at hand. Once you've nailed down your priorities, you'll learn essential tools and tactics for critical activities from voting to lobbying to campaigning and campaign contributions. Plus, advocacy is a marathon, not a sprint—so we'll also talk about how to make your engagement sustainable over the long haul.

- By **Part III**, you'll have the information and tactics needed to establish clear and attainable advocacy goals. Still, you can't create meaningful change if the system itself is stifling that change. Unfortunately, our democracy today doesn't work for everyone the way it should. Because of a whole range of obstacles—like the outsized influence of money in politics, gerrymandering, and voter suppression—there are very real barriers that prevent full participation and political engagement of all Americans. We will address how to build a future in which everyone is fairly represented and able to use their voice to shape the issues they care about.

Plus, at the end of each section, there will be a **Workbook** to help you get specific about what all of this means for *you*, with practical tools and resources to help you go deeper.

One of the most exciting yet most infuriating things about driving change in politics is that there are no hard-and-fast rules for exactly how to do it. There's no straightforward path or playbook. But if you're clear on your issues, clear on how the system works (and where it's broken), you'll always have a way forward. My goal is to show you that it is possible to wield political influence outside of the voting booth—in ways that work for your hectic life. Political engagement should not just be about duty and sacrifice. It can also be energizing and rewarding.

And no magic tricks. I promise.

Part I

LET'S GET CIVIC-AL

CHAPTER 1

....

GENDER GAPS IN
AMERICAN POLITICS

[W]omen don't need to find a voice: they have a voice. They need to feel empowered to use it, and people need to be encouraged to listen.

—Meghan Markle, during the first annual
Royal Foundation Forum (2018)

Why write this book for women specifically? Isn't smarter, more sustainable civic engagement important for . . . well, everyone?
Today, women are more educated than ever—in fact, millennial women are significantly more likely than their male peers to have college degrees. This generation of women is both ambitious and altruistic; they're more likely than men in their age group to volunteer on behalf of nonpolitical groups. And, in general, women want to see the gender gaps in leadership closed: according to a 2015 poll, 78 percent of women say more women in leadership would improve the quality of life for all women. Yet none of this has translated into full and equal participation in political life for women. Despite our education, our desire to improve the world, and the fact that we want to see more women in positions of power, today in

the United States we simply do not have gender equality when it comes to either political leadership or political participation. Every year, the World Economic Forum measures the Global Gender Gap; as of 2020, when it comes to gender equality in political empowerment, the United States ranks *86th* in the world.[1] This is a big problem, and an unacceptable reality.

As English scholar and classicist Mary Beard writes in her book *Women & Power: A Manifesto* (recommended reading if you're interested in the long history in Western civilization of women being silenced and excluded from arenas of power):

> A number of studies point to the role of women politicians in promoting legislation in women's interest (in childcare, for example, equal pay and domestic violence) . . . I certainly do not want to complain about childcare and the rest getting a fair airing but I am not sure that such things should continue to be perceived as "women's issues"; nor am I sure that these are the main reasons we want more women in parliaments. *Those reasons are much more basic: it is flagrantly unjust to keep women out, by whatever unconscious means we do so; and we simply cannot afford to do without women's expertise, whether it is in technology, the economy or social care* [emphasis mine].[2]

Women's voices matter equally to men's because we are equal citizens. Yet women are underparticipating politically compared to men on every issue and topic and are underrepresented in political leadership. Putting aside voting for the moment (American women overall have voted at higher rates than men in the US since 1980),[3] there are gaps in three especially crucial areas: political knowledge, political confidence, and political voice (more on each of these in a moment). The barriers that prevent our full participation are unique as well. For example, research shows us that women require more knowledge and more information than men before we feel we are ready or worthy of participation.[4]

Let me repeat that: women, on average, want *more knowledge and information* before participating politically. Data from the Harvard Public Opinion Project, a national poll of 18- to 29-year-olds facilitated by the Institute of Politics (IOP) at Harvard Kennedy School, shows that women are more likely than men to say they need more practical information about politics before getting involved.[5] The same trend extends to knowledge about particular political issues as well. Research conducted by the American University Women and Politics Institute and the Barbara Lee Family Foundation in

2020 found that, despite comparable levels of reported news consumption, women are *three times more likely* than men to select "I don't know enough about political issues to get involved" as their top reason for not getting involved in politics.[6] To be sure, it's a wonderful instinct to want to be more informed—it's why this book will include a whole lot of civics info. But we can't let the irresistible need for "just a little more research" stop us from acting or from using our voices. We do not have to be perfect to participate.

As mentioned, the only significant metric of political participation for which women outperform men is voting. Voting is crucial (after all, it's what determines who represents us at every level of government), and we'll talk a lot more about voting and elections in the chapters to come. However, as professors Tali Mendelberg and Christopher Karpowitz have written, "While voting is an exception, the most leader-like activities—offering opinions, attempting to persuade, feeling that it is possible to effect change or make a difference—show little progress despite the dramatic rise in women's position in society."[7] Until women equally leverage all tools of political influence, we will not have the impact that we could.

Some argue that women's political participation matters because women are more likely than men to negotiate, work across the aisle, and generally be more effective and get things done once they're elected to office. Or, as Beard notes, because research shows that women are more likely to advocate for what we've historically thought of as "women's issues"—things like equal pay, childcare, prevention of gender-based violence, reproductive health, and maternity leave, whether we're serving in public office or as political advocates—if we have more women participating, the implication is that we'll have more voices advocating for those important issues (and potentially make greater progress on them). And we certainly have work to do there: after all, the US ranked last in a 2016 OECD study on the national paid maternity leave policies of its member countries, as just one example.[8]

Yes, these outcomes are very important. We need a better functioning democracy and more elected officials who are motivated to get things done to improve their communities. But that's not the responsibility of elected women alone—men are equally responsible here (they do make up over three-quarters of Congress). And of course we need policies that are more responsive to the needs of *all* citizens; yes, for women, but also for others who have been historically disenfranchised or ignored. But what the heck is a "women's issue," anyway? Almost all issues or policies affect women, because women make up half of the country—and many of them *disproportionately* or *uniquely* affect women, even if they aren't historically thought of as "women's issues." For example, as Elizabeth Warren discussed in a 2002 article in the *Harvard Women's Law Journal*, women are the largest demographic group in bankruptcy, outnumbering men by about 150,000 per year.[9] Or consider a public health crisis like the COVID-19 pandemic: 85 percent of nurses and 89 percent of paid caregivers—people fighting on the pandemic's front lines—are women.[10] Moreover, the federal Bureau of Justice Statistics reports that 82 percent of domestic violence victims are women;[11] with women isolated in homes with their abusers given shelter-in-place orders all over the country, not to mention the sudden inaccessibility of safety nets like domestic violence shelters, the COVID-19 crisis had a disproportionate impact on women's health and safety.

The argument for women's political participation in the US from the very beginning was often framed with the idea that women are "better" than men (in a moral sense) and the moral stalwarts of their communities, like when women successfully lobbied for Prohibition.[12] But women are not inherently better than men. As Jane Addams, Nobel Peace Prize winner, said, "I am not one of those who believe—broadly speaking—that women are better than men. We have not wrecked railroads, nor corrupted legislatures, nor done many unholy things that men have done; but then we must remember that we have not had the chance."[13] Or as Chimamanda Ngozi Adichie wrote in her essay, *Dear Ijeawele, or A Feminist Manifesto in Fifteen Suggestions*, "Women are as human as men are. Female goodness is as normal as female evil."[14]

We shouldn't use these arguments—that women are naturally moral, or more collaborative, or more community- or family- or women's issues—oriented—as our first or best arguments for why women's participation matters. Ultimately, those arguments lead to expectations for women political leaders that we do not have for men, and these expectations could influence, even if only subconsciously, the kinds of issues women are expected or "allowed" to have a say on. The many dimensions of our experiences shape the things we care about—we should be able, expected, and encouraged to speak with equal credibility on all of them. As professors Tali Mendelberg and Christopher Karpowitz have written, "Women will not be viewed as equal in that basic sense of worth until they carry equal authority in the public discourse that governs their community."[15]

Let's break down what the research says about those three critical gender gaps in political participation: political knowledge, political confidence, and political voice.

POLITICAL KNOWLEDGE

Research shows that, in general, young men tend to have more political knowledge than young women. One study found that 36 percent of young men (ages 15–25) know it takes a two-thirds majority to override a presidential veto compared to only 24 percent of women. That same study also found that 28 percent of men know which party has a majority in the lower house of their state legislatures compared to only 17 percent of young women.[16] Yet another study found that 54 percent of men could correctly name their governor's party affiliation compared to only 43 percent of women.[17] This finding holds when it comes to political events as well. A 2020 AIT survey found that, leading up to Super Tuesday, men were more likely to say they knew when the presidential primaries were taking place than women—a gap that was especially pronounced for younger women compared to younger men.[18]

These gaps in knowledge may, in part, stem from the fact that men are more likely than women to report paying regular attention to political and public affairs, and to believe that paying attention is important. The Harvard Public Opinion Project, which biannually polls men and women aged 18 to 29 on their political views and participation, found in 2020 that 19 percent of men say they "very closely" follow news about national politics, compared to 11 percent of women.[19]

What gives? Maybe you're tempted to guess, "Well, women just don't like politics. And who could blame them? It's dysfunctional and contentious." But that's probably not why. In fact, one study found that men are twice as likely to say they "dislike" or "don't do" politics than women.*

The gap in political knowledge may have to do, in part, with the type of information women are encouraged to pay attention to. The gender gap in

---

* Thirty-five percent of young men compared to 16 percent of young women; Krista Jenkins, "Gender and Civic Engagement."

political interest has traditionally been attributed to gendered socialization processes—that is, women are often (subtly or not-so-subtly) discouraged from political interest or involvement.[20] The disparity between men and women in political leadership likely further reinforces the notion that politics is not a space for women; since 1798, women have made up only 2.9 percent of all members of Congress.[21] Ever!

But what we perceive as a gap in *knowledge* could also be due to a gap in *confidence*. Importantly, many of the "political knowledge" questions that men tend to do better on have answers with a fifty-fifty chance of being right or wrong (Yes/No, True/False, Democrat/Republican). Some researchers hypothesize that men are more likely than women to guess if they're not sure of the answer.[22] And it's hardly a stretch to imagine that not being encouraged to care about politics, along with not seeing many women serving in political office, could have an impact on confidence. So let's dive into that political confidence gap.

POLITICAL CONFIDENCE

Millennial women tend to be less confident than millennial men in their own political competence. Of course, conversations about the gender gap in confidence certainly extend beyond the sphere of politics. Girls *as young as six* say that boys are generally smarter than girls.[23] This is heartbreaking.

On one hand, understanding the limits of our own knowledge can be healthy. When we are not totally committed to our way of viewing or thinking about the world, we're more open to other perspectives. This is a more productive way of approaching conversations and leads to a deeper, more nuanced view of the world. But when a lack of confidence makes it less likely that women will speak up or participate at all, it becomes a problem.

Indeed, women will say they don't participate in politics because they're "not informed enough," while men say they don't participate because it's "hard to get reliable information."[24] For women, the informational obstacle is internal: *they* don't know enough. For men, the challenge is external: it's the *information itself* that's too hard to access or not readily available. A former colleague once told the following joke, which I think illustrates this point: A man and a woman go golfing; neither play well. After they finish, the woman says, "Geez, that was terrible. I really need to take some golf lessons." The man's reaction? "Geez, that was terrible. I really need new clubs."

The fact that so many members of the most educated generation of women in American history don't feel informed enough to get involved is a reality we cannot accept. We need to equip ourselves with the fundamentals of our political system, while also remembering that we do not need to know everything to engage in the political process.

Compounding this issue is the fear of being criticized: young women are nearly *two times* as likely as men to say avoiding criticism is a reason for not getting involved in politics.[25] Every day, we see women raked over the coals and held to "different" standards (read: higher, damned-if-you-do-damned-if-you-don't standards) than their male counterparts. Criticism has become a weapon to erode confidence and to silence women; our society has created a bar for women so high that it impacts our ability and willingness to participate politically.

Despite all this, we remain optimistic. Women aren't more likely than men to say that previous involvement in politics has left them disappointed; they're not more likely to say that politics isn't relevant to them (women are actually more likely to say it *is* relevant to them), or that politics has become too partisan, or that officials don't have the same priorities as they do, or that their vote won't make a difference. Indeed, young women are actually *more* optimistic than young men that their engagement will make a difference.[26]

Brittany Packnett Cunningham, an activist who served on Barack Obama's President's Task Force on 21st Century Policing and cofounded Campaign Zero, a police reform campaign focused on reducing police violence, gave an *amazing* TED Talk on the importance of confidence in 2019 (watch it if you haven't). She says, "Confidence is the difference between being inspired and actually getting started, between trying and doing until it's done. Confidence helps us keep going even when we failed."[27] Confidence, and lack of confidence, Packnett Cunningham argues, shouldn't take a back seat to "hard skills" like knowledge. It's crucial.

Lack of confidence may prevent many of us from using our voices to weigh in on the issues or causes we care about most, and from holding our representatives accountable and shaping the policies that govern our lives. If we can address that confidence gap, for example, by equipping ourselves with the information we need, by supporting and encouraging other women to get involved, by shining a light on female role models, and by calling out gendered stereotypes around confidence, we'd also likely help close the third political gender gap we'll discuss: political voice.

POLITICAL VOICE

To me, this is the most troubling gender gap in politics—and of course it's connected to the gaps we see in political knowledge and confidence. After all, if you don't feel you have the information you need to be effective, you likely won't have the confidence you need to speak up and use your voice on behalf of the political issues you care about. And if you fear that you will be criticized for expressing your views, it is all too easy to step back.

Research shows that, outside of voting, women are less likely to speak up across a range of political activities. A 2006 study found that Congress receives an estimated *two million more letters and phone calls* from male constituents than female constituents every year,[28] a fact that is especially shocking when you consider the fact that women are more likely than men both to be registered to vote and to show up at the polls.

The year 2006 may seem well in the past, but these gaps appear to have persisted. Take a look at the numbers in the critical political activities below from the 2020 Youth Poll, a national poll of 18- to 29-year-olds facilitated by the Institute of Politics (IOP) at Harvard Kennedy School:[29]

Activity	Men	Women
Participated in a government, political, or issue-related organization	13%	11%
Volunteered on a political campaign for a candidate or an issue	11%	8%
Attended a political rally or demonstration	18%	15%
Donated to a political campaign or cause	20%	13%
Sent an email/letter advocating for a political position or opinion	19%	16%
Signed an online petition	41%	44%

As you can see, the only activity in which women are outparticipating men is in the signing of online petitions, which is one of the *least* effective ways to have influence on an issue you care about (more on that in Chapter 7). While the percent differences are fairly small, consider that women are more likely to vote than men—which means there's an even *greater* drop-off for women between voting and other political activities than there is for men. And consider that the difference of even a few percentage points translates into hundreds of thousands or even millions fewer women than men participating.

Women's voices are missing from the broader public discourse as well. Let's take op-eds as an example. Op-eds are opinion pieces, similar to letters to the editor, published in newspapers, and they can be submitted by anyone (not just journalists). In 2008, the *Washington Post* tracked op-ed submissions for five months and found that 90 percent of all op-ed submissions came from men.[30] Why is this important? Well, political officials and their staff read op-eds, and not just the op-eds of the *New York Times* or *Wall Street Journal*. They read the op-eds of the local papers to understand the perspectives their constituents have on specific issues (more on that later, too). Another way elected officials understand the priorities and needs of their constituents is through town halls—but a study of 1,389 town hall meetings in Vermont found that, although women made up 46 percent of attendees, on average they accounted for 28 percent of the speaking turns.[31]

The people elected officials hear from matter—a lot. According to research by Professor Kristina Miler, author of *Constituency Representation in Congress: The View from Capitol Hill*, the constituents that members of Congress hear from impacts *who they think of as constituents*—and ultimately shapes their decision-making in terms of what bills they introduce and how they vote. As Miler said in a C-SPAN interview, "What we're all taught in elementary school, high school—write to your congressperson—actually matters. And the way that I would argue it matters is that it shapes who they think is in their district. It shapes their perception of who their constituency is, and then they can use that later on . . . to shape their conscious, deliberate decisions like how to participate, how to vote, what bills to sponsor."[32] Moreover, it's *regular* contact that really matters: the more frequently we contact legislators, the more likely it is that they will have us in mind—whether during committee hearings, during votes, or at floor debates. On the flip side, if a member of Congress is *not* hearing from certain constituents, those constituents are not going to be considered when they think of how certain legislation would impact "their constituents." Whom members of Congress are receiving campaign contributions from, according to Miler, has the same effect.

An adage commonly attributed to Thomas Jefferson claims, "We in America do not have government by the majority. We have government by the majority who participate." Considering that Jefferson and the other white male framers of the Constitution systemically and deliberately excluded women and people of color from full democratic participation, if Jefferson ever made this remark, his chiding tone seems ironic today. But he wasn't *wrong*; if we don't participate, our government won't work for us as it should. Of course, there are many systemic barriers that limit the power and influence of particular groups. It would, for example, be naïve to think that there aren't social biases that diminish and dismiss women's voices even when we do speak up. And that's not even getting into the lessons that popular culture unconsciously (or consciously, if we're assuming the worst about humanity) teaches us. The first movie I ever saw in theaters was Disney's *The Little Mermaid*. I grew up loving Ariel, a rebellious, curious, brave young woman who pushes the boundaries of her family's expectations and rejects the traditional path that is set for her. I even dressed up as Ariel for Halloween (complete with long underwear underneath my outfit—snow at Halloween was a common occurrence growing up in New Hampshire). It didn't occur to me until I was a teenager that the price for her dream, her existence on land, and her ability to be with Prince Eric, is her *voice*. What kind of a lesson is that, that the price of your dreams is your voice? But if we opt out and *don't* lobby and advocate for the changes we want to see, if we don't participate or pull the levers that are available to us now, that makes it even worse. Our voices and interests can't be represented if we don't make them known. Whatever you think today about politics or politicians, if you fundamentally believe that women's voices are important, that *your* voice matters, you need to get involved. Get engaged. Get active.

A FEW IMPORTANT NOTES

Before we continue, a few important things to keep in mind.

First, the focus of this book on women broadly is *not* to say that there aren't important differences in participation and voice across race/ethnicity, generation, socioeconomic status, education, and other dimensions. Women are far from monolithic, and for too long we have painted "women's experiences" with a broad brush, not taking into account intersectionality (a concept introduced by civil rights advocate, lawyer, and scholar Kimberlé Williams Crenshaw to describe how race, gender, class, and other characteristics "intersect" and overlap, specifically to describe limitations of the law in considering sexism and racism) and the complexity inherent in women's experiences and in the barriers to full participation. As self-described "black, lesbian, mother, warrior, poet" Audre Lorde once wrote, "There is no such thing as a single-issue struggle, because we do not live single-issue lives."[33]

To be sure, there are also differences in political participation between groups of women, for example across lines of race and ethnicity. Leading up to the 2018 midterm elections, for instance, women of color were more likely than white women to mobilize friends and family by encouraging their engagement in the midterms.[34] Black women were most likely to mobilize friends and family to vote (84 percent compared to just 66 percent of white women). There's no doubt that this important work of women of color leading up to the midterms contributed to the fact that turnout in the 2018 elections increased by more than 30 million voters compared to 2014.[35] And research shows that on many key political actions, women of color are more politically engaged than white women; more likely, for example, to attend a march, rally, or protest; more likely to donate or raise money for a political campaign or issue; and more likely to contact an elected official about an issue.

So while gender is certainly far from the only factor at play when it comes to patterns of political participation (or, indeed, the barriers to political participation—as we'll talk about more in Part II, women of color congressional candidates are less likely to receive campaign contributions from donors than men of color and white congressional candidates, and continue to be significantly underrepresented in positions of political leadership), important gender participation gaps seem to persist across multiple dimensions of identity as well. Take, for example, contacting your elected officials, which, as we've discussed, is a particularly critical political activity. A 2019 AIT survey of 1,000 registered voters found that white men were by far the most likely group to have contacted their elected officials (at least once) in the past. Across categories of race, education, and age, this gap persisted.*

---

* Fifteen percent of white men respondents said they had contacted an elected official in the past, compared to 10 percent of white women, 10 percent of Black women, and 9 percent of Latinas. Men in college were more likely than women in college to say they had contacted a representative (19 percent versus 11 percent); same for men and women out of college (11 percent versus 9 percent). Young men were more likely than young women to have contacted an official, and the gap held for older men and women, too. All In Together National Online Survey crosstabs, August 2019 (conducted by GBAO).

Second, creating a system of full and equal political participation is not solely about individual attitudes or actions. Fixing a broken, sexist system that diminishes women's voice and power cannot be the responsibility of women alone—not if we're serious about finding a solution. There is absolutely work to be done when it comes to the structural and systemic biases that inhibit women's voices. However, that won't be the primary focus of this book. This book is focused on what women, individually and collectively, can do to turn our political interests into policy. There are so many women across this country, from cities to small towns, doing truly groundbreaking things in their communities—wielding political power and influence on a huge range of issues. Their stories so often go untold—the unglamorous work of civic action—and deserve to be highlighted here, both to celebrate their accomplishments and to serve as a blueprint for how we can similarly make change. Plus, if we don't understand how our democracy works, and if we aren't fully participating, we won't be able to articulate exactly where the system is broken and where structural versus individual action and change is required. Systemic change takes time. And there are levers of power that we can use to our advantage *now*.

Third, there will be readers of all gender identities for whom the purpose of this book might resonate. If you don't feel, for whatever reason, that you have the information or tools you need to get involved, or you feel sidelined or excluded from using your voice to engage on the issues you care about, welcome! This book is for you, too.

Finally, this book is *not* going to tell you what issues you should care about. That is 100 percent up to you. American women are as diverse as our country; our interests, passions, and experiences run the gamut. You will know better than anyone what your issues are. They're what make you "you." This book will give you a bunch of things to think *about*—but won't tell you *what* to think. There's enough of that out in the world already.

What this book *will* do is help you translate your interests, passions, and voice into real change. I'll share a framework to help you narrow down what those issues might be for you, as well as tools and tactics from women advocates that showcase the most effective ways to have influence on them— plus we'll look at some systemic and nonpartisan issues that prevent many citizens from having full voice. You'll create an action plan that allows you to be an engaged citizen in a sustainable way, regardless of whether "your party" is in office or not.

Women are not all going to agree on every issue, and we don't need to. In a democracy, conflict has the potential to lead to better outcomes; more competing, diverse perspectives can create better, more nuanced solutions. But we *do* all need to engage and to do the hard work of citizenship because it's our responsibility, as well as our privilege, and because women's power and perspectives are worthy of equal weight to men's.

So, it's with Chimamanda Ngozi Adichie's words that we begin our advocacy journey: "Your feminist premise should be: 'I matter equally.' Not 'if only.' Not 'as long as.' I matter equally. Full stop."[36]

If you take one thing from this book, let it be this: your voice matters. Use it, as loudly and as often as you can.

Advocate in Action: Rachna Choudhry, Cofounder, POPVOX[*]

After 10 years of advocacy and lobbying for several nonprofit organizations, Choudhry cofounded POPVOX, a nonpartisan platform for civic engagement, based on her experiences connecting with lawmakers. Through POPVOX, she offers grassroots advocacy strategy to organizations, helping them engage their supporters and amplify their voices. She also serves on the board of PLEN, which trains women for policy careers. She holds a BA in political science from UCLA and a master's in public policy from Georgetown University's McCourt School of Public Policy. She's based in Washington, DC.

On barriers to women's political participation—and how to address it:

When I worked for the National Partnership for Women & Families, I lobbied on issues like paid leave, an issue directly affecting women. But so many women didn't feel confident enough to talk to lawmakers about it, and I found that really interesting—how much more of an expert can you be when you're trying to juggle your sick kid and your work? You're in it, and therefore you are an expert, but they didn't feel that way.

Women, whatever issue it is that they're struggling with, might not feel like it is a social or political problem. They might feel it's only their problem. The case of sick pay is almost too easy: nearly half of people don't have a single paid sick day in this country. But when your kid is sick, you ask yourself, "Oh my God. What am I going to do?" You feel it's your problem to fix. You don't think of it as political. But how many other people are having this same conversation in their mind? It's not just your problem. Taking it from the personal and reframing it as a political issue is important.

On why it matters to be consistently engaged on your issues—not just "one and done":

The 2012 school shooting at Sandy Hook Elementary was a horrific tragedy that could have been prevented in many ways. In the aftermath, we watched so many people become politically active in a way that we hadn't seen with gun control campaigns in the past. On POPVOX, we saw an incredible increase in people participating by writing letters to their lawmakers. What we saw among people supporting stronger gun control legislation was that they wrote a letter to Congress about how frustrated they were about the lack of background checks or why we

---

* Rachna Choudhry, interview with the author, March 25, 2020.

needed an assault weapons ban. Afterwards, they felt like their work was done, and it was up to the lawmakers to do the right thing. But nothing happened—neither the Assault Weapons Ban of 2013 nor the Manchin-Toomey amendment, which would have required universal background checks for firearm sales, were passed by the Senate despite broad support.

Meanwhile, opponents of stronger gun control legislation, let's just call them the Second Amendment supporters, thought that this was going to be the moment when not only would more restrictions on access to buying guns be passed into law, but also that guns might be taken from their homes. As a result, many of them wrote letters to Congress about almost every single bill that was introduced that might restrict gun rights in any way, because they didn't trust that their lawmaker would do what they wanted them to do. The end result was that even though polls showed that majorities of people supported background checks, the amount of engagement, and the intensity of engagement, was much greater from gun control opponents.

There's this assumption that, "Oh, Congress is going to take care of it because everyone knows it's an issue," and that's a big tactical error that people make when thinking about advocacy. If you're not telling your lawmaker about it, then perhaps your neighbors aren't either. Technology actually makes this problem worse with easy tools that lure you in with "Text this message" with one click or "Sign this petition" to Congress. Most of that goes nowhere. If your lawmaker can't figure out if you're a bot or an actual constituent, then you're actually not going to influence them.

Creating new laws or changing existing laws are long-term fights, so you have to stay on top of it and not feel like you're being pesky. Administrations come and go, and new members of Congress are sworn in every two years. People think it's a flawed system that every new Congress, you start from scratch, and a bill has to be reintroduced and go through the whole process all over again. It feels like Groundhog Day. But that's put into place intentionally so that the system doesn't produce hasty lawmaking. Movements take time, so you have to find small victories. You've got to find ways to keep people engaged. And that could mean changing things up. Maybe one month focus on one thing, like writing letters to your lawmaker, and the next month focus on another tactic, like letters to the editor. That way, it won't feel like you're just banging your head against a brick wall.

On the power of building relationships:

Find somebody on the "inside," meaning someone in the mayor's office or in the city council office or in your member of Congress's office, that is passionate about your issue, or at least interested. Women are really good at building relationships. When I was a lobbyist, I was working on work-life issues, like paid sick days, paid leave, but staffers would call me asking if I knew any issue experts around, for example, postpartum depression. A lot of times staffers are looking for regular people who can testify or who can frame an issue for them. So you can be that person on the ground who can provide detailed information that they can't get from a poll or focus groups.

CHAPTER 2

. . . .

FEDERAL GOVERNMENT

*Our children should learn the general framework of their govern-
ment and they should know where they come in contact with the
government, where it touches their daily lives and where their influence is exerted on the government. It must not be some distant
thing, someone else's business, but they must see how every cog in
the wheel of a democracy is important and bears its share of the
responsibility for the smooth running of the entire machine.*

—Eleanor Roosevelt

I f one of the biggest barriers to upping your political game is feeling like
you don't know enough, these next three chapters will be just what you
need. They provide an overview of how our government is structured,
walk you through how the legislative process works at all levels of government, and, most importantly, help you identify and learn about the public
officials who represent you. Because the United States is a representative
democracy, we (the people) directly elect political officials to represent us
in office—with the exception of the Electoral College in presidential elections. Knowing who represents us and understanding our opportunities and
obligations to influence and hold them accountable is critical to driving
policy change.

First, it's important to remember that we have multiple layers of representation: in addition to the federal representatives who take up so much of the media's (and our) attention, we're also represented by state and local elected officials. But most Americans don't know their state senators or city council members. In fact, a recent survey of 18- to 34-year-olds found that more than three-quarters of respondents couldn't name one of their senators at the *federal* level.[1] The problem with this is that it's impossible to hold our representatives accountable if we don't know who they are. After the 2016 election, there were so many calls to action that encouraged voters to reach out to representatives that were key to certain votes or political appointments—even if those representatives didn't represent them. That's not the most effective strategy. Political officials who don't represent you are not going to be as receptive to your interests or demands as those who do. After all, voting is how we hire or fire representatives; the system was designed that way to ensure that representatives would be responsive to their constituents. If you can't vote in a certain representative's election, they have little incentive to respond to your concerns; they care most what their own constituents think.

In other words: To create change on the issues you care about, you need to know who *your* representatives are, what their responsibilities are, and when they are up for reelection—not to mention what they stand for, and whether they're representing your interests. Not having this information puts us at a disadvantage. Plus, we run the risk of engaging in political activities that don't make the most of our (very precious) time. Getting smarter about how the system is structured, and what it can and can't do, helps us to be more effective.

The next few chapters are part civics class (think of it as a brushup, since you likely last took civics back in middle school) and part history lesson. We'll walk through how our federal, state, and municipal governments are structured, their respective responsibilities and powers, and what it all means for you. This is meant to be a useful overview that you can refer back to as needed for a quick reminder (our system of government is complicated!). But most importantly, these next chapters will include what you really *need* to know—not just what you think you need to know—to participate.

Before we get started, consider these five questions (see answers on page 49):

1. Which body of the US Congress votes on Supreme Court nominations?

2. What is required for Congress to override a presidential veto?

3. How many congressional representatives does your state have?

4. What is the name of your *state* senator (note: this is not to be confused with your US senators)?

5. When is Election Day?

How many of the above were you able to answer? If you knew all of them, that's great! If you didn't know any of them, not to worry. We'll cover all of these questions (and more) in the rest of Part I. And even if it can feel more difficult to get information on political happenings than the pop culture news we're constantly bombarded with, I guarantee you that staying up to date on what your elected officials are doing is way more important than keeping up with the Kardashians. It's critical that we understand the tools of power our elected officials have at their disposal, and then stay up to date on what they do with those tools. The rest of this chapter—and Part I—will help you do just that. Let's start with an overview of the federal government structure.

. . . .

As you may remember from civics class, structurally, the federal government is made up of three branches: executive, legislative, and judicial. At the most basic level, here's how that breaks down:

- **Legislative:** The legislative branch is made up of both houses of Congress (the House of Representatives and the Senate) and is the branch responsible for creating and passing the laws.

- **Executive:** The executive branch includes the offices of the president, the vice president, the president's cabinet, and most federal agencies (like the Department of State, Department of Education, etc.) and is responsible for enforcing or executing the laws.

- **Judicial:** The judicial branch comprises the Supreme Court, the nation's highest court, as well as federal trial courts and appeals courts, and it's responsible for resolving disputes about the meaning and application of the laws.

Each branch also has the power to limit what the other branches do so that, together, the three branches create a system of checks and balances. There are clear processes and mechanisms set up to ensure that if one branch acts improperly, the other two branches have recourse to reset the balance. For example, if Congress passes a bill the president disagrees with, the president can veto the legislation. If Congress feels strongly that the bill should in fact be law (despite the president's veto), they can override the veto if two-thirds of each chamber votes in favor of the bill. If the Supreme Court believes that a law is unconstitutional, they can strike it down. And the president is responsible for nominating the members of the Supreme Court, who are then confirmed (or not) by Congress (specifically, the Senate). These are just a few examples; there are lots of ways that these branches (in theory and in practice) hold each other in balance.

In this first section, we're going to focus primarily on the legislative branch because those are the people we elect to represent us most directly, who can introduce bills that become federal law, and over whom we have the most influence when advocating for our issues. You've likely seen advocacy groups asking you to call your senator in favor of a specific issue—and we'll get to how and why to do that later—but unless you know what your senators can actually *do* with your call, you're at a disadvantage.

LEGISLATIVE BRANCH STRUCTURE

First, let's go over how the legislative branch is structured. The United States has what is called a bicameral legislature—that is, we have two houses that make up our legislative branch. We have a large "lower" house (the House of Representatives) and a smaller "upper" house (the Senate). (The terms "upper" and "lower" are conventions used by political scientists in describing legislatures with two houses or chambers.) While they jointly make up the legislative branch, they were designed both to work together and to fundamentally be at odds with each other. We often complain about partisan gridlock, but that's exactly what the system was designed to create (we'll dig into this more later).

The House, also known as "the People's House," is the larger body, meant to be most responsive to the whims of the voters. In fact, until 1917, it was the only branch of our federal government that was directly elected by the people (senators were originally elected by the state legislature and not by direct vote). In contrast, the Senate was designed to be the "emergency brake" against populism and was intended to be the more deliberative body that allowed for attention and voice to be given to the views of minority positions. In other words, the House is designed so that the majority rules, while the Senate is designed to ensure that policy is not dictated solely by the whims of the majority, and that minority positions are also represented.

While both the Senate and the House can pass legislation, they also have distinct differences in terms of how long each member serves, size, leadership roles, as well as special powers and rules. See pages 32 to 35 for a quick cheat sheet.

Today, the public's trust in members of Congress is *crazy* low. According to the Pew Research Center, only 17 percent of Americans in 2019 said that they could trust the federal government to do what is right "just about always" or "most of the time." When the National Election study began including questions on trust in 1958, approximately 75 percent of Americans said they trusted the government to do the right thing.[2] That's a *significant* drop.

This low level of trust, and its downward trajectory, is likely due to a lot of factors, but I'd argue that one important factor is that there's very little understanding of what a member of Congress actually *does*. How does a member of Congress spend their day? How many hours a week do they work? What do they do when they're in Washington, DC? How about when they're on recess? (Does that mean they're on vacation?) Let's dig into these questions next.

Legislative Branch Cheat Sheet

Note: For both houses, a "Congress" lasts for two years, with each year constituting a separate session. For example, the 116th Congress convened from January 3, 2019, to January 3, 2021. Because of the Senate's longer terms, Senate elections are staggered so that one-third of the Senate faces an election every two years.

	Senate	
Term	Six years (no term limits)	
Size	100 senators (two per state)	
Leadership	Leadership is less formal than in the House (because the Senate is meant to be the smaller, more deliberate and collegial body) and includes: • presiding officer of the Senate (This role is responsible for maintaining order, recognizing members to speak, and interpreting rules and practices, and it's usually filled by the vice president. The Senate also elects a president pro tempore, who serves as presiding officer when the VP is absent.) • the majority leader • the minority leader • the senate majority whip • the minority whip The main advantage of being the majority or minority leader is being allowed to speak first in debate. Unlike in the House, the leaders do not appoint committee members; in the Senate, each party convenes before the start of each Congress to elect leaders and determine committee appointments. Each conference appoints a "committee on committees" to create a list of names it wants to assign to each party's allocated committee seats. Typically, the majority member with the longest tenure on a committee is committee chairperson, although this is always subject to approval.	

House
Two years (no term limits)
435 representatives (distributed according to state population)

Given the size of the House, leadership is much more formal than the Senate (otherwise it would be chaos!) and includes:

- the Speaker of the House (The Speaker is third in line to the presidency, if anything happens to the president and vice president.)
- the majority leader (deputy to the Speaker)
- the minority leader
- the majority whip
- the minority whip

The Speaker and minority leader jointly appoint committees, but committee leaders are appointed at the sole discretion of the Speaker.

	Senate
Special powers	• Votes on presidential appointments (e.g., cabinet members and Supreme Court justices) • Advises on international treaties • Holds impeachment trials (if articles of impeachment have been brought forth and passed by the House)
Special rules	• Filibuster • Cloture • Unlimited debate (More on these later when we talk about legislative norms and how bills become laws.)

A DAY IN THE LIFE OF A MEMBER OF CONGRESS

Regardless of whether you agree with the policies they're enacting, members of Congress are generally working hard. According to research by the Congressional Management Foundation (CMF), members of the House of Representatives work an average of 70 hours a week when Congress is in session, and 59 hours a week when Congress is out of session. And it's not a Monday-to-Friday workweek; representatives are usually in DC from Monday through Thursday, and then back in their districts Friday through Sunday. In fact, according to the CMF, nearly 80 percent of members who participated in the study reported spending more than 40 weekends a year in their districts.[3]

House
• Holds the "power of the purse" (responsible for approving the budget of the federal government) • Brings forth articles of impeachment against government officials
• The rules committee governs the rules under which bills are voted on, and processes are governed by a much more formal set of rules than in the Senate

One common misunderstanding: Many people think that when Congress is not in session (otherwise known as "recess"), members are on vacation. Not so. While recess sounds like fun, all it means for members of Congress is that they're not required to be in Washington, DC, because votes won't be taking place. That doesn't mean they're not still on the job. It just means that, instead of working in DC, members are working back in their districts.

So what do members of Congress actually do when they're in their districts? Or when they're in session in Washington, DC, for that matter?

The following chart illustrates how members of the House of Representatives reported the breakdown of how they spend their time.[4]

- When **in Washington, DC,** members reported spending their time as follows:

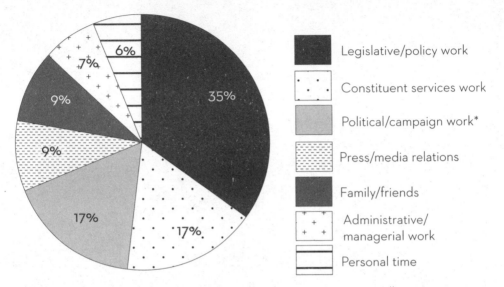

*We'll talk about this more in Part III, but members of Congress are essentially running for office and raising money for their campaigns all of the time.

- When members are **in their districts,** they reported spending their time as follows:

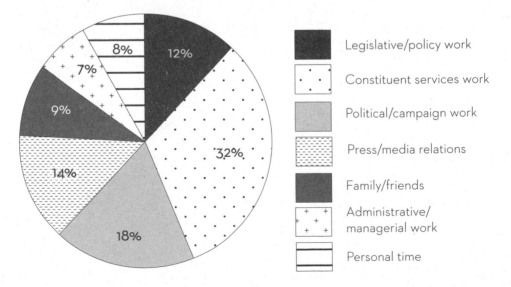

It makes sense that when members are in Washington, DC, the majority of their time is spent on legislation and policy making; after all, when Congress is in session, they're drafting and introducing bills, reading bills, meeting in their respective committees, and of course voting on legislation.

In contrast, when they're back home in their districts, the majority of their time is spent meeting with constituents and working with their communities.

What I think is surprising, though, is how little personal time and time with friends and family members of Congress are able to spend. In fact, nearly 9 out of 10 members feel they spend too little time with family and friends and on personal activities.[5] These are *intense* jobs. And these are people who, in general, work extremely hard and do so because they want to help their communities.

Tonya Williams, former director of legislative affairs for Vice President Joe Biden (*read more from Williams in her Advocate in Action profile on page 189*), says that when working with public officials, "[t]here's no set day. Current events drive what you're doing. The political landscape drives what you're doing. I've never had a day where I did just what I thought I was going to do at the start of it—it's just not how it works." While she notes that there are aspects of working for public officials that are similar to working in more typical organizations (for example, how you organize yourself and your team and get people in the right places to manage their goals), it's also quite different. "There's so much more out of your control," Williams says, "and the problems you're trying to solve are often more systemic and more complex than in an organization. There are emotions and my ultimate service to [the community] is not a return on investment—it is in fact a better life for them, leaving them better than they were when we started."[6]

This, as you can imagine, is incredibly difficult work. People, Williams says, would be "surprised to know how much [public officials] honestly care, and how much of a sacrifice they make to do this work. It's not glorious. There are glorious parts and pieces to it, but for the most part, they travel, they're away from their families, they have to raise a lot of money all of the time, they're constantly bargaining for a better position for themselves, which means better positioning for their constituents . . . They're real people, with real experiences, with real reasons for what they believe. And most of them want to get something done and are frustrated by the fact that they can't." Much of this inaction, Williams notes, is due to the sheer size of the government: "In the federal government, there's only so much you can control. You're talking about a huge bureaucracy. It's like a battleship; you can't just turn it around."[7]

One big change, in contrast to the legislative bodies of yesteryear, is the amount of travel required. Before commercial air travel became affordable, members of Congress typically lived in Washington, DC. While members may have had their disagreements at the office, they often interacted socially: their kids went to school together, and they frequented the same restaurants and social clubs. All of this, one imagines, had the effect of establishing personal, trust-based relationships between members of Congress by making it easier for them to meet and work together face-to-face, even on divisive issues, as well as creating shared, common experiences among people who otherwise might be very different from one another.

However, as air travel became more accessible and affordable, constituents increasingly pressured members to move back to their districts, arguing their representatives could better represent them if they lived among them. Today, members of Congress often rent apartments in Washington, DC (where they stay Monday through Thursday), but have homes back in their districts (where they stay until they leave again for DC the next Monday, and often where their families live full time), providing less opportunity to build personal relationships with their colleagues. This kind of travel time means that members are really only available Tuesday through Thursday, which makes scheduling incredibly complicated and also makes it even harder to build friendships, relationships, and cross-party experiences.

It's important to note that these expectations around travel could also have an important, and disproportionate, impact on women's interest in serving in elected office, particularly women with children. Women today continue to take on the lion's share of childcare responsibilities; the prospect of living away from their families for half the week could be discouraging. Other legislative norms have an impact, too. As Cynthia Terrell, executive director of RepresentWomen, points out, "How legislatures function really impacts women's ability to serve effectively. That's everything from: Are there women's bathrooms? Are there nursing rooms? Can you use campaign money to pay for childcare? From qualitative research, we know this has a huge impact on women's abilities to serve."[8]

But while the responsibilities of a member of Congress change from day to day and hour to hour (and, like any job, have evolved over time), one of their core responsibilities, as we've discussed, is to work on legislation that will help their districts. Now, let's talk about how that actually happens.

Knowing how bills are created and become law is critical to becoming a more effective advocate.

HOW A BILL BECOMES A LAW

The short story: The journey of a bill becoming a law is a *lot* more complicated than *Schoolhouse Rock* makes it out to be. Let's review the grown-up version, shall we?

STEP 1: INTRODUCING THE BILL

Fun fact: Anyone can write a bill—not just a member of Congress. In fact, think tanks and lobbying groups frequently draft bills for legislators to introduce (or adopt as a template, which legislators can build upon). However, only a member of Congress (or multiple members of Congress if the bill is "co-sponsored," meaning that multiple members have endorsed and are introducing the bill) can actually *introduce* the bill. A bill can be introduced in either the Senate *or* the House (but ultimately has to be passed through both chambers, and then signed by the president, to become a law). Once the bill has been drafted, the original sponsor of the bill often works to gather co-sponsor support before officially introducing it. Co-sponsorship of a bill is huge: more names on a bill at the outset signals a higher level of support for the bill, especially if it's clear that there is bipartisan support (in other words, if the bill has both Republicans and Democrats as co-sponsors).

Once drafted, in the House of Representatives, the bill is given to the Clerk of the House (a position nominated by the Speaker and elected by the House of Representatives) by physically placing it into a wooden box called "the hopper," at which point the Clerk gives the bill a number. In the Senate, the bill is either formally introduced on the Senate floor or placed on the desk of the Senate's presiding officer. The first bill of any new Congress is numbered "1," and the bill numbers reset with every new Congress, that is, every two years. Bills also have a special notation depending on the kind of bill it is; for example, the first bill introduced in the House would be "H.R. 1," while the first bill in the Senate would be notated as "S. 1."

Once the bill has been introduced, there is still a lengthy process before it actually goes to a vote. Next, it's sent to a committee.

STEP 2: COMMITTEE REVIEW

Committees are small groups of members of Congress that focus on particular issues. Committees exist in both the House of Representatives and the
Senate, and they cover issues ranging from homeland security to financial
services to the environment. There are often also subcommittees within
the committees themselves. Each committee has a chair (who belongs to
the majority party and leads the full committee) and a ranking member
(who belongs to the minority party and leads the minority members of
the committee).

Which committee a bill is sent to depends on its content and focus. For
example, if a bill is introduced that's all about farm policy, it would likely
go to the agricultural committee. Sometimes, however, it's not clear which
committee a bill belongs in—so the bill may go to multiple committees at
once, or one after the other.

In the House, the Speaker is responsible for assigning a bill to committee. (In 2007, California congresswoman Nancy Pelosi became the first—and
to date, only—female Speaker of the House.) In the Senate, it's the job of
the Senate parliamentarian (a nonpartisan role) to assign the bill.

So, what happens in these committees? In committees, members read
the bill, ask relevant agencies for written comments on the bill, hold hearings
focused on the topic of the bill (at which point experts or even constituents
who have been affected by the issues share statements and respond to members' questions), offer changes to the bill, and ultimately vote on whether
the bill should move forward to a full floor vote.

You've likely seen or heard of congressional hearings, especially when
they're big news. For example, in 2020, Representative Katie Porter received
national attention (and acclaim) for her expert questioning at a House
oversight committee meeting. Showcasing the cost of COVID-19 testing
for Americans (an estimated $1,331), she questioned CDC director Robert
Redfield, asking him if the general public would be able to afford the tests,
as well as if the administration would move to allow free testing.[9] The result?
Redfield committed to make COVID-19 testing free for all US citizens.

Note that most hearings are open to the public and listed on the House
or Senate websites. If you live in DC (or nearby), you can watch the hearings
in person; otherwise, you can typically tune into C-SPAN and watch live

that way as well. If you don't catch the hearing you want to see live, websites like Congress.gov provide *tons* of information about each committee; you can check out the committee schedule and view archived video of committee activity like hearings.

Committees are incredibly important. Given the sheer volume of bills that are introduced in each Congress (according to GovTrack, 13,556 bills were introduced in the 115th Congress from 2017 to 2018)[10] and the range of issues they cover, committees allow a small group of members with expertise on particular issue areas to review and weigh in on a bill so that *every* member of Congress is not reviewing *every* bill. This creates a more efficient process and also ensures that members with the most expertise in an issue area are reviewing the bills on that issue first (at least in an ideal world; committee appointments can be incredibly, for lack of a better word, political).

Committees are also the first place a bill can effectively "die." Remember that the House Speaker is a politically appointed position (the Speaker is a member of the majority party, nominated and voted on by their colleagues in the House). The Speaker can choose not to assign the bill to committee, stalling its progress. If a bill doesn't go to a committee, it simply doesn't move forward. Similarly, committees themselves can decide not to vote on the bill, or vote against the bill—meaning it doesn't move to a full floor vote. If a bill doesn't leave committee during the congressional session in which it was introduced, it officially dies. The only thing that can be done to revive the legislation at that point is reintroducing the bill all over again in the next Congress . . . where the entire process would start from the beginning. The Equal Rights Amendment, or ERA, for example, a proposed constitutional amendment to guarantee equal rights regardless of sex to all Americans, has been reintroduced in every session of Congress since 1982—and has never been passed.

In the House of Representatives, if a committee sits on a bill, there is another way forward: members can introduce what's called a "discharge petition," which the majority of House members need to sign to bring a bill out of committee and onto the floor. In the Senate, however, there's no such petition process. The only check on the power of Senate committees is voting in new members or a new majority party.

If the bill *does* make it through committee, the next step is to bring it to the floor of the House or the Senate.

STEP 3: BRINGING THE BILL TO THE FLOOR

Once a bill has left committee, the process is a bit different for the House and the Senate. Let's break it down by chamber.

- **House of Representatives:** The Speaker of the House decides when a bill will be voted on (yet another way that the Speaker has *huge* influence on the likelihood of legislation moving forward). The bill also goes before the rules committee, which determines the parameters for debate in the House (e.g., if amendments can be offered to the bill, how long debate on the bill can last). These rules are seen as critical in the House given the large number of members—if, for example, unlimited debate were allowed, or if the committee didn't restrict the number or type of amendments allowed, the process of debating and voting on bills could be endless.

- **Senate:** The majority leader decides when the bill will be voted on. In stark contrast to the House, there are no rules determined for debate—senators can debate a bill as long as they'd like, and add any number of amendments (which could be on any topic, as opposed to in the House, where amendments, if allowed, have to be "germane" or relevant to the content of the bill). Unlimited debate has always been a key feature of how the Senate operates, and senators can also use it as a way to delay a vote, which is called filibustering. There will be more information on the filibuster later in this chapter; for now, all you need to know is that senators can use the filibuster to delay a vote on a bill that has come to the floor, and that the only way to "overcome" a filibuster is through cloture, a petition that must be signed by 60 percent of the Senate.

In either case, if the vote is delayed for the entire congressional session and never brought to the floor, it dies and must be reintroduced in the next Congress to be considered. If it *is* brought to the floor, however, then members of Congress vote on it.

STEP 4: VOTING ON THE BILL

Once a bill has been introduced, passed through committee, and actually brought to the floor for a vote, it is then and *only* then that an actual vote takes place. Whew! In the House, the Speaker of the House calls the vote, and representatives vote by an electronic device where they insert a card into a reader and hit a green button to vote yes and a red button to vote no. Given that there are only 100 senators, in the Senate the vote is a little different. The presiding officer of the Senate calls the vote, and, often, the Senate uses a voice vote, where a senator's name is called and they say "aye" to vote in favor of the bill or "nay" to vote against it.

If the bill passes, it goes to the other chamber—in other words, if the bill originated in the Senate and passes in the Senate, it then goes to the House, where the bill is assigned to the relevant committee there and has to go through the entire process again. If it originated and was passed in the House, then it is reviewed and assigned to a committee in the Senate. Either way, it's a long road.

While this is the general process, note that rules governing how votes are cast can change. For example, in 2020, the House of Representatives changed voting rules to allow remote voting and virtual hearings, in response to the COVID-19 crisis (an enormous change considering that, since 1789, members of Congress have been required to be present for votes and hearings).[11]

STEP 5: PRESIDENTIAL ACTION

Only after a bill has passed in both chambers of Congress does it go to the office of the president. And this is assuming that the language of the bill wasn't changed at all in its journey through the second chamber. If the language of the bill *has* been changed, the bill goes to what's called a conference committee. Senior members of the House and the Senate review the bills to decide on a final version that reconciles the differences (if any) between the versions that passed in the House and the Senate. And *then* the bill goes to the office of the president.

At this point, the president either signs the bill—in which case it becomes law—or vetoes it. If the president vetoes the bill, it *can* still become law, but to do so, it has to go back to both chambers again for a vote. If two-thirds of each chamber votes in favor of the bill, it becomes law despite the president's veto.

Alternatively, the president can do nothing. If the bill is left on his or her desk for 10 days without action, it automatically becomes law—*unless* Congress adjourns before the 10 days are up. If this happens, the bill doesn't become law; this is what's known as a "pocket veto."

THE FILIBUSTER: A BRIEF OVERVIEW

As promised, let's dive a little deeper into the filibuster. First, a quick definition: A "filibuster" is essentially anything that might block legislative action—for example, delaying a vote on a particular bill or delaying legislation from being introduced to the floor.[12] Although the word "filibuster" wasn't coined until the 1850s, the process of using delaying tactics to block legislation, a rule change, or an executive-branch nomination is an approach as old as the Senate itself.

On its face, the filibuster isn't necessarily a bad thing; the Senate is meant to be an emergency brake that allows for a cooling-off period, ensuring that there is moderation in the legislation passed, and a balance to the more populist House. By initiating a filibuster, the minority could potentially force the Senate majority to moderate a bill in order to gain the votes needed to end the filibuster. The filibuster was historically also sometimes used as an educational tool, especially when senators deployed a "live" filibuster—this is the filibuster most often portrayed in popular culture, where a senator stands up and lectures, not giving up the floor, until he or she essentially runs out the clock.

As mentioned earlier, the mechanism used to stop a filibuster is called "cloture." The support of a minimum of 16 senators is required to even introduce a cloture petition. Then you need 60 votes to approve the petition and actually "invoke" cloture. Once cloture is invoked, the clock starts—the Senate has 30 more hours to debate the bill, during which they can't introduce any new amendments, and then they must vote. The Senate used to require 67 votes to invoke cloture, but the requirement was lowered in 1975, in part because of a series of filibusters used throughout the 1960s to keep civil rights legislation from the floor.[13] Today, some argue that the filibuster gives the minority in the Senate *too* much influence; because of the votes needed to invoke cloture, 21 states, representing only 11 percent of the population, can potentially prevent the majority from getting 60 votes.

At a conceptual level, if the Senate is meant to be a body of unlimited deliberation and debate versus majority rule, tactics to slow that debate seem in line with that purpose. The issue today is how the filibuster is *deployed*. As the Congressional Institute points out, the most significant change in the filibuster over time has been the frequency of its use. As Congress has grown more polarized, use of the filibuster in the Senate has become more common.*

Filibusters have also become a heck of a lot easier to execute. For example, many filibusters these days are "virtual"—in other words, senators do not have to hold the floor to prevent a vote; they can essentially filibuster just by telling the Senate majority leader that they're planning to do so. Today, the filibuster has led to the ability of the minority to veto a bill without it even reaching the floor for debate—likely not something the founders intended.

To address these challenges, experts have developed ideas to reform the filibuster. These include:

- eliminating the filibuster completely;

- eliminating the "virtual" filibuster (raising the bar for what's required to filibuster by forcing senators to actually hold the floor when they are filibustering, which might discourage some from using it as a tactic);

---

* It's tricky to count how many times a filibuster is "used" because senators are not *formally* required to register their objections to end debate (often just knowing that at least 41 senators oppose cloture is enough to stop a vote from even being scheduled), but the Congressional Institute uses the number of cloture petitions as one indicator (after all, cloture petitions are used to "unstick" the Senate when a filibuster is being used). The last Congress that did not introduce any cloture petitions was the 85th Congress (1957–1958); the number of cloture petitions peaked in the 113th Congress (2013–2014) with *252* in just one year. A lot of legislation that's been favored by the majority of the US population has found itself stalled because of the filibuster—including campaign finance reform, which we will cover in Part III (Molly E. Reynolds, "What Is the Senate Filibuster, and What Would It Take to Eliminate It?" Brookings Institution, October 15, 2019, https://www.brookings.edu/policy2020/votervital/what-is-the-senate-filibuster-and-what-would-it-take-to-eliminate-it/).

- eliminating the filibuster only on "motions to proceed" (this would preserve the use of the filibuster in voting on bills, but not on whether bills should be brought to the floor in the first place);

- lowering the threshold to invoke cloture.

It is more than reasonable to advocate for filibuster reform—today the filibuster regularly prevents important legislation from being enacted (and in extreme cases, from even being formally considered). As mentioned, the filibuster enabled a handful of politicians to block civil rights legislation for nearly a century. At the same time, as Brown University professor of political science and public policy Wendy Schiller has written: "[S]enators also use the filibuster to slow down or halt legislation that they believe will be harmful to individual rights. For example, when the Patriot Act was up for reauthorization in 2005, both Democratic and Republican senators used the filibuster to obtain more protections against government intrusion on privacy and surveillance of individuals."[14] If the filibuster were eliminated, Schiller asks, "[H]ow could ordinary citizens, companies, or states stand up for their own interests in a majoritarian system of government?"

In any case, as experts have pointed out, any reform to the filibuster should be done as part of broader legislative reforms to reinforce civility, deliberation, and bipartisanship. This is because, by fixing the filibuster, we might only be fixing a symptom of a deeper problem. Yes, the filibuster has been weaponized to prevent bills from even reaching the floor, but many experts are not convinced that fixing it would restore the Senate to a more civil and deliberative body.

KEY TAKEAWAYS REGARDING THE LEGISLATIVE PROCESS

So there's your refresher on how a bill becomes a law. It's a lot! And even this doesn't explain all of the nuance and complexity. Bills with bipartisan support, for example, follow a slightly different (and faster) process. These bills range from the symbolic, like renaming a post office, to the more complex, like passing a spending bill. In the House, there's a suspension of the rules, which lets the House fast-track a bill to a vote. In the Senate, there's a unanimous consent agreement, which similarly lets a bill go right to a direct vote. Here are a few important takeaways from this process:

- **Party control matters a *ton* . . .** Think about it: the party in control of the House of Representatives gets to determine the Speaker of the House. The party in control of the Senate determines the majority leader. These roles have enormous impact on when (or indeed even if) a vote on a bill takes place. In addition, the Speaker of the House assigns committee leaders (who decide the other members of each committee), which impacts which experts and community members are called in for hearings, what changes are made to a bill, and if a bill even makes it out of committee. And in both the House and the Senate, the majority party of the chamber dictates which party has a majority in each committee. In other words, if the Republican Party is the majority party in the House, the majority of members of *all* committees in the House will be Republicans, and the committee leader of each committee will also be a Republican. Finally (and perhaps most obviously), the party with the majority can determine the outcome of votes on a bill once it comes to the floor. The majority rules in the House, where a bill passes with 50 percent plus one vote. In the Senate, it's a little more complicated, but given the current way the filibuster works, a bill essentially needs 60 percent support to pass. And remember that the Senate is also responsible for the confirmation of cabinet positions and federal judges . . . just another way that party control really does matter.

- **. . . which means that most things don't happen without compromise.** Because party control means so much, unless one party has a wide margin of control in both chambers, compromise is required to get much of anything done. In today's polarized environment, compromise is increasingly rare. But working with members of both parties and finding common ground (or at least identifying areas that are negotiable) is critical.

- **The system is meant to move slowly.** Given the deliberate, layered process—from a bill's introduction, to committee review, to debate and a floor vote, then repeating the process in the other chamber, and finally going to the president—there are a *lot* of places a bill can be derailed. Indeed, of the 13,556 bills introduced in the 115th Congress, only 442 (or 3 percent) were signed into law.[15] (By the way, these bills aren't one-pagers; the average bill enacted in the 115th Congress was 17.8 pages long.[16]) But the founders actually *wanted* to create a system where change only occurred when public opinion and the political elite were largely in concert with each other. Of course, today the influence of money in politics and special interests has certainly affected that balance (more on that in Part III), but if it sometimes feels like nothing happens quickly in Congress, that's because it doesn't—and that's intentional.

Okay! So there you have it: how a bill generally becomes a law. Obviously, there's a lot more to the federal government that we could go into. But the information we've reviewed should help you better understand the legislative branch of the federal government, what your members of Congress actually do on a day-to-day basis, and how policy comes to be—all critical things that will serve as a foundation for understanding how to influence your representatives' work and drive effective change.

Quiz Answers

1. The Senate.
2. A two-thirds vote in favor of the bill in both chambers (Senate and House of Representatives).
3. Depends on your state; representation is proportional to state population.
4. Depends on your state; consult a website like Ballotpedia or Common Cause (or even your state government's official website) to confirm.
5. Typically, the first Tuesday in November. It takes place every four years for presidential elections (in even years), and every two years for congressional elections (in even years). State and local elections are typically held on the same days for the sake of convenience and cost savings, although some states hold state or local elections during odd-numbered years and may also hold special elections for offices that have become vacant.

Advocate in Action: Katie Kottenbrock, Congressional Staffer*

Katie Kottenbrock is a congressional staffer in Minnesota who focuses on health care and gender and sexuality equity issues. She completed undergraduate degrees in political science and women and gender studies as well as the Masters of Advocacy and Political Leadership program. With a passion for ending gender-based violence and promoting access to quality health care, she works to ensure that all her policy work is completed through an intersectional equity lens.

On her journey to Congress and passion for advocacy:

I grew up in North Dakota in a pretty small town. In my government class in high school, we were conversing about same-sex marriage, debating it. One of my classmates was the only person who had come out as homosexual or gay in our class and really our entire school. He had been outed by others and was struggling to navigate this issue and his own self-identity. I remember our government teacher kept talking about how same-sex marriage was the same as legally allowing people to marry a horse. I was too young to grasp all of the concepts and the harassment that my classmate was experiencing but remember being quite sad that the leader of the conversation was actually just perpetuating a discriminatory and hostile viewpoint.

I studied political science and international relations in college and also earned a second undergrad degree in women and gender studies. I had amazing, strong women as professors, and they changed my life. I ended up working as a Medicare counselor and started to recognize the intersectional feminism at play. There are so many vulnerable people operating within many complex systems. I started working with county staff to help them understand how Medicare works within their local community. Even if the policy was already in place, it wasn't always implemented in a way that helped the folks who were most at risk.

I applied for a job in Congress and was hired as a constituent service representative, focusing on health and human services. I've been able to work for two members of Congress who believe that policy should prioritize marginalized communities. I now work as the LGBTQ+ and gender equity outreach director, which involves ensuring that folks who are trans have equal rights and equal access to health care.

---

*   Katie Kottenbrock, interview with the author, March 27, 2020 (adapted for clarity).

On effective advocacy—and getting started:

The first step is determining where you can get the most traction with your issue. I think a lot of people overlook what their city council member or county commissioner can do. Building those relationships will help you learn what policy levers you can pull.

I have the opportunity to hear individual stories from advocates about how different policies impact their lives. When you're able to make something personal for any politician at any level of government, it helps bring that issue home and leads to better conversations.

You also need to find something you feel you can move the buck forward on and focus your heart and your energy on that. It's hard when there are a hundred things that need to change and you're passionate about all of them—engagement won't be sustainable until you define where you want to commit your energy.

On barriers to women's full and equal participation:

The biggest barrier is still sexism. With the women Democratic presidential nominees in 2020, the conversation was, "Are they electable?" Why is that the conversation we're having around women candidates? And why are men more electable? We have a long way to go where it's not a gender dichotomy in that conversation, too. We address those barriers by supporting each other and ensuring that women's voices and the voices of folks who are queer, or gender nonconforming or nonbinary, are uplifted.

CHAPTER 3

. . . .

STATE GOVERNMENT

*Politics is not just about voting one day every four years. Politics is
the air we breathe, the food we eat, and the road we walk on.*
*—Unita Blackwell, in her memoir Barefootin': Life
Lessons from the Road to Freedom (2006)*

I
t's all too easy to forget that we have multiple levels of government, and
representatives at each of those levels. Our laser focus on the federal
system is reinforced by the fact that our main news sources are so often
national and not local—we only hear about what's happening at the state
level when it could be considered national news. It doesn't help that local
newspapers today are in crisis; according to a 2019 Brookings Institution
report, 65 percent of Americans live in counties with only one local news-
paper, or none at all.[1] And between 2003 and 2014, the number of full-time
statehouse reporters that were sent to the state capital by their newspapers
fell by *35 percent*.[2]

But if state-level policymaking doesn't get the same attention as what
goes on in Washington, DC, it's not because state government is unim-
portant! It would be a mistake to think of the federal government as the
major leagues and state and local government as the minor leagues. In many

cases, state and local policymaking is *more* important—it's likely your state government that has the most day-to-day impact on your life.

For example, consider what is printed in school textbooks. Textbook content might not seem like a political issue on its face, but as a 2020 *New York Times* analysis of Texas and California social studies books for eighth and eleventh graders showed, it certainly can be. The analysis found that the textbook editions differed in key ways, despite having the same publisher. These differences, *New York Times* journalist Dana Goldstein wrote, "can be traced back to several sources: state social studies standards; state laws; and feedback from panels of appointees that huddle, in Sacramento and Austin hotel conference rooms, to review drafts."[3] Those panels are chosen by *state political leaders*. Goldstein explains that "[a]ll the members of the California panel were educators selected by the State Board of Education, whose members were appointed by former Gov. Jerry Brown, a Democrat. The Texas panel, appointed by the Republican-dominated State Board of Education, was made up of educators, parents, business representatives, and a Christian pastor and politician."[4] The differences identified in the textbooks are subtle, but they reflect familiar partisan divides: in the discussion of women's fight against workplace discrimination, for example, only the California textbook mentions the role of birth control in "allowing women to exert greater control over their sexuality and family planning."[5] And as the article points out, you can imagine how these differences, no matter how subtle, can influence students' worldviews.

Here are a few more examples of important state-level legislation from 2018 and 2019:

- **Nevada** passed a law automatically restoring the voting rights of felons in Nevada after their release from prison, permitting an estimated 77,000 people who would otherwise have been prohibited from voting to cast their votes in the 2020 presidential election. The prior law required that released felons wait two years before restoration of their voting rights.[6]

- **California** passed the California Consumer Privacy Act, which requires companies to disclose information they collect on or about consumers, and allows consumers to opt out of having their data sold.[7]

- **New York** introduced paid family leave, which by 2021 will allow parents to take 12 weeks of paid leave at 70 percent of their average salary financed by the state, not by the parents' employers.[8]

- **New Hampshire** passed a law requiring school districts to provide free pads and tampons in women's and gender-neutral bathrooms in middle schools and high schools. (By the way, this legislation was spearheaded by high school student Caroline Dillon, who had this to say about the experience: "I think the thing that stuck out to me the most is that you can make an impact and actually do something without being eighteen, without running for office. You can make your voice heard and participate in the process.")[9]

Each of these pieces of legislation has an *enormous* impact on the lives of people living in these states. In fact, in some cases, state laws can even affect people living in other states—or other countries. Take the California Consumer Privacy Act mentioned above. In order to comply with that law, many companies will likely begin providing opt-out rights to users regardless of location, rather than going through the trouble of identifying users in California and providing a specialized opt-out only to them. And regardless of how companies handle their obligation to provide an opt-out right for Californians, the public disclosure of the kinds of personal information companies collect is a benefit for users located outside the state, too.

Another broad benefit of laws enacted at the state level is that they provide an incredible opportunity to innovate. As Supreme Court Justice Louis Brandeis wrote in his dissenting opinion in *New State Ice Co. v. Liebmann*, "[I]t is one of the happy incidents of the federal system that a courageous state may, if its citizens choose, serve as a laboratory; and try novel social and economic experiments without risk to the rest of the country."[10] Policymakers in all 50 states can theoretically be conducting these kinds of "social and economic experiments" at the same time, and if one of the experiments pays off, other states or even the federal government can enact a similar law.

For people involved in state politics, it is often the potential for having an immediate impact on people's lives that attracts them to the work they do. New York state senator Alessandra Biaggi, who represents New York's 34th District (including portions of the Bronx and Westchester), was elected in 2018. A lawyer by training, she also worked as associate general counsel in

Governor Cuomo's Office for Storm Recovery and, in 2016, served as deputy national operations director for Hillary Clinton's campaign. But these are just her formal qualifications; Alessandra Biaggi is also a force of nature. In just her first six months in office, she introduced 80 bills, 17 of which were passed, and four of which have been signed into law by the governor (at the time we spoke, a fifth was poised to be signed into law as well). When I asked her why state government mattered so much, here's what she said:

> The representatives that most directly impact your lives in a very significant way are at the state level, and that is because the legislation that is passed and the money that is brought back to the districts for specific programming is a direct line. The federal government has a significant amount of power, but their impact, while large and for everyone in the country, takes so much longer because of how big it is.
>
> At the state level, you go to your state capitol, and if you pass a law, it literally impacts every single person in the state of New York. That is huge. Someone in Congress? It could take them 10 years to pass their first bill.[11]

Speaking of significant pieces of legislation, one of the bills that Sen. Biaggi sponsored has become one of the strongest workplace sexual harassment and discrimination laws in the country. In rewriting the laws that were previously on the books in New York, the legislature voted to change the standard of what it will take for someone to bring a case against someone who's harassing others. "[The previous] standard for someone to win in court was 'severe' or 'pervasive,' which is a very high threshold, and some of the most egregious things were not even found to be 'severe' or 'pervasive,'" explained Biaggi. "That's a very scary thing. And the standard was being confused by very educated male judges to be severe *and* pervasive . . . so people were having an even harder time proving their case and no abuser was being held to account in New York. We changed the standard to 'petty slights' or 'trivial inconveniences,' and it's going to make a big difference in New York."[12]

Don't just take a state senator's word that state government matters, though. Sherry Leiwant is cofounder and co-president of A Better Balance, an organization that works to "promote equality and expand choices for men and women at all income levels so they may care for their families without sacrificing their economic security."[13] They accomplish all that by advocating for policies that help families, such as paid sick leave, family leave, pay equity, and others (*read more about Leiwant in her Advocate in Action profile on page 161*). For A Better Balance, engaging at the state and local level first is a core part of their strategy. "Our theory of change, if you will, is that starting with localities and states, you can engage people and you can make changes that are difficult to make at the federal level. So it's a good place to start,"[14] says Leiwant.

But what powers does a state government have, and how do they differ from the federal government? The Tenth Amendment to the US Constitution mandates that all powers not explicitly granted to the federal government are reserved for the states and the people. Unique powers held by states include the power to conduct elections (this, by the way, leads to huge variability in how voting and elections take place from state to state—more on that later); to provide for public safety, health, and welfare; to maintain a militia; to establish local government; and to ratify amendments to the US Constitution.* Shared responsibilities include things like law enforcement (depending on whether the crime is at the federal or state level), taxation (you pay taxes to both the federal and state governments), and eminent domain (the right to take land for public use).

Arguably, one of the most important roles state governments play is in congressional redistricting. But before we dive into redistricting, let's quickly talk about the census (something you've likely heard a lot about, given that it was most recently conducted in 2020). The US was the first country to constitutionally mandate a national census, which is conducted every ten years and provides critical information about the US population. Specifically, it counts the number of people living in every US household (defined as the group of people who spend most of their time at that home), regardless of citizenship or immigration status. It's a simple concept, but this population count has profound implications, and two of the most important are representation and federal funding:

- **Representation**: Remember that in the House, representation is proportional to population; changes in state populations could result in redistribution of the House's 435 federal representatives. The census determines how many representatives are allocated to each state, as well as how many electoral votes each state gets in presidential elections.

---

* Congress has to introduce a constitutional amendment like other bills; however, before it becomes law, it has to be ratified by three-fourths of the states.

- **Federal funding**: The census also informs how much federal funding each state gets—here, *billions* of dollars are up for grabs. To allocate the proper funding for roads, hospitals, schools, and more, you need to know how many people there are, as well as where they are. If you *don't* know, you run the risk of underfunding incredibly important state-run services.

As you can see, the results of the census have some very serious consequences. And here's where we come back to redistricting. Once representatives have been apportioned to each state, based on the census's population numbers, the state needs to be divided into voting districts. The process of redrawing these lines is called redistricting (and it's a fairly time-bound process; generally, redistricting must be completed by the filing deadlines of the next primary election for federal and state legislators, although some states do have specific redistricting deadline).[15] When redistricting is done in order to benefit one party over another, that's partisan gerrymandering. We'll discuss partisan gerrymandering in more detail in Part III, but what you need to know for now is that it's typically the state legislature, with the governor's approval, that decides how those lines are (re)drawn. If one party has a majority in the state legislature and, at the same time, they control the governorship, redistricting can be (and often is) used for partisan gain.

Like the federal government, all state governments have three branches: executive, legislative, and judicial—although the specifics often look quite different from state to state. At the state level, the governor plays the executive role, similar to the president at the federal level (vetoing bills, appointing some judges, facilitating pardons, and directing the state National Guard), and the lieutenant governor plays a role similar to the vice president (i.e., they're next in line if anything happens to the governor). Many argue that because of the executive nature of the governor's role, it's great training ground for a future president—and indeed, 17 former governors have gone on to become president, compared to 16 senators and 18 House representatives.[16] That so many governors have become presidents is especially impressive since senators and representatives are much larger pools; at any one time there are 100 senators and 435 House representatives, but only 50 governors. Indeed, four governors ran to be the Democratic nominee in the 2020 presidential primary. Other state leadership roles that typically serve in the executive branch at the state level include the attorney general and secretary of state, as well as auditors and commissioners.

The structure of the judicial branch at the state level, as well as the process for judicial elections or appointments, also varies from state to state, and is determined by the state constitution or by legislation. That said, state judicial systems broadly resemble the federal structure, in that a state supreme court hears appeals from lower-level state courts—although, because naming conventions vary, this can get pretty confusing. For example, in New York state courts, the *lowest-level* trial courts are actually called New York supreme courts, whereas the *highest-level* court (typically what we think of as a "supreme court") is called the New York Court of Appeals. There can also be courts at the state level that deal with specific kinds of issues, such as traffic court, or courts that hear only lawsuits involving relatively small amounts of money, called small claims courts. The best way to figure out how your state's judicial system is organized is likely by looking at your state courts' website—just Google your state (e.g., "Washington") and "courts" and it should come right up!

Finally, there's the legislative branch. The legislative branches of state governments approve state budgets, introduce and pass legislation, and write articles of impeachment for state-level positions. Every state but Nebraska has a bicameral legislature like the federal government: a small upper house (the senate), and a larger lower house (often called the house of representatives but in some cases called the assembly or house of delegates, depending on the state). State legislatures vary significantly from state to state not only in naming conventions, but also in size, members' term lengths, and other procedural rules. Every state has its own constitution, which lays out these details. As of late 2020, state legislatures also vary wildly in terms of gender representation.

On the next page are a few examples from the states I've lived in over the past 15 years (New Hampshire, New York, Washington), as well as the states my mom and sisters live in (Michigan, Florida) to give you a sense of the diversity of naming conventions, size, term length, and women in leadership, as of early 2020 (prior to the 2020 elections).[17]

It's important to note that, while there are differences in terms of gender diversity, none of the states above have reached parity. And women of color are especially underrepresented; as of 2020, women of color made up only 7.4 percent of state legislators serving nationwide, and only 25.3 percent of women state legislators,[18] despite constituting nearly 40 percent of women in the US population.[19]

Name of state government	Number of state senators	Senate term lengths	Number of state representatives	Representative term lengths	Overall legislature gender diversity
Florida Legislature	40	4 years	120	2 years	29% women 71% men
Michigan Legislature	38	4 years	110	2 years	36% women 64% men
New Hampshire General Court	24	2 years	400	2 years	34% women 66% men
New York Legislature	63	2 years	150	2 years	32% women 68% men
Washington Legislature	49	4 years	98	2 years	40% women 60% men

A DAY IN THE LIFE OF A STATE LEGISLATOR

As we just discussed, state legislatures operate very differently from state to state. In some states, being a legislator is a part-time role; in others, it's a full-time job. There are also huge differences in how often legislatures meet, and in the size of the legislatures themselves (all determined by what's in the state constitution).

See the opposite page for a side-by-side view of some of these features for Florida, Michigan, New York, New Hampshire, and Washington, to give some color as to how they can differ.[20]

As you can see from the table, for New York state senators like Alessandra Biaggi, the legislative session runs from January through June. Then, from the end of June through December, legislators are back in their districts during recess (though, as we know, this doesn't mean that they're not working!). Sen. Biaggi has a large team in both locations, but they have different responsibilities: "In Albany, [the team's responsibilities are] mainly legislative and budget issues; in the district, it's constituent affairs."[21] This is similar to the experiences of members of Congress, who are mostly focused on legislating while they are in Washington, DC, and on constituent engagement

	Type of role for legislators (full-time/part-time)	Legislator salary	Total number of state legislative staff working in the state legislature[22]	2020 session calendar (exact dates vary year to year)[23]
Florida	Hybrid (estimated 70% of a full-time job)	$29,697	1,613	January 14 through March 19
Michigan	Full-time	$71,685/year (plus $10,800/year expense allowance for session and interim)	817	January 8 through the end of the year
New Hampshire	Part-time	$200/two-year term (or $100 per year)	150	January 8 through June 30
New York	Full-time	$110,000/year	2,865	January 8 through the end of the year
Washington	Hybrid (estimated 70% of a full-time job)	$48,731/year (plus $120 per diem while in session)	793	January 13 through March 12

when they're back in their districts. In fact, legislators across the country have to strike this same balance between operations in their home districts and those in the capital, whether that capital is Washington, DC; Albany; or, as for New Hampshire state representative Safiya Wazir, Concord, New Hampshire (*read more about Rep. Wazir in the Advocate in Action profile on page 68*).

For Rep. Wazir, an Afghan American representative and one of the first former refugees to serve in the New Hampshire Senate, her "main job is to represent the people of Ward 8, District 17, in Concord, New Hampshire. I am constantly talking to people, answering emails, and researching issues that range from honoring veterans to safety issues. I have testified at many hearings before my own committee (for example, on my colleague Cassie Levesque's bill to raise the marriage age) and other committees. I serve on the Children and Family Law committee, so I attend meetings there, listen to testimony from people, which can be heart-wrenching at times, and research the issues being presented."[24] Once bills make it out of committee, they "go to the full legislature for hearings and votes, and you can find me there, voting on hundreds of bills."

Keep in mind that part-time legislators like Wazir are paid extremely little for their service; as you saw in the table on page 61, it's just about $100 a year for New Hampshire state legislators. For these reasons, Wazir says, "it can be hard to get young people to serve. I am fortunate to have family help with childcare. Still, it requires a lot of very hard work to hold down a paid job, serve in this important elected public position, and juggle important family responsibilities." For Wazir, however, it's worth it: "Although it's hard to raise three children while serving as a state representative, I think my children and others will see the big possibilities in their own lives and futures by seeing my example. Ultimately, it's worth overcoming the challenges."[25]

The pace of a state leader's day, especially while in session, can be relentless. Here's how Sen. Biaggi explained her "typical day" when in session:

> The reality is, from January to June, when I'm in Albany, what the day looks like is you wake up and you go to the capitol, you sit in something called a conference, which is basically just a meeting of all the Democratic senators in a room. You talk about the agenda for the day; you talk about the issues coming up; you talk about our specific issues that we care about. You basically are lobbying for your own [legislation] to move and to get passed, and you're in that room sometimes for an hour, sometimes for two, sometimes for ten. And then you go to the floor to vote, and you could be there for, again—we spent 18 hours in there one night. During the budget season, which is in March, you could have twenty-hour days.[26]

She also shared the very personal cost of a legislator's intense schedule and responsibilities:

> When you're in Albany and the demands on you are to be vigilant, to pay attention, to make sure that things don't get put into the thousand-page budget that shouldn't be in there, that things aren't getting removed that *should* be there, you have to follow the games

and who's aligning with who and what's going on—it takes an incredible amount of energy . . . to stand up and be thoughtful, to be on the record, to speak eloquently about your district and how this [legislation] impacts it or to speak against things because that's also very important. It takes all of you, all of the time.

In my first session . . . I did a town hall almost every weekend. I would come home and do events, and it wasn't enough. It was basically seven days a week, sometimes twenty-hour days, most of the time fourteen-hour days, and it still wasn't enough. And I kept pushing and pushing and pushing myself, to the point where at the end of the year, I got really sick. There's a picture of me on the front of the *New York Times* passing the sexual harassment legislation, and it took every piece of me . . . I had nothing left to give. So there's a picture of me on the cover of the *New York Times*, hugging the [senate majority] leader, but I had just thrown up in a garbage can.[27]

Our elected officials are there to serve us; how can we help *them* so that they can better fulfill this goal? First, we can understand when they're in session (and why they can't always be in our district), and better understand what they're doing when they're there. We can continue to push and advocate for the change we want to see, while also understanding that our elected officials are working hard on many competing priorities. Second, says Biaggi, is to show more patience and kindness—which I think is advice that everyone can get behind.

HOW A BILL BECOMES A LAW AT THE STATE LEVEL

At the state level, the process of a bill becoming a law is much the same as at the federal level. First, the bill is introduced in one of the two chambers, goes through committee, and comes to the floor for a vote. Then, depending on its passage there and in the other chamber, it goes to the governor, who signs it into law (or vetoes it). Each state has slightly different rules and processes (and Nebraska has just one legislative chamber!), but in general, the procedures should feel familiar.

Here's a quick overview of the legislative process in New Hampshire, my home state, to give you a sense of how state legislative processes are similar to, but can also differ from, the federal one:

STEP 1: BILL INTRODUCTION

The legislator introducing the bill (whether they serve in the house or the senate) files the bill with the Office of Legislative Services, and the bill is submitted to the clerk's office. The senate president or house speaker assigns the bill to the appropriate committee.

STEP 2: ACTION BY THE COMMITTEE

The assigned committee holds the necessary meetings. New Hampshire has a rule that public hearings must be announced to citizens at least 72 hours in advance and be listed on the state's official website.

At the federal level, House and Senate leadership may choose to assign a bill to a committee—if they don't assign it to a committee, the bill can die in that legislative session. But in New Hampshire, every single bill that gets introduced is required both to be assigned to a policy committee and later to be sent to the floor for a full vote. The members of the committee review the bill, then present it to the full house or senate along with a recommendation—that the bill pass, that it be amended, that it be referred back to committee for additional study, or that it be defeated. All bills move to the floor, along with the respective committee's recommendation, for a full vote; unlike at the federal level, there's no such thing as a bill dying in committee!

STEP 3: FLOOR VOTE

The bill is brought to the floor for a vote, where the committee presents its recommendation for the bill (i.e., whether it should be made it into law). This is followed by full-floor debate. The flow of the discussion on the floor has rules: to ensure fair airing of pros and cons, those who oppose the committee's decision must alternate speaking with those who support the committee's decision. After the floor debate, the full body votes on whether to accept the committee's recommendation; typically, they do.

If the bill is defeated or referred back to the committee for additional study, the bill does not move to the other legislative chamber—but if it passes, it is referred to the other chamber, where it undergoes another committee hearing and another floor vote.

In New Hampshire and many other states, this process for going from one chamber to another has a deadline; there is a designated "crossover day" that serves as the date by which all house bills have to go to the senate, and all senate bills have to go to the house. The exact date varies from state to state. New Hampshire's crossover day, for example, is March 26, about midway through the legislative session. If the legislatures don't meet that deadline, the bill cannot be moved along for a vote.

STEP 4: GOVERNOR'S DECISION

Once the house and senate both pass the bill (and agree on an amended version, if the versions of the bill passed in each chamber differ from one another), the bill goes to New Hampshire's governor. The governor has five days to veto the bill; if the governor does nothing in those five days, the bill automatically becomes law. The veto can be overridden by a two-thirds vote in both houses.

As you can see, New Hampshire's legislative process is pretty similar to the process at the federal level, with just a few important differences: for instance, the rules governing floor votes, "crossover day," and the timeline for gubernatorial vetoes.

During this process, there are many opportunities to get involved in shaping state legislation on a wide range of topics. Your state government works on a *lot* of diverse legislation. You can take a look at your state legislature's hearings schedule to see what I mean, or the schedule of votes, or the schedule of meetings. To illustrate, here's a list of meetings that took place at the New Hampshire state legislature on September 16, 2019. Take a look at the range of issues state-elected officials were discussing that day:[28]

- Commission to Study the Environmental and Health Effects of Evolving 5G Technology

- Committee to Study Tiny Houses

- Commission to Study Career Pathways from Full-Time Service Year Programs to Postsecondary Education and Employment

Opportunities in Support of New Hampshire's Future Workforce Need

- Committee to Study Providing Certain Health Care Services While Ensuring Increased Access to Affordable Health Care Services in Rural Areas of the State

- New Hampshire Drinking Water and Groundwater Advisory Commission

- Commission on Aging

- Committee to Study the Use of Tax Incentives for Promoting Development of Dense Workforce Housing in Community Centers

- Mushroom Foraging Study Commission

- Committee to Study the Effects of Past New Hampshire Trust Code Legislation

- Division for Children, Youth, and Families Advisory Board

Tiny houses! Drinking water! Tax incentives! Employment opportunities! Mushroom foraging! As you can see, the state legislature studies, introduces, and enacts bills that affect all kinds of things. And that's just one day of what's going on in one state house. If there's an issue you care passionately about, I can almost guarantee you that there's an opportunity to engage your state government to work on it.

THE IMPORTANCE OF STATE-LEVEL ENGAGEMENT

What I love the most about state legislatures is illustrated by the following advice on New Hampshire's state legislature website, on the actual, official explanation page for how a bill becomes a law:

You have many opportunities to impact this process, including testifying at hearings, writing letters or making phone calls to your representatives, or working with organizations to create awareness of the possible impact of a piece of legislation. You should know that New Hampshire's "citizen legislature" is a great source of state pride, and that Representatives and Senators welcome phone calls at home since many of them don't have offices at the State House, and have little to no staff to help them gather information.[29]

Not only does this lay out ways for you to influence policy, it encourages you to engage because your involvement will also make the policy *better* and the state legislators *more informed*. It's a source of state pride! Granted, I don't think this means that legislators want people calling their home incessantly or at all hours of the day and night, but it does demonstrate the importance of being part of the process.

While I've used a New Hampshire example here, the takeaway remains the same, regardless of what state you're from: your participation in state-level government is critically important. This means knowing your state legislators and knowing how the system works, particularly around how decisions get made—after all, those decisions have the power to change lives.

Advocate in Action: Safiya Wazir, New Hampshire State Representative*

Safiya Wazir is an Afghan American community activist and politician, and a member of the New Hampshire House of Representatives. Prior to elected office, she worked with the Heights community of Concord as a director of its Community Action Program and a vice chairwoman of its Head Start Policy Council. Wazir is one of the first former refugees to serve in the New Hampshire State House.

On running for and serving in office:

I graduated from college and became increasingly involved in issues affecting my community, focusing mostly on children. I got involved with Head Start, a program that advocates for early childhood education, and soon began serving on their policy council. Later, I joined the board of the Community Action Program of Belknap-Merrimack Counties, which offers more than 70 programs helping people from children to senior citizens. After I received an Unsung Hero Award from the New Hampshire Children's Trust, friends and peers began to encourage me to run for office.

I knocked on many doors, talked with hundreds of people, beat the incumbent in a primary election, and went on to win. I am thankful to have been part of this year's efforts to eliminate the death penalty, move paid family and medical leave forward, work on the state budget, testify on implementing a minimum wage in the state, and so much more important work to make sure New Hampshire is a great place for everyone, young and old, long-term resident and newcomer, to live.

On the importance (and challenges) of getting more women's voices in state leadership:

Sadly, I have seen male legislators mock women who were testifying for "clutching their pearls" over gun safety issues. About 34 percent of legislators in New Hampshire are women, so our numbers are still small, but we have had women in leadership positions. I was especially inspired by my state's first all-female US congressional delegation. Women have wisdom to share on issues that men, primarily retired men, do not. We want to speak on workplace issues, economic issues, and more. I think women are seeing more role models, but we need to encourage more of them to run for office.

---

* Safiya Wazir, written interview with the author, September 22, 2019 (adapted for clarity).

I gave birth to my third child last January, just at the start of our session, so I sometimes brought my new baby with me when I went to the State House. It's great to see other young parents like myself serving in the legislature. A few years ago, the average age in the New Hampshire legislature was 66 and it was declared the "oldest" legislature in the country. That has changed.

Don't be shy about getting started. Once I reached out, I received tremendous support and training from organizations (for example, New Hampshire Young Democrats, Emily's List, the New Hampshire Democratic Party). I raised money for signs, fliers, and more, most from people who had been strangers. Be a good listener. Show respect, even to your opponents. Respond to people's concerns. Be grateful, generous, and always thank those who help you.

On how to better engage your state representatives:

Where I live there are amazing grassroots organizations (for example, the Kent Street Coalition) that people can get involved in. For me, it started with Head Start's board. Join an organization. If there isn't a group, start one.

I've had people email me, write to me, or ask me to have a cup of coffee. I've met people over lunch in the State House. Mostly, when I was knocking on someone's door and they shared a story of personal struggle and then put the ball in my court. I would look into their issue, reflect on it, remember it, and get back to them.

Ask your officials what they are doing; tell them how something affects you and those you know and ask them to get back to you with information and an update. They work for you!

CHAPTER 4

. . . .

LOCAL GOVERNMENT

We know there is power when [women] serve on boards and commissions. We know there is power when we are at the table making the decisions that impact our lives ... when we come together and vote, we make magic happen. We make change happen.
                    —London Breed, Mayor of San Francisco, in a speech
                    kicking off Women's History Month (2020)

Local governments aren't the minor leagues any more than state governments are. These, too, are important bodies that shape policy and provide important services that often have more impact on your day-to-day life than the federal government. (For instance, as highlighted by responses to the Black Lives Matter protests, local governments often control police budgets and policies.) Numbers back up their importance: in fiscal year 2016, local government expenditures totaled $1.6 *trillion*—compared to state government expenditures of $1.4 trillion.[1] And while the federal expenditures for the same year were $4.3 trillion, consider that about *two-thirds* of federal expenditures are simply transfers to individuals or state and local governments.[2]

There is no explicit power carved out in the United States Constitution for county or municipal (i.e., town or city) governments, so a local government must be granted power by its state. Services that are impacted by local government include:

- Emergency services (e.g., police and fire departments)
- Hospitals
- Public housing
- Parks and recreation
- Libraries
- DMVs
- Local roads and highways
- Prisons
- Public transportation
- Public schools
- Zoning
- . . . and more

Local government, defined by the US census, falls into two categories: general purpose governments and special purpose governments.

GENERAL PURPOSE GOVERNMENTS

County, municipal, and township governments are all considered "general purpose governments," whereas school districts and special districts are "special purpose governments." It's a fairly complex system (and, surprise, surprise, varies considerably across the country), so let's dive into each, one by one.

COUNTY GOVERNMENT

If you didn't know that you had public officials at the county level, you're not alone. As County Commissioner Angela Conley, who serves Hennepin County in Minnesota (*learn more about Commissioner Conley in her Advocate in Action profile on page 79*), said, "A lot of people just didn't know what a county commissioner even was when I was running for office. The main question we'd get was: *She's running for what? What do they do?*" Rather than see this as a challenge, for Commissioner Conley, this was an opportunity. "We started explaining to people: *This is what a county commission is responsible for; this is what we do; this is the impact we have on your lives.* You have a county road outside your home, and it's dangerous and your kids are afraid to cross it? Well, you need to contact your commissioner about road safety on that county road. You're living in or experiencing poverty or know someone who's going hungry? Well, our health and human services, that's where people go to apply for benefits to get back on their feet. We're in charge of the county jails, so if you're thinking about mass incarceration and the ways that Hennepin County can put a stop to it, you want to go to your county commission ... As commissioners, it's our jobs to be paying attention to these things."[3]

These aren't small operations, either. For example, in Hennepin County, the budget is $2.5 billion.[4] Organized county governments are found in every state in the US except for Connecticut and Rhode Island—although they're known as "boroughs" in Alaska and "parishes" in Louisiana.[5] In addition to county commissioners, other elected county officials vary from state to state but can include roles like the county clerk (who oversees voter registration and potentially verifies election results), the county sheriff, or treasurer.

MUNICIPAL GOVERNMENT

In addition to counties, local government is also organized at the municipal level. These are towns and cities, and they lie *within* the counties (although they can technically cross county boundaries).[6] Municipal governments can be structured in a number of ways. The executive role at the municipal level is typically a mayor, who is either elected directly by the people or appointed by an elected council. The mayoral position might be filled by the same person for the duration of the position's tenure, or it might be filled by various members of the council on a rotating basis. The legislative branch of municipal government is typically some sort of city council, and the people on that council can be called council members, freeholders, trustees, selectpersons, or commissioners. Municipal charters lay out the powers and organization of the municipal government, similar to how powers and organization of the federal government are laid out in the US Constitution.

According to the National League of Cities, the five most common forms of municipal governments are:[7]

- **Council–Manager (*most common*):** An elected city council sets the budget and creates policy, and the mayor is often chosen from the council and serves on a rotating basis. Phoenix, Arizona; Topeka, Kansas; and Rockville, Maryland, all use this form of government.

- **Mayor–Council (*second most common*):** An elected council makes policy and introduces legislation, but the mayor is elected separately from the council. Often the mayor has significant authority, although it depends on the municipal charter. New York, New York; Minneapolis, Minnesota; and Houston, Texas, all use this form of government.

- **Commission (*oldest form*):** Voters elect commissioners to a small governing board, with each commissioner responsible for one area of focus, like the police or public works. One of the commissioners is designated as chairperson or mayor. Less than 1 percent of cities use this form of government today; examples that do are Sunrise, Florida, and Fairview, Tennessee.

- **Town Meeting:** Voters themselves meet on an ongoing basis to determine policy and then elect officials to execute those policies. As you can imagine, this system is only practical with a relatively small population. For example, Marblehead, Massachusetts (with a population of just under 20,000[8]), uses this form of government.

- **Representative Town Meeting:** Voters choose a large number of citizens to represent them at town meetings, and those elected citizens serve as the legislative body (although all citizens are permitted to attend the town meetings). Similar to the town meeting model, a smaller group of elected officials are then responsible for implementing those policies. Typically found in New England municipalities; Bowdoin, Maine, and Lexington, Massachusetts, both use this form of government.

Given that municipal government structures can vary so much from place to place, it's best to take a look at your official town or city website to understand what it looks like where you live (there typically will be a section on your local government as well as various agencies and departments). How is *your* municipal government structured? Take a few minutes to research what *your* municipal government looks like—after all, you can't influence local outcomes without knowing the structure and the process for how policies are introduced and passed.

For an example of what can be done at the municipal level, take the work of former city councilwoman Julissa Ferreras-Copeland. From 2010 to 2017, she served on New York's city council and was the first Latina to be elected to political office in Queens. She was also the first woman, first person of color, and youngest person to be elected to the council's finance chair, where she oversaw New York City's $82 billion annual budget. While in office she expanded paid sick leave to ensure that survivors of domestic abuse, stalking, sexual assault, or trafficking can take time off of work without worrying about their financial security[9]—the first such legislation to pass in any city in the country. She also brought to light the fact that there was a *luxury* tax on feminine hygiene products sold in New York City. I don't know about you, but I definitely don't consider things like pads or tampons to be luxury items, and I don't even want to imagine the conversation among old white dudes that had to happen for that to be the law of the land. To address this, she sponsored legislation to get rid of the luxury tax *and* legislation that guaranteed access to menstrual hygiene products in schools, prisons, and shelters.[10]

Nothing minor league about any of that!

TOWNSHIP GOVERNMENT

The final category of general purpose local government you need to know about is a township. Sometimes counties are divided into townships; those townships can comprise many towns and are often governed by an elected board of three to five trustees.

States with township governments include Connecticut, Illinois, Indiana, Kansas, Maine, Massachusetts, Michigan, Minnesota, Missouri, Nebraska, New Hampshire, New Jersey, New York, North Dakota, Ohio, Pennsylvania, Rhode Island, South Dakota, Vermont, and Wisconsin—20 states in total. As you can see, townships tend to be most common in the Northeastern and Midwestern states.[11]

SPECIAL PURPOSE GOVERNMENTS

Now that we've gone through the forms of general purpose government, let's review special purpose governments.

SCHOOL DISTRICTS

In the US, there are two types of school districts: independent and dependent school districts. Dependent school districts are *not* counted as separate governments; instead, they're agencies of local, county, or state governments. Independent school districts, on the other hand, have been designated by state law as having sufficient administrative and fiscal autonomy to qualify as a separate, special purpose government.[12] This means that they're able to operate in a similar way to a municipal government in the sense that they're accountable for the services they provide, and they may exercise powers of taxation and eminent domain.

Boards ranging from 5 to 15 members typically run these districts. The board is responsible for things like setting policies and appointing a superintendent (who is responsible for school administration). The majority of board members are elected, although in some cases they are appointed. In Oakland, California, for example, out of the ten board members, the mayor appoints three, and seven are elected. In Baltimore, Maryland, on the other hand, the state government and mayor jointly appoint all members.[13]

SPECIAL DISTRICTS

Last but not least, there are special districts. As of 2017, the most common form of special district was for fire protection (5,975 in total).[14] Why would this type of district exist? Wouldn't county or municipal governments be responsible for fire protection?

Here's an explanation from the US census:

> In some cases, states create [special districts] to provide services to newly developed geographic areas. In other cases, the special purpose activity or services already exist, but residents expect a higher level of quality. For example, a state may have fire protection services. However, the established governmental structure may not legally allow the fire district to raise enough funds to maintain the desired level of quality services. That's when a state may choose to create a special district. Most special districts can levy additional property or sales taxes and may borrow money to buy or build facilities by issuing bonds. Some districts are only active for a limited time, usually as long as it takes to pay back a debt.[15]

Wherever you live, you almost *certainly* have general purpose local governments: you likely have representation at the *county* level (unless, of course, you live in Rhode Island or Connecticut), as well as a more local form of government (be it at the *municipal* or *township* level). You also *may* have *special purpose* governments; for example, you may have an independent school district. Who knew local government could be so complex?

I currently live in the city of Seattle, Washington, which is part of King County. I have elected officials at the county level, as well as in the city of Seattle; our city government is governed by a mayor (our city executive) and city council members (all of whom are elected by Seattle residents). In Seattle, the city council acts as the city's legislative body.

Now let's look at an example where the municipal structure is totally different: I grew up in Stratham, New Hampshire, where I also had county-level officials (Stratham is part of Rockingham County). But, unlike Seattle, Stratham is governed by a town board of three elected members, and day-to-day operations are run by a town administrator, who is selected by the town board. In Stratham, it's actually the *voters* assembled at the annual town meeting who act as the town's legislative body, rather than a city council.[16]

In short, there's no one form of local government. It really does vary tremendously from place to place.

FINAL THOUGHTS ON FEDERAL, STATE, AND LOCAL GOVERNMENT

Perhaps the most important thing to remember as we wrap up this section is that state and local government are often where you can have the most impact, because the public officials who serve at this level are closer to their constituents; similarly, the policy that is enacted at these levels often has greater impact on your life. It's unfortunate that activity at these levels of government gets comparatively little attention, but the good news is: that same lack of attention can also be an opportunity! It's an opportunity to learn a lot (if you don't feel you know much about state and local government today), as well as an opportunity to get involved where there is relatively less constituent engagement (in other words, less competition).

As we move into Part II, on tips and tools for your own advocacy, you'll need to think hard about which level of government has the greatest influence on the issues that you care about most. For example, if your issue is that pothole in your street, you'd likely want to engage with your local government, since that would probably be under their jurisdiction. If your issue is K through 12 education, and you have independent school districts, you would want to engage the school board that serves in that district. Or if you care about prison reform, that would likely involve advocating at both the local and/or the state level, as the majority of inmates today are incarcerated in local (e.g., county) or state jails. If you care about safety on interstate highways or foreign policy, however, you'd likely want to engage your federal representatives. Understanding who is in charge of the policy that is impacting you or your community is critical to having influence on it.

And even if you're really eager to drive federal change, remember that a lot of important legislation introduced at the federal level is tested out at the state and local levels first. Take the Affordable Care Act, for example, which was based largely on universal health care legislation introduced in Massachusetts in 2006 (after it was hugely successful there), or marriage equality (Vermont in 2009), or what's happening now with marijuana legalization (Colorado and Washington in 2012).

I know all of this can seem overwhelming (our government is complex!), so don't feel like you need to memorize all of it. The past few chapters are meant to serve as a reference guide for when you need to quickly brush up on the details, or when you move to a different state or city and need to figure out your state and local government all over again. But understanding that there are multiple levels of government, what's happening in each, and having a complete picture of who represents you at all levels is critical—all of which we'll pull together in the Part I Workbook.

Advocate in Action: Angela Conley, County Commissioner for Hennepin County, Minnesota*

Angela Conley is county commissioner for Hennepin County, Minnesota, where she serves as the first African American elected to the Hennepin County Board. Prior to winning elected office, she worked for over 20 years in public services at the state and county levels. She received a bachelor's degree in social work from St. Catherine University and a master's degree in public administration from Hamline University. In office, she holds numerous leadership positions, including as Hennepin County Health and Human Services Committee chair, Heading Home Hennepin co-chair, and Hennepin County Housing and Redevelopment Authority vice chair.

On changing the system from the Inside:

For me it was always, "What can I do at the ground level to bring about change?" I never saw myself in politics, much less elected office. Minnesota is not a very diverse state. Typically our representatives are very white and that can be a big turnoff for many community members. I was so tired of seeing government make decisions that were not guided by the voices of people that have actual experience in the issues.

We had never had any person of color elected to county leadership even though people of color made up 40 percent of Hennepin County at the time I first ran. That percentage was even larger in the city of Minneapolis. I remember the county board went on a retreat to talk about racial disparities—this was an all-white board. When I expressed how upset I was about this retreat, my friends were like, "You need to run for office." I was still doubting myself until someone else announced their run and my friend was like, "Do you see this? You need to begin now." What ultimately made me decide to run was seeing the failures of the system and feeling like I had no voice.

On the importance of organizing and engaging the community:

I was—still am—an activist, but I felt like my real power was listening to folks who are directly impacted by the issues and treating them like the experts. I was an organizer, activist, protester. When I was running for office, I was very unapologetic about calling the system broken—and that I intended to get in there and start chipping away at the levels of institutional oppression that put us in the same position year after year after year.

---

* Angela Conley, interview with the author, September 30, 2019 (adapted for clarity).

When I chaired the Bryant neighborhood organization on the South Side, we shifted to a community-values platform. We surveyed our neighbors, drafted questions, and called a mayoral forum. There were questions about reparations and land use, about what they could do to give back to communities that have historically been stolen from. It took organizing around these issues so that we could call out our elected officials to do more. The organizing is huge.

On prioritizing your issues:

I was asked the question once, "Angela, you care about so much, how do you focus?" For me, it's: think about the one issue that hits you the hardest, that hits you in your gut. And that's the issue you rally around. For me, that was housing and homelessness, specifically unsheltered homelessness. It doesn't have to be a laundry list of things you want to fix. Yes, the system is incredibly broken, but movement happens one step at a time.

On empowering others:

The thing that touches me the most is that there have been so many young Black women who have met with me or called me or sent me thank-you letters because we inspired them to run for office. When I say "we," I'm talking about myself and everyone who came out to volunteer with me, knock on doors with me, organize with me. It was a people-powered campaign. This job and career I have now is a people-powered career. As the first Black Hennepin County commissioner in history, I was very visible, but I said during the campaign: I don't care if we win or lose— internally, I did care—as long as we showed young girls, young women of color, that this is possible, that if you run with your full self and stick to your issues, you can do this; it's not out of reach for you.

I wanted people to see a Black woman with a huge Afro running for office, and ultimately we won. Now that I am in this role, I am part of this system and it's my responsibility to change the narrative, to ask the tough questions that have probably never been asked before, to push and push against the status quo and continue to do that every single day.

PART I WORKBOOK

At this point, we've walked through federal, state, and local government structures, their key responsibilities, and how legislation gets passed. Now it's time to bring it all together and look at our overall representation.

I live in Seattle, Washington. Based on the congressional and legislative districts I'm part of, the next page lists who my political officials are as of October 2020, and some basic information about them, including gender, party affiliation, and committees on which they serve (the committees your officials serve on can give you a good indication of what issues might be a priority for them, or on which issues they have the most expertise/influence, so it's important information to know).

	Elected office	Name	Gender
Federal	Senator (1 of 2)	Sen. Maria Cantwell	F
	Senator (2 of 2)	Sen. Patricia Murray	F
	Representative	Rep. Adam Smith	M
State	Governor	Gov. Jay Inslee	M
	Lt. Governor	Lt. Gov. Cyrus Habib	M
	State Senator	Sen. Rebecca Saldana	F
	State Representative(s)	Rep. Sharon Tomiko Santos (Position 1)	F
		Rep. Eric Pettigrew (Position 2)	M

Party	Years served in office	Committee assignments
D	2000–present	• Commerce, Science and Transportation (Ranking Member) • Energy and Natural Resources • Finance • Indian Affairs • Small Business and Entrepreneurship
D	1992–present	• Health, Education, Labor & Pensions (HELP) (Ranking Member) • Appropriations • Budget • Veterans Affairs
D	1997–present	• Armed Services (chair)
D	1993–present	N/A
D	2016–present	N/A
D	2016–present	• Transportation (vice chair) • Labor & Commerce • State Government, Tribal Relations & Elections
D	1998–present	• Education (chair) • Capital Budget • Consumer Protection & Business
D	2003–present	• Appropriations • Public Safety • Rules • Rural Development, Agriculture & Natural Resources

	Elected office	Name	Gender
Local	**County Executive** *(e.g., county executive, county manager, or county mayor)*	County Executive Dow Constantine	M
	County Representative *(e.g., county commissioner)*	Council Member Girmay Zahilay	M
	Local Executive *(e.g., mayor)*	Mayor Jenny Durkan	F
	Local Representative(s) *(e.g., city council member, town board member)*	Council Member Tammy Morales	F

So, what does all of this tell me?

Gender diversity: One of the first things that I can see from this table is the gender of my representatives—you can probably guess that I'm excited and proud to have such a large number of women political officials representing me. (They're considerably overrepresented in leadership in my district compared to the average, considering women make up approximately 20 percent of leadership in federal and most state governments.) An incredible wealth of role models!

Tenure: As we discussed earlier, term lengths vary for each body (for example, one term for a senator is six years, and one term for a

Party	Years served in office	Committee assignments
D	2009–present	N/A
D	2019–present (first term)	• Law and Justice (chair)
D	2017–present (first term)	N/A
D	2019–present (first term)	• Community Economic Development (chair) • Sustainability & Renters' Rights (vice chair) • Public Safety & Human Services • Transportation & Utilities • Select Committee on Homelessness • Select Committee on Labor

representative is only two years), but even so, I can see that there's quite a bit of diversity in how many terms (and years) my political officials have served. For those who have served for a substantial period of time, there is likely quite a bit of evidence for me to look at with regard to their past voting records, their public statements, and legislation they've introduced or sponsored. Lots to dig into to better understand their priorities.

Interests and influence: Committee assignments often reflect members' interests or expertise (especially for those who are chairs or ranking members). But it's also important to remember that people serving on a particular committee have a lot of *influence* when it comes to those issues in particular. Committees are crucial to weighing in on potential legislation and whether it moves forward for a floor vote. So if the issue that you've prioritized maps to a committee assignment of your elected officials, this is important to note as you begin your advocacy efforts.

One critical thing this information does *not* tell me, however, is my representatives' level of representative-ness. Even if it's the case that you're a Democrat represented by Democratic officials, or you're a Republican represented by Republican officials, it would be a mistake to assume shared party affiliation means you're all set and your work as a citizen advocate is done. Just because your representatives share your party does not mean that they are representing your interests—especially when it comes to the issues that you care about *most*. To evaluate that, you need to know not only who your representatives are, but also their priorities, their activities in office, and what makes them tick.

Now it's your turn! Use the section on pages 88 to 89 to create your own reference guide for how your government is set up, particularly at the state and local level, and then who represents you across all levels, as I did above. Even if you feel like you already know this stuff, don't skip it! Use it as a test for yourself—fill out as much as you can, and then check your answers with a little online research.

Remember, local government can look pretty different across different cities and towns, and names of elected positions may not be consistent from place to place. Do some research to figure out what your local government looks like: Is there a county board or a council? Does your town or city have a mayor? Is there a city council or town board? Use this information to fill out the questions later in the workbook about who represents you as well.

Here are a few resources that may help, especially as you learn more about your state government:

- **National Conference of State Legislatures, or NCSL:** Includes resources for bill tracking at the state level, session calendars, "legislatures at a glance" (with information on the size of each state legislature, term limits, state legislature size, house and senate state leadership, and an overview of gender and racial composition of state legislatures), and more.

- **StateScape:** Provides detailed, helpful overviews of how your state government is set up and operates, including the legislative process in your state, a look at your state's political landscape (e.g., which party has control at the state level, session schedules, key deadlines like bill crossover and bill-signing deadlines), and more.

- **Your state legislature's official website:** What's included here will vary state to state, but it will have lots of important information about your state government, from where the state house and state senate are located, to biographies and contact information for legislators, to dates and logistics for upcoming hearings, to your state's constitution. Often, your state legislature website will have educational resources on ways that you can have influence on the legislative process as well—a critical resource.

Okay, so you've got a better sense of the overall structures in your state and city or town. Now, who represents you in your district? Fill out the section on pages 90 to 93.

Here are some resources you can use to fill in the table:

- **Ballotpedia:** Provide your home and email addresses, and Ballotpedia will provide an overview of who represents you in Congress and statewide offices (including judges and commissioners, your state senator, and state representative), as well as local information.

- **Common Cause:** Similar to Ballotpedia, providing your home address gives you access to your federal and state representatives, as well as links to their official websites, phone numbers, Twitter accounts, Facebook pages, and even their YouTube channels.

- **Other resources: IssueVoter.org, Congress.gov**, Google, or your elected officials' websites (many elected officials, if not all, will have individual websites that talk about their experience, qualifications, and what they've done to date). State and local government official sites have this information as well, if you need help figuring out who represents your district.

Your Government Structure

		Number of officials total	Term length
Federal	**Senators**	2	6 years
	Representatives		2 years
State	**State Senators**		
	State Representatives		
Local	**County Officials**		
	Township Officials (if applicable)		
	City/Town Officials *(e.g., mayor, city council member, as applicable)*		

Term limits	Part time or full time	Annual salary	Time in session
None	Full time	$174,000*	All year
None	Full time	$174,000*	All year

* There are some nuances in terms of salaries in the federal government for those in leadership positions. For example, the president pro tempore of the Senate earns $193,400, as do the majority and minority leader of the Senate.

Your Representatives

	Elected office	Name	Gender	
Federal	Senator (1 of 2)			
	Senator (2 of 2)			
	Representative			
State	Governor			
	Lt. Governor			

	Party	Years served in office	Committee assignments

	Elected office	Name	Gender
State	**State Senator**		
	State Representative		
Local	**County Executive** *(e.g., county executive, county manager, or county mayor)*		
	County Representative *(e.g., county commissioner)*		
	Local Executive *(e.g., mayor)*		
	Local Representative *(e.g., city council member, town board member)*		

Party	Years served in office	Committee assignments

As you look at the entire table, how do your representatives stack up in terms of gender diversity? Tenure? Any other observations or things you notice about your elected officials? Note that this is *not* an exhaustive list of elected officials that serve at the federal, state, and local levels. Other important positions include judges, sheriffs, attorneys general, district attorneys, and secretaries of state, to name just a few. It's important to know who these folks are, especially if it's a position that has influence on an issue that you care about. You can use the above resources to identify all elected officials at each level of government, not just your representatives.

Gender diversity (could also include other important dimensions of diversity, e.g., race/ethnicity)	
Tenure	
Other observations	

Once you've filled out the above and have a better understanding of your representation at all levels, here are ways to keep the momentum going:

- **Dig deeper.** Now that you have a little more information about your representatives and who they are, don't stop there! Read about their backgrounds, what they were doing before they got into politics, and what seems to motivate them (buy their books if they've written them!). Use **OpenSecrets** to take a look at what organizations and causes are donating to their campaigns. We'll talk in the next chapter about how all of this knowledge can be channeled into power and influence. If you're unsure of their issue positions, call their offices. And don't worry if it seems hard to find unbiased information about representatives, especially on key issues. We'll talk about this in Part II.

- **Create ways for updates to come to you.** Now that you know who your representatives are, make it easy to keep track of what they're doing. If you're on social media, follow them there. Sign up for their newsletters. This may not be the most unbiased information, but it will let you keep tabs on them with minimal effort. If you're looking for a more in-depth picture of their activities, create a Google alert with their name that automatically collects all articles mentioning or about them and sends them to your email inbox; you can choose to receive these alerts daily, weekly, or as articles are published.

- **Make sure you understand how legislation gets enacted at the state and local levels.** We walked through how a bill becomes a law in New Hampshire, but make sure you understand the basic mechanisms for how bills become law in your state and city/town. You can't influence the process if you don't understand how the process works! **StateScape** and the official state legislature website are good places to start at the state level. Similarly, your city or town almost certainly has an official website that lays out the process for your municipality (and, at the very least, your city/town official's name and contact information). I grew up in a town with a population of a little over 7,000—and even we had a town website with basic information!

Finally, if you identify with a particular party, there are plenty of clubs and communities to engage with, especially at the local level. Do a little research to learn more about them, where they operate, who their leaders are, and meeting opportunities. (Google is a great resource for this. Just googling "Democrats of Seattle" led me to sites for Washington Democrats, Metropolitan Democratic Club of Seattle, and King County Democrats, to name a few! "Republicans of Seattle," similarly, directed me to the Washington State Republican Party and King County Republican Party websites. All of these had "Events" or "Get Involved" sections on their sites.) Oftentimes there are even volunteer opportunities with these groups! You can usually find like-minded groups to meet with even if you don't affiliate with one of the two major political parties.

Your Local Clubs and Communities

	Groups	Leadership/ organizers	Engagement opportunities
County level			
Legislative district level			
Municipal level			

PART II

TOOLS FOR INFLUENCE

CHAPTER 5

. . . .

YOUR ISSUES, YOUR VOICE

When I dare to be powerful—to use my strength in service of my vision—then it becomes less and less important whether I am afraid.
—Audre Lorde, *The Cancer Journals* (1980)

Many of us think that, to be an effective political advocate, we have to be an expert on everything: the details of every bill, every member of Congress, and every issue up for debate. This is not only untrue, it's unrealistic.

Of course it's good to be informed. Knowing more will help you advance the issues that matter most to you. Having a basic understanding of how the system is set up and works will enable you to navigate that system more effectively and have more influence within it. That's why we covered how government is structured and key processes (e.g., how bills get enacted) in Part I.

But should not knowing *everything* stop you from participating at all? As we've already established: absolutely *not*. For many of us, our goal should not be expertise as we traditionally think of it. After all, we have full lives: jobs, families, friends, hobbies, and volunteer commitments. If the bar for participation is being an "expert," we're setting ourselves up for failure. Many women (myself included) have a hard time wrapping their heads around this. We *want* to be experts, to have all the facts, to get the A+. While at CTI conducting research and focus groups, I heard over and over again that women wouldn't throw their hats in the ring for a job or promotion unless they met 10 out of 10 of the job requirements *already*. (Men, on the other hand, will apply with just half of the requirements.) But not only is this instinct damaging to our careers, it can prevent us from speaking up entirely, especially about the things that directly affect our lives. Besides, who knows more about your own personal experiences than you? You are already an expert on those issues, whether or not you think of it that way. You don't need to "know it all" to be a highly effective advocate for the issues that affect you and the communities in which you work and live. In fact, many women elected officials and professional, full-time advocates and activists I've spoken to originally became politically active because of *one specific issue* that was personally affecting them, their families, or their communities.

And make no mistake: the things that affect you personally *are* political issues. Your entire life has been shaped by the decisions of those in political office. Whether it's the sidewalk on which you learned to ride a bike as a kid, the financial aid that helped you pay for college, or the health care you rely on—so many things can be traced back to decisions made through and paid for by different levels of government.

The key to having impact on the issues you feel most strongly about is prioritization and focus—and zeroing in on the things that you care about most personally and most passionately is a good place to start. Inevitably, the issues most important to you will shift and change as the world changes, and as you change and have new life experiences. That's okay! As you build your political muscle and your issues evolve, you'll be able to shift your engagement; the tactics we'll walk through in this part of the book can be applied universally to *any* issue you care about.

As we get started, I want to point out that sometimes it's easy to miss the ways politics affect the issues that mean a lot to us—I can relate! Some of my most meaningful personal experiences and priority issues have been impacted by politics, and I wasn't fully aware of *how* at the time.

Here's an example: Growing up, sports had never been my "thing." Coaches, initially excited about my potential because of my height, would watch on the sidelines in horror at tryouts as I tripped over my feet in soccer, accidentally hit girls at bat in softball when I was pitching, or missed the backboard entirely when taking a shot in basketball. Every time, I would shuffle off the field or court and retreat gratefully back into my books.

When my ninth-grade English teacher suggested I try out for the rowing team, I was skeptical but did it anyway. During the two-mile tryout run, I trailed behind everyone. After a day with the oars, the skin on my hands blistered and tore, making washing my hair in the shower the next morning a painful experience. Everything hurt. But I stuck with it, and for the first time, I made the cut. By the end of the year, I was the fastest freshman on the team. Two years later, I was invited to the USRowing Under 19 Selection Camp, where I had the opportunity to row all summer with some of the best junior rowers in the country and tried out for the team that represented the US at the World Rowing Junior Championships.

Through rowing, my body became powerful and strong. It allowed me to tap into my competitive nature—who knew that the mild-mannered, quiet kid in class who had been described by teachers since the second grade as an "old soul" would become someone unable to play board games without alienating family members with my competitiveness? But more importantly, I began to see myself differently. I became increasingly confident. I stood taller. I spoke up in class more. I loved the egalitarian nature of rowing: the harder you worked, the better you got. Eventually, I was named captain of my high school team and even had the opportunity to row in college. I thought of myself more and more as a leader. And in college, juggling a twenty-hours-per-week training schedule with a full course load made me an expert-level project manager. I learned to work smarter (a necessity when literally every hour of my day needed to be scheduled and planned for).

The lessons I learned through rowing continue to serve me well (excluding, perhaps, my inability to take any kind of competition lightly). I've seen firsthand the power of teamwork and how the seemingly impossible can happen when a group of individuals work collaboratively in pursuit of a singular goal. I deeply believe in the importance of mentorship and coaching—both seeking it out and passing it on. Hard work, staying organized, and performance are necessary but insufficient without the guidance and support of others, especially when things get tough. And I believe that when someone is empowered to see herself as a leader, as successful, as powerful, in one (however small) dimension of her life, it can spill into and influence other dimensions. It did for me.

Here's the kicker: none of this would have happened for me without Congress passing Title IX in 1972.

A quick refresher on Title IX: It was the first time the United States government expressly guaranteed equal opportunities for women in school.

It states, in part: "No person in the United States shall, on the basis of sex, be excluded from participation in, be denied the benefits of, or be subjected to discrimination under any education program or activity receiving federal financial assistance."[1] In other words, in order to comply with Title IX, schools had to ensure women had the same opportunities that men had, including when it came to sports.

For me, the effects and opportunities offered as a result of Title IX absolutely changed the trajectory of my life. And these opportunities are firmly cemented in the realm of the political—their existence, after all, is the result of the passage of a bill introduced by politicians (more on that in a minute). When I graduated from Princeton in 2010—an institution that, only 41 years prior, had been completely closed to women—my graduating class consisted of 49 percent women.[2] I also graduated a four-year NCAA Division I varsity athlete. Without Title IX, the resources required for female athletes like me to compete most likely would not have existed.

My experience is not unique. The impact of Title IX, at least when it comes to women's increased participation in sports, has been far-reaching. Since Title IX was enacted, the number of women participating in college athletics has increased about sixfold[3]—and women now receive approximately 48 percent of grants-in-aid dollars at Division I schools (before Title IX, women's athletic scholarships were nonexistent).[4] This is real, measurable progress. There also seems to be a direct connection between women's participation in sports and their confidence and leadership: a study of 400 women executives found that 94 percent had participated in sports, with nearly two-thirds claiming that their involvement in sports had contributed to their career success.[5]

As *Guardian* columnist Moira Donegan pointed out following the dominance of the US women's soccer team in the 2019 World Cup, their success would not have been possible but for the opportunities created by Title IX. In 1972, there were approximately 700 girls playing soccer nationwide.[6] In the 2018–2019 season, there were 394,105 high school girls playing soccer.[7] Not to mention, opportunity begets opportunity: given the widespread and visible success of the US women's soccer team, it seems likely that even more young women will sign up to play.

As Donegan writes:

Nearly 50 years after Title IX became law, a generation of women has reaped the benefits of institutional support, professional development and education that the law provides, and many of them have gone on to successful athletic careers. Those careers were made by policy: Title IX effectively turned the American education system into the world's most successful women's sporting development organization. The success story of women's sports under Title IX shows how marginalized groups can be given opportunities through policy interventions; how the talents and passions of individuals can be fostered when they have institutional support.[8]

The enactment of Title IX also speaks to the importance of having at the decision-making table both women and men who support gender equality. Reps. Edith Green (D-OR) and Patsy Mink (D-HI) drafted the Title IX legislation, which Birch Bayh, a male senator from Indiana, then introduced in the Senate. On the Senate floor, Bayh said: "[This is] an important first step in the effort to provide for the women of America something that is rightfully theirs—an equal chance to attend the schools of their choice, to develop the skills they want, and to apply those skills with the knowledge that they will have a fair chance to secure the jobs of their choice with equal pay for equal work."[9]

It also speaks to the importance of the activism of individuals. In drafting the bill, Rep. Green relied on the work of Bernice Sandler, an educator who had personally experienced discrimination; she was rejected from several teaching jobs, in one case being told she was "just a housewife who went back to school."[10] She responded by working with the Women's Equity Action League to file complaints against colleges and universities regarding sex discrimination. As part of her research, she collected data and stories of women and academia, as well as built relationships with members of Congress—including Rep. Edith Green. As Green held congressional hearings on women's education and employment, Sandler herself served on the subcommittee staff. Those hearings, informed in large part by the work of Sandler, became the basis of the Title IX legislation. Sandler became known by many as the "Godmother of Title IX."[11]

Political action has *huge* potential to help (or hurt) us personally. Sometimes the experiences that we take for granted, experiences that we don't necessarily think of as "political," in many cases are. Whom we choose to represent us matters. What they do once we elect them matters. We have to pay attention and hold them accountable—but we also have to set our own priorities. One of mine is to fight for gender equality in all arenas.

From my time as a rower on a team of strong, powerful women to my job today, I've always worked and operated in a community of women dedicated to fostering a culture of mentorship and inclusion. I've always felt supported and encouraged by them. This, however, was in direct contrast to what I saw not only in the research I was part of while at CTI, but also in conversations with my female friends and peers who were coming up against obstacle after obstacle as they tried to advance in their careers: sexist bosses, vague feedback from managers loaded with bias (unconscious or otherwise), finding themselves responsible for taking meeting notes even when they were far from the most junior person in the room.

Title IX expanded numerous opportunities for women. That's great news. But there are still numerous challenges women face in college, even as women make up the majority of college graduates. Research shows that women's confidence actually *decreases* while at college, whereas men's increases. A study conducted by Princeton University found that women at Princeton were more likely than their male peers to make self-deprecating remarks, more likely to undersell themselves, and less likely to speak up in class.[12] Women are still far less likely to be represented in leadership positions on campus; the numbers have hardly budged since women began enrolling at Princeton in the late '60s (women constituted 8.6 percent of leadership positions in the 1970s, compared to just 17.1 percent in the 2000s).[13] Another study of 2,100 college campus students found that only 5 percent of women had held student government positions, compared to 8 percent of men.[14]

The prevalence of sexual assault on college campuses is another horrific reminder of how far we have to go when it comes to creating a college environment that fosters inclusion and equality: studies show that 23 percent of women on college campuses are sexually assaulted—that's *one in four* women.[15] (Under Title IX, discrimination on the basis of sex can include sexual harassment or sexual violence—and schools that fail to respond to and remedy a hostile environment are at risk of losing federal funding.) In 2019, students at Princeton protested inadequate implementation of Title IX protections at the school, calling for transparency of Title IX processes and decision-making procedures, as well as increased access to services for survivors, among other demands.[16] And the inequities of course don't end with college: women continue to face barriers in the workplace and in our broader society as well. These disparities, especially when they harm and limit women, must be addressed.

For many, the kinds of advantages, opportunities, and work environments I've had the privilege of being a part of do not exist. So it's important to me to support and do whatever I can to amplify women's voices—so, so critical but far too often sidelined, unheard, ignored, interrupted. It's what I worked with corporations to do while I was at CTI, and it's why I cofounded the All In Together Campaign. It's why I wrote this book! This is my issue.

So, you see that the personal is often rooted in the political—that even the things we take for granted as a part of our personal experiences are tied to the decisions of politicos and policy makers. You've heard about some of my priorities and what's shaped them. But we, as women, are not all the same, and the issues we care about aren't either. As you've likely already picked up from the Advocate in Action profiles, there are very specific issues that were catalysts for the women leaders featured throughout this book, whether they're advocates or elected officials. For County Commissioner Angela Conley, it was unsheltered homelessness. For New Hampshire state representative Safiya Wazir, it was issues affecting children. For cofounder and co-president of A Better Balance Sherry Leiwant (whom you'll hear from later), it was economic justice, particularly through a gender lens. The examples go on and on.

So the most important question is: What is *your* issue? For many of us, this is hard to answer, especially when everything feels like it's on fire. It's impossible to even sign into Twitter or Facebook these days without being bombarded by what's happening in the world. And it seems embarrassing to admit that this experience even feels like a bombardment: after all, knowing what's happening is important. But that avalanche of information can feel overwhelming. How do you choose the issues on which to stay informed and on which to act? It can be tempting to tune out completely.

What I've heard again and again in the workshops I've facilitated across the country is that we don't give ourselves the time or space to think about what our core, highest-priority issues are. We don't create the space for ourselves to be deliberate and strategic regarding how we engage—instead, we just add our names to the petitions that fill our inboxes, or reshare posts on Facebook, because it's easier.

So in this part of the book, we're going to prioritize. When everything feels like it's on fire, think of this as the equivalent of a fire escape plan. Prioritizing issues doesn't preclude us from engaging on new ones as they arise, but rather will serve as a foundation on which we can build.

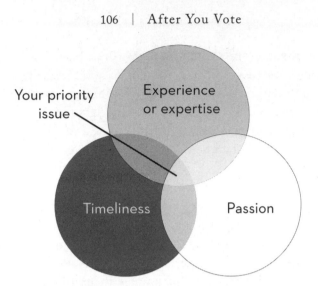

To help you prioritize *your* issues, we're going to use the framework above.

It may already be glaringly obvious to you what your priority issue is. Even if that's the case, I still recommend going through the following exercise to articulate your connection to that issue and why it's so critical to address now. These will be important inputs as we move onto the advocacy section.

To fill out each of the buckets, you'll write your responses to each of these questions in the Workbook section of Part II (see page 191):

Experience/Expertise
This is your unique perspective or "value add" to the issue. Perhaps it's because the issue has affected you personally or because of other knowledge or insight you have on the topic.

Answer these questions:
- *Personal experience:* What issues have personally affected you? Your family? Your community? What have their impacts or outcomes been?
- *Expertise:* On what issues do you have professional expertise or knowledge? Maybe you've studied an issue in depth in school or worked in a specific field for years.

Why this matters:

If you feel overwhelmed by all the issues facing us as a country, just imagine how many things your political officials are juggling. They're expected to have not just knowledge but an informed opinion on an astonishing array of topics. Also, the staff members typically responsible for intake (responding to constituents' emails, answering phone calls, etc.) are often twenty-two-year-old interns. If you reach out to a political official's office or schedule a meeting with them and can share a unique perspective—maybe you're a marine biologist and have special insight into the way a proposed environmental bill will affect marine wildlife, or maybe your family has been negatively impacted by new voter registration laws—you can become a valuable, ongoing resource to them and their staff.

Passion

This is your "fuel." It's what keeps you going, keeps you motivated, to keep fighting on behalf of this issue.

Answer these questions:

- What are your main voting issues? In other words, what issue, if a candidate didn't support it, would make you consider not voting for them?
- What kinds of charities do you donate your time or money to?
- What gets you fired up?

Why this matters:

Tapping into the things that you really care about, that drive you, that give you energy, is the *only* way to be a lifelong citizen advocate. Advocacy and engagement take effort—and time. In fact, some pieces of legislation take *years* to come to fruition. Think of your passions as your fuel; this is what will keep you going when it gets difficult to stay motivated and engaged. Plus, excitement is contagious: your passion will ignite the passion of others.

Timeliness

This is your call to action, and your answer to "why now?" Why is it import-ant to address this issue now instead of later? This could be because it's an urgent issue, like the Flint water crisis, or because there's public momentum on behalf of the issue, or because a bill is coming up for a vote.

Answer these questions:
- On the issues you care about most, which needs to be acted on now rather than later? Which is the most urgent? For what reasons might this be the time to address this issue?
  For example:
  ◊ Is there a bill coming up for a vote?
  ◊ Is something currently affecting you and/or your community that needs to be addressed *now*?
  ◊ Is this issue timely for a different reason (e.g., an important anniversary for this issue is coming up, or there seems to be a groundswell of interest on behalf of this issue that could be lost in the future)?

Why this matters:
Timeliness means you're more likely to be able to get attention and resources directed toward your issue. Typically, it takes the resources of a political official's entire office to deal with all the issues and bills at hand. If a bill is coming up or an issue needs to be addressed immediately for specific reasons, you can give your political official something tangible and actionable. Not to mention, your political officials are extremely sensitive about reelection—if an election is coming up, that also might be a way to create urgency around an issue, especially if that issue is important to many of their constituents.

One thing I've heard from some people upon completing this exercise is that their passion—the thing that really drives them—does not line up with their experience or expertise. That's totally okay. It just means your action plan will be a little different than for those whose passion and experience or expertise do align. Rather than immediately creating an advocacy plan, you might instead find opportunities to build your expertise on that point of passion (reading, volunteering for organizations focused on that issue, etc.). Congresswoman Alexandria Ocasio-Cortez will often post on Instagram to help her constituents (and whoever else follows her!) understand how Congress works, and what they can do to influence their members. In one of her posts, she talks about the importance of reading. "When people ask, 'What can I do?'—READ! . . . The better-read you are on the issues you care about, the better the decisions you'll make and the better your advocacy becomes. Reading is one way you don't have to rely on people telling you what to do. Reading refines your inner compass."[17] It will also mean ensuring that you're really engaging with and listening to others who have had more personal experiences with those issues, to ensure that you're really empowering those who have been directly affected. (This, by the way, is important to do even *if* you already have experience on the issue! We'll get to that later.) Remember: Expertise doesn't mean that you need to know *everything*. It does, however, mean that you need to put in the groundwork and leverage tools of political persuasion (which we'll cover later in the forthcoming chapters).

When it comes to translating all of this into action, what's happening politically at the moment can affect which of these factors (passion, timeliness, or experience/expertise) is your primary motivator for getting involved, as well as the actions you take. If a bill or piece of legislation comes up that you disagree with, or if an issue is causing suffering in your community, urgency might be the reason you engage and get involved on that issue. On the other hand, if there's nothing *immediate* happening on behalf of an issue you care about, your expertise might direct how and when you engage. For example, you might focus instead on building relationships with staffers at your representative's offices, helping to inform them on the issues, bringing things to their attention, and establishing yourself as a long-term resource on the topics.

Here are a couple examples of how these motivators can play out. In 2016, frustrated with what was happening at the federal level, I started looking for ways to get more politically active closer to home. Doing so made me realize I had been paying zero attention to what was happening locally; there was so much I didn't know. So, I started doing my research. I found out that I wasn't alone—that local civic associations had been in decline for decades as citizens started opting out of local political activities.[18] I also found that women's representation in local city government was particularly pathetic (as of 2020, only 12 of the 51 council members were women).[19] As a result, I got much more involved with local city council races in New

York City to help improve diversity on the city council. I got in touch with campaigns to volunteer my time, because I believed my skill set was valuable, and made campaign contributions to women running for office across New York City because I believe that gender diversity in leadership leads to better outcomes. I tapped into something I felt was urgent, given the upcoming elections, while also pursuing my passions and lending my expertise to a cause I believed in—namely, electing more women into local office.

Here's another example on a different kind of issue (again, our politics and our priorities are personal!). One of my best friends, Ameneh, is a rock-star corporate attorney in NYC. In January 2017, midway through her first year as an associate at a megawatt Manhattan firm, she got an email. President Trump had just signed an executive order banning refugees and immigrants from seven countries: Iran, Iraq, Syria, Sudan, Libya, Yemen, and Somalia—and many people with green cards and valid visas were landing in the US to find they were unable to enter the country (instead, they were detained and/or sent back). The email she received was a request for lawyers to come to JFK airport to provide legal counsel to those unable to enter.

Now, I don't know if you know any first-year corporate attorneys, but their schedules are almost always *terrible*. The week prior, she had texted me at 4 AM from her taxi headed home from the office (and again at 7 AM when she went back to work). She had also gotten married less than a year before and was doing her best to balance her workload with being a good partner. In other words, she was exhausted. It was the worst possible time to be asked to do something outside the scope of her day job. But she also recognized the urgency of the situation. And in combination with her unique skill set and passion for this issue, she made the choice to engage. As she told me, "I had this thought—even though I'm not an immigration attorney—that if I don't do this, and I don't do it because I'm tired, I've done something really wrong. This is needed right now. I can't do this on another day. It's today or never. I believe in the collective action problem: you have to be the one to take care of something if you believe in it."[20] So she got in a cab and headed to JFK airport.

Over the next eight hours, she got to work—and quickly realized she was able to add value because she could tap *all* of the skills she'd gained over the course of her career. She had been a theater director, where she learned management. She had worked in a hospital, where she learned compassion and quick thinking. As a lawyer, she knew the impact of advocacy. Her mother is from Iran and she's proficient in Farsi, so she was able to help translate between Farsi and English. Plus, this was an issue she cared deeply about—both morally and from personal experience (her parents are both immigrants). "The idea that my mother could have been on a plane 40 years ago, landing at JFK and being told she couldn't enter the country—that was personally upsetting,"[21] she told me.

So, this was an urgent issue that she was able to really support because of her expertise and skill set—as well as one that she personally cared about. Because of this, she was able to engage in meaningful ways and see firsthand how she was able to make a difference. I asked her if getting involved changed the way she thought about the issue, and here's what she said: "I think it's impossible to ignore [an issue] when you have a personal connection to it. It's absolutely true that because I was there that day and I saw people, saw what was happening, touched their hands, it was much more meaningful and more important to me that this ban not be put in place. Here, I saw people's lives being impacted and so have paid more attention to that issue."[22]

Let me reiterate again that prioritizing your issues is not about choosing one or two issues and sticking to them for the rest of your life or ignoring issues that you are not affected by personally. It's about finding and using a framework that allows you to focus, to overcome the initial paralysis that prevents you from getting started by identifying something that resonates deeply with you. In addition, if you're new to political advocacy, having an initial focus will enable you to build your political advocacy muscles, creating a baseline that you can expand upon as you become an advocacy expert.

Staying connected to that passion, according to New York state senator Alessandra Biaggi (who we heard from in Part I), is core to being an effective advocate:

> In order to do this work, to do any work that's going to impact people's lives, each and every one of us has to be rooted in the belief that we are smart enough, good enough, important enough, valuable enough to do the work. And every one of us is.
>
> However, every one of us is going to have different ways of sustaining that confidence and that foundation. And if we don't fill those things first, what starts to happen is the noise, which is probably louder [in politics] than in most jobs or industries, will consume you. Part of doing that is being clear—I am rooted in my values, I'm fighting for these things, no one is going to take me off that track—and being totally unapologetic.

It's very hard, but it's also necessary. That could literally be for a very big thing like *I'm going to stop harassment around the world* to *I want to plant trees in my community because we want to capture carbon* . . . You have to believe that planting that tree is the most important thing that you could be doing as a human at that very moment because when you believe that and when you are rooted in that, other people believe, too. It's infectious.[23]

Amen to that.

Here's what my filled-out framework looks like:

Experience/Expertise

- **Personal experience:** Legislation with the goal of creating equal opportunities for women (like Title IX) has had a major impact on my life and allowed me to better understand how the political and personal intersect. My mom started her own business, and I have two younger sisters; all of them deserve opportunities that are nothing less than equal to the ones their male peers have.

- **Expertise:** In college, I wrote my thesis on how social movements affect women's rights. While at CTI, I conducted research and ran programs for private-sector companies on the barriers to advancement in the workplace (and beyond) for professional women. Since cofounding AIT, I've also done significant research on and facilitation of women's civic engagement and political participation.

Passion

Because of my personal experience, it's extremely important to me that I do what I can to make sure my mother and sisters (and all women) are able to reach their full potential. I am driven to support equal representation and equal opportunities for women and girls in the US, specifically when it comes to their professional and political participation. This is particularly important for women who have been historically disenfranchised; I recognize how very, very lucky I am in my personal circumstances. For example, I graduated from college with no student debt, which was a huge factor in enabling me to leave my job and start AIT. My lack of debt meant that I was empowered to take some financial risks. It's important to address the disparities that exist for women in the US as well; I'm very aware that not everyone has had the opportunities (or enjoys the privilege) that I've had.

Timeliness

Progress for women has stalled in the US and, by some measures, we're actually moving backward. In 2020, we celebrated the anniversary of the 19th Amendment (which gave women the right to vote, although in practice this only applied to white women—so much of the 19th Amendment was, and remains, incomplete), and, while it's worth celebrating progress, it's also important to understand the disparities that remain, from civic engagement to corporate leadership. In recent years, we've also seen a huge uptick of women's interest in politics and political mobilization; if we harness that momentum, we can create change.

In using this framework in the Part II workbook, hopefully you have a clearer sense of the one or two issues you want to use to kick-start your political engagement—that's a huge step!

What can you actually do to have influence on those issues? Let's dig into that next.

Advocate in Action: Bianca Jackson, Chief Development Officer, New Friends, New Life*

Bianca Jackson is the chief development officer for New Friends, New Life, a nonprofit that restores and empowers formerly trafficked girls and sexually exploited women and children, where she is responsible for overseeing donor cultivation, budget growth, and strategic communication plans for the organization. Prior to New Friends, New Life, Jackson served as senior director of fund and community development at Genesis Women's Shelter & Support. Jackson holds a bachelor's degree in public relations from Temple University and is a 2015 graduate of Dallas Baptist University, where she obtained a master's degree in organizational communication.

On the importance of telling your story:

I'm from Freeport, Grand Bahama, which is one of the islands that were absolutely decimated by Hurricane Dorian in 2019. You get one side from the national news, US news, about how terrible it is—which it is— but it's my family and local connections who are telling a fuller story of what's happening and about how people are coming together to have barbecues at the churches every night. There's so much more hope coming out when you look deeper.

What are your sources of information on whatever topic you're focusing on? It is so important that you seek out local information. You can get involved in your city, in your community. Where is your local sex trafficking agency, or who is the regional nonprofit that's working on domestic violence? Some issues can really vary geographically; the symptoms show up in different ways. It's not that bigger news sources aren't useful; they're just not complete. They can't be. If you want the whole story, you have to be a little closer to it.

On the importance of enthusiastic engagement:

As a Black female immigrant in the US, I was so excited when I became a citizen, because the two things you get to do as a citizen are vote and sit on a jury. Literally two weeks later, I got my first jury duty summons. All of my friends and colleagues asked, "How are you going to get out of it?" And I was like, "What do you mean get out of it?" You can't effect change if you're not in the room. I want to be able to sit on a jury. I want to be able to vote. You can't change anything if you're not there. To be able to vote and to be able to have a voice in that room, that's the only

---

* Bianca Jackson, interview with the author, September 19, 2019 (adapted).

way you can make a difference and maintain that power. If not, you're at the mercy of everyone else.

On staying committed to the issue (even when it's not convenient):

What I have learned and what I am learning is as the advocate, as the citizen, as the community member concerned about an issue, you have to commit to the right side of the issue every single time. Whenever there's a prominent figure involved in domestic violence, sex trafficking, or sexual assault cases, there are always people who attempt to excuse or downplay the crime because of the person's wealth or stature, as if the same rules don't apply. But we can't pick and choose when it's a good time to be an advocate. If you are concerned about this issue, you have to stand for the victim every single time. So that's one lesson that I learned; your voice cannot be dictated by circumstance. You have to be so clear: this is what I believe, and it doesn't matter who is committing the act or the crime. I still have the same belief.

On keeping perspective:

When you're not from here, America is held up as a beacon. You know you've made it if you can get there, be there, study there, whatever. But when you're here in America, knowing we have so many systemic and social issues, it's hard to see the good, but we don't have these resources and agencies in every country. Not every country has domestic violence agencies and sex trafficking agencies. There is not always social support and mobilization. I think about that all the time. Here in America, we have the freedom to voice these dissents and differing opinions; that's not even possible everywhere, and there's so much value in that. That's not a given. When the days look dark, and you feel like nothing good is happening, just remember that.

Chapter 6

....

VOTING

I think we have to vote our values and we have to vote for the people who are standing up for us. We can't vote for someone just because of a label, of a party.
—Dolores Huerta, in an interview with *Latino USA* (2016)

In these next three chapters, we're going to talk about tools for influence—what you can do to engage your representatives and create the change that you want to see (not to mention how to make the most of your precious time). We'll walk through what really works when it comes to citizen advocacy, covering three categories: (1) voting, (2) advocating for your issues and influencing your elected officials, and (3) campaigning for candidates or causes (or even considering running for office yourself!). Keep in mind that these are just some of the tools for your political advocacy toolbox, *not* a checklist of everything you can or must do to be an engaged, effective citizen. These chapters will help you understand some of the tactics at your disposal to fight for the issues you care about most—and remind you that you don't need to be a professional advocate to make real change and engage effectively. But what your personal engagement looks like will also depend on your time and resources. My own civic engagement looked very different when I had a more flexible job compared to a job where I worked eighty-plus-hour weeks; so trust me, I've been there. And political engagement can be exhausting no matter the circumstances, especially when change moves at a snail's pace (or when things seem to be moving backward). So, in the final chapter of Part II, we'll look at how you can engage in ways that are sustainable for you in the long term.

As citizens, there is a lot that we can do to advocate for our interests. It's one of our most protected and sacred rights as Americans. You probably know that the First Amendment includes the right to free speech, freedom of the press, and freedom of religion. But it also includes the right of people to petition the government and to peaceably assemble (i.e., peacefully protest). In other words, a citizen's right to engage their representatives and government and to hold them accountable for what they're doing—or not doing—is written right there in our Constitution. It's been granted to us. Now you have something to say to your drunken uncle at Thanksgiving when he won't stop talking about how protestors and activists are disrespectful and un-American.

And, speaking of rights, let's talk about one of the most fundamental: voting.

Whether you vote in every election (even special elections!) or you're *not* a regular voter today, this chapter is for you. Yes, voting is table stakes to political participation—but it can also be complicated. Most people who vote are confronted with ballots full of issues and elections they don't know much about (I know I have been). When it comes to voting, there's almost always more to learn and do. In this chapter, we'll cover the prep and research you need before heading to the polls, what to expect when you get there (like so many things in our political system, this will vary significantly by state), and how to encourage and mobilize others to do the same. Voting is a right that many have fought for—even given their lives to obtain and protect. Let's celebrate their memory by taking full advantage of this right in all the ways in which we're able, and help others to do the same.

PREP AND MAKE A PLAN

When it comes to voting, preparation is key—and the first thing you need to do is to register. Maybe you're not sure if you're registered to vote. Or perhaps you can't remember if you reregistered with your new address the last time you moved. I knew when I moved across the country that I would need to reregister as a voter in my new state, but even when I moved from the Upper West Side of Manhattan to Brooklyn (a whopping six miles), all of my political officials changed—except, of course, my senators—and I had to register to vote with my new address so I could vote for the political officials that represented me in my new district.

If you think this could be you, too, never fear! This is an easy thing to confirm, and there are many resources that can help. I like **Vote.org**, which takes all of 30 seconds to confirm if you're registered to vote at your current home address. It's also a great resource to check in on your voting status in general. All you need to do is to enter your name, date of birth, and address, and it will tell you if you're registered. **When We All Vote** is another great resource and another place you can confirm your status.

If you find that you're *not* registered to vote in your current district, it's time to fix that. The exact steps you need to take will differ from state to state, but online resources can help there, too. Not only will **Vote.org** walk you through the registration process for your state, it'll also give you all the information you need about the current voting laws in your state. As of January 2020, 39 states (plus the District of Columbia) allow you to register to vote online, so chances are it will be straightforward process.[1]

Note: If you're a first-time voter, you'll need to show an ID when you register to vote—or, if you registered online, bring ID with you when you vote. This is true regardless of where you live and what voter ID laws look like in your state.[2]

If you've moved to a new state, note that DMVs in many states are required to provide you with the opportunity to register to vote when you get a license. This way, you can kill two birds with one stone: get an up-to-date license that reflects your new home address and register to vote at the same time. Boom.

If you *are* registered to vote, that's great news—and it will give you peace of mind when Election Day hits and you panic, wondering if you'll show up to the polls and not be on the voter rolls. It's good to check no matter what, but especially, as mentioned, if you've moved recently. Even if you've stayed in the same city, district lines are invisible; you might have crossed one without realizing it—which not only affects which polling place you'll go to on Election Day (if you're voting in person), but also the other prep work you'll do (e.g., deciding whom you're voting for). You're busy enough as it is; you don't need to add the headache of running around town between polling places if you can avoid it.

Once you've registered to vote (or confirmed your status), the next piece of voting prep work is *research*. And luckily, this research won't just help you make informed choices at the voting booth; all the things you'll look into as you get ready to vote will also help you with other kinds of engagement and political involvement in the future. For example, if you have a working knowledge of the candidates on your ballot and what they stand for, you'll be in a better position to hold them accountable for their promises—or to lobby against them if you disagree with their policy positions.

Here's the information you'll want to research ahead of Election Day—a simple who, what, when, where, and how:

- **Who** you'll be voting for. Which candidates are up for election in your district (at the federal, state, and local levels) and for which positions? Which candidates will you be voting for, of those running?

- **What** is on the ballot. Many states have what are called "propositions," or legislation that you're being asked to weigh in on as a citizen, which has the potential to become state or local law.

- **When** you need to vote. Election Day isn't always predictable. Federal elections are always the first Tuesday after November 1 in even years, and many local elections are the first Tuesday after November 1 in odd years. But there are also elections that don't always follow these patterns, known as "special elections." Special elections typically are held when there are vacancies before the end of an official term (e.g., if an elected official resigns, passes away, or is recalled).

While voter turnout tends to be higher in years with presidential elections, remember that so-called midterm elections are also critical. The entire House of Representatives and one-third of the Senate are up for reelection during midterm elections, not to mention numerous state and local positions! And as we saw and discussed in Part I, state and local government often has more influence on your day-to-day than the federal government does.

- **Where** you need to vote. Your district will determine your polling place, and knowing where that is ahead of time lets you make a concrete plan (maybe even carpool or meet neighbors or friends there if they live in your district!).

- **How** you'll vote. What options are available to you in order to vote (e.g., early voting, vote by mail, in-person voting the day of the election), and which will you choose? There are often different deadlines and rules for different forms of voting, which is why it's important to figure it out ahead of time, as it varies significantly from state to state.

So now you have your voting prep checklist. But executing it can feel easier said than done. For example, I know it can be difficult to feel like you're getting unbiased information about political candidates. So here are a few tips and tricks for each step.

WHO

Research which positions are up for election at the federal, state, and local levels, and make sure you understand the core responsibilities of each position. There will probably be plenty of positions and candidates you recognize, but perhaps others that you don't, like federal judges or town clerks.

Next, research who is running to fill those positions. In primaries, there may be a lot of candidates! Here are some good ways to learn more about both the positions that are up for election, and to find out about those running to fill them:

- Research what will be on your ballot. **BallotReady** and **Ballotpedia** are both great resources for this. BallotReady, for example, will include a full list of who's running for each position, their stances on issues, biographies, and endorsements (more on those in a minute) based on which district you live in. You simply need to enter your address and you're off to the races (literally).

- Visit the campaign websites of the candidates running and better understand their platforms. Yes, this information will be more biased, but also more personal and in their own words.

- Help information about candidates and their campaigns come to you by following candidates on Facebook, Instagram, or Twitter, and sign up for their newsletters (all candidates and campaigns will have them). Note that during an election season, you will also get a *lot* of requests for donations, so brace yourself.

- Check out a candidate's endorsements. Endorsements are a really good way to quickly vet a candidate. Keep an eye out for which candidates have been endorsed by newspapers you read or care about. More importantly, check out if candidates have been endorsed by issue-specific organizations, especially those that you trust or that work on issues that you feel strongly about. Some organizations will go a step further and rank candidates based on their records or platforms on certain issues, from the environment to health care. These organizations are often made up of experts on their respective topics who spend a lot of time researching and understanding candidates' stances on them, so their endorsement will do a lot of the legwork for you and can be a helpful gut check. While of course you shouldn't rely totally on the opinions of others, using endorsements and ratings can be a useful shortcut, especially when there are a lot of candidates in the field, or candidates are running for positions that you know less about, like a county clerk or comptroller.

- If a candidate running for office has served in the past, check out their record. This is where your issue prioritization can be especially handy. You don't need to look at their record on every issue or every bill (although you're certainly welcome to!), but if you can, take a peek at how they've voted on particular priority issues for you in the past. If their voting record is confusing, you still have questions, or you just want more details, call their offices and ask! Staffers are more than happy to help inform and educate you on their candidate's stances.

WHAT

Sometimes there are more than just candidates on the ballots—as mentioned above, in some states or local jurisdictions, you may be asked to vote on legislation, often called propositions, as well. Not every state allows propositions on the ballot, but if you live in a state that does, propositions are extremely important to know about and research. There are three types of propositions[3]:

- **Initiative:** Citizens can initiate a statute on the ballot for a vote (provided they collect a minimum number of signatures from other citizens supporting the statute—this minimum is set by the state constitution), essentially bypassing their state legislature. If that statute is passed, it becomes law.

- **Referendum:** There are two types of referendums: legislative and public. A legislative referendum is when the legislature refers a measure to the voters for their approval; a public referendum is when voters petition to have a measure appear on the ballot, similar to an initiative, but specifically to approve or repeal an action of the legislature.

- **Recall:** Citizens can submit a petition to recall politicians currently in office; if successful, a recall election is held. These are very rare! Only 19 states permit recalls, and there have only been two successful recalls in history (including the one that resulted in Arnold Schwarzenegger becoming governor of California).[4]

The cool thing about propositions, whether introduced by citizens or by a legislature, is that they allow voters to weigh in on legislation directly. It's a way to introduce and potentially pass legislation that's being ignored by the legislature or stalled due to partisan gridlock.

There are, however, downsides to propositions. First, the public is often not well educated about the propositions heading into Election Day. Second, the language explaining propositions on the ballot is written by the state attorney general's office and can be quite complicated and even politicized. For these reasons, it's incredibly important to know what you're getting into when it comes to propositions *before* you get into the voting booth. You might end up voting against your own interests if you're reading a proposition for the first time on Election Day; the language of a proposition can be incredibly confusing (and, at worst, intentionally misleading, to get voters to vote a certain way). Here's a recent example from Washington State, Washington Initiative 976, that showed up on my ballot in 2019:

> Initiative Measure No. 976 concerns motor vehicle taxes and fees. This measure would repeal, reduce or remove authority to impose certain vehicle taxes and fees; limit annual motor vehicle-license fees to $30, except voter-approved charges; and base vehicle taxes on Kelley Blue Book value.

On its face, this sounds pretty good, right? Fewer vehicle taxes and fees? The majority of voters thought so, too; the initiative passed. But what *wasn't* noted in the ballot measure were the implications—which included an estimated loss of $1.9 billion and $2.3 billion to state and local governments, respectively, over the next six years, and less funding for highway maintenance and construction, ferry support, and public transportation projects.[5] Maybe not so good, after all. Knowing what propositions will be on your ballot, and what they actually *mean*, is critical.

Similar to candidate prep, do your research on propositions ahead of time. What is the real issue at hand? What do advocates and opponents say about the bill? Who has endorsed it? It's a lot harder for an informed, prepared citizen to be manipulated or tricked by the system. In addition to candidate info, **BallotReady** will also include information about propositions in the upcoming election, if your state has any.

WHEN AND WHERE

Look up when and where your upcoming elections will be! You could even make it a tradition to list all the year's elections every January 1, so you can plan effectively. **Vote.org** has a lot of great information, not just about the timing of elections themselves, but also deadlines for voter registration, absentee voting, and more, as well as state-by-state information that allows you to easily find your polling place based on your name and address.

Once you know when and where an upcoming election is, make an appointment. Put it in your calendar, as you would anything else! If you're using a calendar app on your phone, be sure the calendar appointment will send you a notification or reminder as well. Include the election date and polling place address in the calendar entry. From your phone, it will then be super easy to use Google Maps or another navigation app to find the best way to get to your polling place.

You can also make sure that information comes to you, rather than you having to hunt it down every time! For example, you can sign up for alerts using tools like **TurboVote**. Once you've signed up, you'll receive text reminders about voting and even other opportunities for civic participation like participatory budgeting, a process by which members of the community decide how local funding should be allocated. (In New York City, for example, participatory budgeting is used for New Yorkers to propose and vote on projects in the city council districts.[6])

HOW

There are three questions to ask here.

First, what do you physically need with you when you head to your polling place? What's required in order to cast your vote? There's huge variation in voting requirements from state to state; some states have stricter requirements around voter identification than others. Make sure you know the requirements in your own state—both so you know what you need in order to vote (for now), and so you can, if you feel they're too restrictive, advocate for changing them (for the long haul). We'll talk about the challenges and barriers to voter participation in more detail in Part III. That said, states are required to provide alternatives for voters who do not have an ID on Election Day.

- **If you don't have an ID and your state doesn't have "strict" voter ID laws:** You'll be able to cast a ballot that will be counted without any further action on your part. You might be asked to sign an affidavit or vote on a provisional ballot; after the close of the polls, officials will determine via signature or other verification whether the vote should be counted.

- **If you don't have an ID and your state does have strict voter ID laws:** You can vote using a provisional ballot (which you won't need an ID to do), but you may be asked to visit an election office within a few days after the election and present an acceptable ID to have your vote counted. If you don't show up, your provisional vote won't be counted. The amount of time you have to do this varies, but it can be as little as three days after the election (for example, in Georgia).[7]

Second, in what way will you cast your ballot? If you know you'll be away or traveling on the day of the election, check to see if your state allows early voting or absentee voting. (It's also important to note if your state has restrictions around absentee voting; some states have "no excuse" absentee voting, meaning you can vote absentee for any reason. Other states require an excuse such as physical absence or disability.) When I was a consultant, I was often out of town on Election Day, so I would vote absentee.

Third, if you're voting in person, how will you get to your polling place? Subway? Bus? Driving? Walking? Biking? See what options are available to you. Ridesharing companies like Lyft sometimes offer discounted rides to polling places. You could organize a group of neighbors to take a Lyft with you or carpool to reduce costs. If you have kids, bring them with you! It's good for them to see you participating so they'll grow up with strong civic habits.

WHY

Last but not least: remember *why* you are voting. You care about who represents you and about the policies they'll enact, because those policies have the potential to change your life and the lives of your family members, friends, and neighbors. It's your responsibility as a citizen.

MOBILIZE AND ENLIST OTHERS

We've covered the who-what-when-where-how-why (whew!) of voting prep, which will make you powerful in the voting booth. Here are a few ways to help empower others, too:

- **Make it social (media).** Research shows that social pressure is an effective motivator for voting.[8] Take a selfie with your "I Voted" sticker and share it on Facebook, Instagram, or Twitter. Even if this feels like a humblebrag, the research backs this (and you!) up as an effective tactic for voter mobilization.

- **Share your knowledge.** Another easy, nonpartisan way to help educate others is to use social media to share any resources that you found helpful as you prepared to vote (for example, how to check on where your polling place is). Want to go a step further? If you think all that prep you did as you got ready to vote (checking out candidates, endorsements, and ballot measures) would be helpful to your family and friends as well, put it in an email and send it to them.

- **Volunteer your time.** There are lots of organizations out there, like the **League of Women Voters**, that are always looking for volunteers to help support in-person voter registration drives. You can typically find information about these opportunities on their websites and sign up to volunteer there, too.

  You could also sign up to be a poll worker on Election Day (for which you will be paid, in most cases). Just keep in mind that this will likely require advance training, so it can be a more time-intensive option.

- **Throw a party!** We think of the voting booth as a traditional element of voting in America, but the private voting booth wasn't how early Americans voted. In fact, the private voting booth was an idea that Americans took from Australian elections, and even then, not until the 1890s.[9] Voting used to be a public act. Voters would gather in the street, play music, drink, eat, and cast their votes publicly—it was an incredibly celebratory activity.

  Of course, the public nature of voting back then also meant that votes could be bought, because those buying the votes could confirm that people had voted the way they had paid them to because they could *watch* them vote. The secret ballot was originally introduced to help reduce violence and corruption and by the nineteenth century had been adopted almost everywhere in the

United States. While it did succeed in reducing violence and corruption, the introduction of the secret ballot also coincided with states introducing literacy tests, poll taxes, grandfather clauses (which exempted people from requirements like poll taxes and literacy tests if they had the right to vote before the Civil War, and which applied to any of their descendants), and other voting requirements that disproportionately disenfranchised Black voters.[10] Gone, too, was the celebratory aspect to voting. Overall, voter turnout dropped.

We're probably not going to bring back public voting, but we *can* make it more celebratory. Host a BYOVS (Bring Your Own Voting Sticker) party, even if it has to take place over videoconference! Make a civics party playlist (there are also tons of playlists already created on Spotify—just search for "Election Day")! Voting is important and has serious consequences—but we can also recapture some of the joy we should all feel in the freedom of expression that voting gives us.

- **Work with your company on voter mobilization.** Increasingly, it's not just nonprofits and governments that people expect to support voter mobilization. More and more for-profit companies are starting employee voting initiatives, including organizations like Patagonia, Gap, and Target.[11] Since 2016, for example, Patagonia has closed for business on Election Day for major elections and given all employees paid time off to vote.[12] Check to see what your company provides (some hold voter registration drives or voting celebrations) and, if you think it could be doing more, talk to your manager or leadership team to see if it's possible to launch an initiative.

Key Takeaways

1. **Do your research.** Understand who (and, in some cases, what) you're voting for on Election Day. Don't be caught unaware!
2. **Make a plan.** Like everything else that's important to you, don't leave voting to chance. Make a specific voting plan in advance.
3. **Engage others.** Share your knowledge with others on the importance of voting in every election and consider volunteering your time to make sure you can help others get to the polls.

As we've established, voting is critical, but it's also just a first step. Can you imagine hiring someone for a job and then not talking to them again until their year-end review? Or following the draft for your favorite sports team but then not tuning in for any games? Didn't think so. We hire our representatives to do a job; it's then our job to make sure they do it. And that means learning how to advocate for your issues. As the title of this book suggests, what happens after you cast your ballot is equally—if not more—important.

Advocate in Action: Eve Reyes-Aguirre, Community Organizer and Advocate*

Eve Reyes-Aguirre is an Indigenous grassroots community organizer and community advocate. She lives in Phoenix, where she does community organizing and advocacy work at Tonatierra Nahuacalli, An Embassy of Indigenous Peoples. As an Indigenous woman, she also represents the women in her Calpolli (traditional community) annually at the United Nations Permanent Forum on Indigenous Issues, as well as at the Global Indigenous Women's Caucus. Reyes-Aguirre has served as the co-chair for the Global Indigenous Women's Caucus and currently serves as the special rapporteur. She ran for US Senate in Arizona in 2018 as a Green Party candidate.

On the importance of political education and knowing the system:

Political education is something that's sorely lacking at a grassroots and community level. Grassroots organizers are very well versed in how to execute protests or workshops, but when it comes to advocating around policy to those in positions of power, there's not enough information for us as women, especially about what the processes are. It can make or break your campaign. We're mothers, or grandmothers; we are women who have experienced injustice and want to have a voice and bring light to those issues, and the only way that we feel like we can move that forward is through the political arena. Protesting has gotten us a lot over the decades, but we need to understand policy, not just at a community level, but on a national and even an international level. We already know we have to be involved, but we also need to know how to be involved, so that we're not just participating, but creating effective engagement.

At the UN, there's a certain process you need to follow in order to write interventions and present them. It took me 10 years to learn. You have to know whether or not the issues that you're bringing up have been addressed before and what the follow-up was. It's the same when it comes to local politics. You have to know what's been done, what's already happened. You can't come forward and say, I need you to change this because they can turn around and say, Well, we've already done that, and it didn't work. So, you have to know going in what you want and how to do that in whatever arena it is that you're advocating in.

---

* Eve Reyes-Aguirre, interview with the author, March 2, 2020 (adapted for clarity).

On the power of community engagement:

Establishing a relationship with the community and, most importantly, receiving feedback from those who are directly affected, is really important. Often you have these bigger, well-funded organizations that come in and want to dictate the agenda without consulting or even understanding the issues and the dynamics around the issues, especially with women. When you're working with the community face-to-face and they know you and they know your families and they know that you're going to be at a certain place at a certain time every week, that's when people really open up. And it gives other women the courage to do the same thing. I've seen women who were afraid to leave their home go out and protest and bring their children along with them. It's really powerful to have that consistent face-to-face relationship with the people you are representing.

On shifting from local to global advocacy:

About 21 years ago, I moved to Phoenix, newly married with two young children, and started volunteering at a community center. I was helping out with the weekly food bank. I started meeting with members of the community, most of them mothers, a lot of them migrants. We started organizing different workshops and started talking about health care and different things that they could do to help their family.

And then Arizona SB 1070 passed. Because of that, there was a lot of racial profiling happening, not just to people from the south, but also to Native people who lived in the state of Arizona. And so the advocacy work that I did around that turned into more of a "know your rights" work. There is a forum that happens at the UN every year called the Permanent Forum on Indigenous Issues, and I was chosen to be the representative for my community. Suddenly I was advocating on a global scale, which also involved issues around gender-based violence, especially around Indigenous women. Back then we were shedding new light on the issue of missing and murdered Indigenous women. People also don't realize how much trade and foreign policy affects different regions, and especially women at the community level.

But I never put all my eggs in one basket. I don't go to the UN and think all my problems are going to be solved. You have to raise your voice in every arena so that we can make sure that our concerns and issues are being uplifted.

CHAPTER 7

. . . .

LOBBYING AND ADVOCACY

I want people to feel hopeful about how to make change happen.
I want them to have the tools that they need to make that change
happen. I want them to feel their power. Every single one of us has
enormous power. We have to know that and really allow ourselves
to dwell in that place and then use that power to create good that
matters for the world.
　　　　—Pramila Jayapal, in an interview with *ELLE* magazine (2020)

S o, you made it to the polls and voted for your candidates. Now, one of two things has happened: they won, or they lost. Either way, your job as an effective citizen advocate stays the same: You engage. You advocate.

If a candidate you voted for won, now is the time to hold them accountable, especially on the issues that matter to you the most. It's no secret that politicians don't always follow through on their campaign promises. Indeed, some may be hoping that after the election is over, you'll disengage and forget about their commitments to you. But even politicians who want to keep their promises can't do it alone. They need your support and full engagement to make those promises a reality, especially if they're new ideas or controversial measures.

It can be tempting to disengage if your candidate didn't win, too—you're no doubt frustrated, disappointed, upset, or maybe even fearful. It is *so* easy to tune out and focus on other things, especially considering how busy we all are. But disengaging now is the worst thing we can do. Not engaging means we are giving our political opponents full rein to do as they please; the next opportunity to vote them out of office is too far away to prevent them from enacting policies that could have a tremendous impact on your community.

Whether your candidate won or lost, the basic tools that you'll use to engage your representatives and advocate for your issues are mostly the same, and this section is about understanding the tools in your toolbox and how to use them to advocate for the kind of change you want to see take place. Think of this chapter as Advocacy 101, as it is not an exhaustive list of every way you can have influence on the issues you care about (we won't, for example, go deep into community organizing). But we'll walk through three critical activities: understanding the landscape, lobbying for your issues, and building broader awareness by participating in public discourse.

Remember, this is not meant to be a checklist of all the things you need to go do all at once. I know you're busy, and the worst outcome would be for you to feel so overwhelmed that you decide it's hopeless to do anything at all. Everyone's activism is going to look different, depending not just on your time and resources, but on what is required to solve the problem your community is facing. Influencing elected officials isn't easy, but you can take it slow and steady. As Maria Castro, community organizer for the migrant justice organization Puente Human Rights Movement based in Arizona, says, "[Advocacy] is a practice that takes a lot of work in the same way that you go to the gym and you practice and you train to build those muscles."[1]

Time for boot camp.

UNDERSTAND THE LANDSCAPE

In order to advocate for an issue effectively, you need to look at the landscape of what's happening with regard to that cause, and at which level of government it's best to engage. Even if you already have a lot of experience with the issue you're advocating for, it's a good opportunity to refresh your knowledge. No matter what tactics you decide are the best to influence your elected officials, this is always a good place to start!

- **Look at the issue from multiple sides.** See what people who disagree with you are saying. Remember in school when you were debating and were assigned to one side of an issue—and had to argue for that side, regardless of whether you agreed with it? Think of this first step like that. Read articles that present different sides of an argument; you might realize that what you think is the strongest argument "for" an issue isn't even what's being discussed by opponents of the issue. Avoid confirmation bias (our tendency to seek out or interpret information to reinforce what we already believe) by really taking a critical eye to what you're reading. This is a good idea both to sharpen your own understanding and also so you know what representatives are hearing from the "other side."

- **Engage with and listen to others.** This may be the most important step to better understand an issue and what solutions are most likely to help. By engaging and gathering outside input, you'll have a better sense of what solutions you need to advocate for—solutions that are better and more inclusive, because they address how the entire community (not just you) is affected by an issue, as well as understanding how groups are differently or disproportionately affected by that issue. In Maria Castro's view, "Eighty percent of [community organizing] is listening. For me, whenever I'm thinking of an issue I'm passionate about, I think about the people that I love, the people in my community, and I sit down and talk to them, and dream about what are the possible outcomes."[2] Maria says that what surprised her when she first started doing this work was that "the best ideas were already in my community. Everything we need to win, to create the change we need in our lives and in our communities, is already *in* the communities we're participating in. It's important for us to have a global understanding, but more important to have a local and focused solution."[3]

- **Determine which level of government you should target (e.g., federal, state, or local).** Where you need to engage depends a lot on your issue and the kind of outcomes you're looking for. If your main issue is that pesky pothole, your local government would be the best place to start. If your issue is about higher education, you may be better off starting at the state level. If it's about health care, it might require targeting a mix of both state and federal. Given your area of concern, where's the best place to start? Knowing the right level of government to engage will also help you zero in on which elected officials you should target to lobby for your issues. More specifically, you're looking for who has decision-making power on your particular issue.

One way to figure out where to start is to seek out your local political party headquarters (for example, New York City Democrats) and ask them. They'll likely have a comprehensive understanding of the political landscape, and they'll also have lots of important inside information, like member and staff contact details, ongoing mobilization on key issues, and more.

If you're not sure where to start, my advice, generally, is to start at the most local level of government possible. If the issue you care about is outside of their jurisdiction, they'll tell you! They'll also likely have some good advice about where you should engage (they're political insiders, after all). And as we talked about in Part I, the more local you go, the better chance you have of getting a faster response and more attention. Building relationships within government can help you navigate the government more effectively over the long term as well.

- **Understand where your representatives fall on your priority issues.** If you did your voting prep, chances are you already have a good baseline for what your representatives think (or how they've voted in the past) on your issues. But if you haven't brushed up on their policy priorities recently or don't have a good sense of their stance, here are a few suggestions:
    ◊ Check out your reps' voting records on your priority issues. There are lots of helpful online resources to do this, including **IssueVoter**, **Vote Smart**, and **POPVOX**.
    ◊ Read articles that discuss your representatives' views on your issues. To make this easier to track on an ongoing basis, set up a Google alert with your representatives' names and the particular issues you want to keep tabs on.
    ◊ Call your representatives' offices. Pick an issue and ask to talk to the member of the team who is responsible for policy

related to that particular issue; some offices are large enough that there might be one person focused on health care, for example. (Later in this chapter, we'll talk about tips and tricks for how to make these phone calls effective.)

◊ Take a look at any professional or personal reasons your representatives might have a special interest in your issue. For example, your representative might serve on a committee focused on your cause, which means this is something that matters to them a lot. Your issue may also be one that your representative personally cares about as well (after all, they're people, too!).

Here, it's also good advocacy hygiene to follow the money. Websites like **OpenSecrets** can help you understand if there are any special interest groups focused on your issue that are making financial contributions to your representatives (which could sway how they vote). **Vote Smart's Political Galaxy** allows you to choose a federal representative and a specific issue, and then provides an overview of how that person has voted on the issue, speeches they've made on the topic, an overview of any groups that have made donations to their campaign that may have special interests with regard to the issue, and more.

• **Gain a basic understanding of what's happening with regard to your issue.** Is there existing or upcoming legislation on this topic? Look for existing organizations that are already focused on your topic; in their resources or the "in the news" section of their website, they'll likely have good information on what's happening on your issue from a legislative perspective. If you can make a case to your elected official for why this concern needs to be addressed *now* (whether because there's an upcoming bill or because the issue is being ignored completely, to the community's detriment), you may be able to make this a policy priority for their office.

After you've done all this, make sure you have answers to the following questions (these responses can be just one to two sentences; the point is to help you organize your thoughts and prep for engaging your representatives!):

Goal
- What are your priority issues? What would you like to see happen regarding those issues? Be as specific as you can. This is also where it is critical that you understand what is currently happening on your issues; if there's legislation that's coming up for a vote that is about your topic, your goal might be to have your representative vote "yes" on that bill so that it becomes law.

Background
- Why does this issue matter to you? Your community? Your state?
- What are your representatives' current stances on those issues? Look at past voting records, statements, endorsements, and so on. What is the most compelling information you have that may change their mind?
- Why does this issue need to be addressed now rather than later?

Next Steps
- What's the best way to reach your goals (e.g., which representative should you work with, what advocacy tactic should you use)? (Note that you may not yet know the best advocacy tactic. Not to worry! We'll cover that in the next section.)

LOBBY YOUR REPRESENTATIVES

The word "lobbying" really just means trying to influence government action (although it often has a bad rap, conjuring images of faceless people in expensive suits doing backdoor deals with politicians). And when it comes to making your voice heard and your opinions known to your representatives, as well as trying to influence their decisions and priorities, there are a lot of options for how to do it. These include:

- Calling your representative's office
- Signing petitions
- Writing an op-ed or letter to the editor
- Writing a letter or email to your representative
- Posting on social media
- Meeting with your representative
- Showing up to town halls
- Participating in committee hearings

Okay, that's . . . a lot. How do you decide where to start? Where can you have the most impact, with the amount of time you have available? Suffice it to say all tactics are not created equal. Some of these actions are less effective than others, but all of them benefit from being deployed as thoughtfully and strategically as possible. As a first step, though, let's break this down. Generally speaking, which tactics are more effective than others?

Overall, petitions are less effective when it comes to influencing your elected officials compared to other methods. Of course, petitions can help groups (like nonprofits, for example) identify people who are like-minded and support their organization's key issues—a group that the organization can then mobilize further at a future date. And petitions can also be helpful, for example, when it comes to getting propositions on the ballot, which we discussed earlier in this section (remember that a certain number of people need to sign a petition in support of a ballot initiative for it to appear on the ballot). They can also signal widespread public support for an issue or cause. But petitions on their own aren't very persuasive to individual representatives as an influencing tactic. If you're like me, you've added your name to lots of these over your life (it's so quick and easy!). But your political officials and representatives care most about what their constituents have to say—the people they represent, in their state or district. If a representative's office is unable to verify that you are a constituent (and some petitions only ask for your name and email address), they are able to dismiss the petition as not relevant to their state/district. And nearly half of congressional staffers believe that petitions they receive are sent without approval or permission of the constituents whose names are listed on them.[4] Yikes. Finally, petitions are also relatively impersonal (we'll talk more later in this section about why telling your *personal* story is so influential).

The same goes for form email messages. You may have received information from an organization asking you to take action by emailing your elected official, which also included text or messaging for you to include. When an elected official receives *thousands* of the same email, it dilutes its impact; they don't know why an issue matters to *you.*

Social media is similar. It can be difficult for your representatives to confirm that someone posting on social media is an actual constituent, so unless a demand for a specific action or attention to a specific issue has gone viral, it's really not the most effective way to engage your representatives. Like petitions, social media can be a great way to virtually convene a community of people who agree on an issue, or it can be a way to raise awareness about a concern in your community.

But here are the tactics that work best: individual calls, emails, letters, and in-person visits, as well as op-eds and letters to the editor. Intuitively, this makes sense; these are more personal, one-to-one tactics that invite your representative to engage in a conversation with you, understand why an issue matters to you personally, and make them feel connected to your story in a way that impersonal petitions or email messages that have been copied and pasted may not. Meeting in person? Your representative (or their staffer) can put a face and a name to an issue. A phone call or email? That's in your voice, and from someone they can confirm is a constituent on the call.

The research bears this out. A 2017 OpenGov Foundation report found that "staff and members value high-touch, personal contact over low-effort apps and tools that facilitate easy engagement but provide little meaningful information about constituents."[5] Not only are high-effort advocacy tactics more effective, but some staffers worry that the passive advocacy tools that have become increasingly popular through technology are actually damaging trust between constituents and their members of Congress. As one staffer told the OpenGov Foundation as part of their research, "These apps that constituents use to contact their representative degrade the quality of the conversation. These are low effort, and they have low impact."

The Congressional Management Foundation (CMF), a nonpartisan organization, has done fantastic research defining the advocacy strategies that have the most impact on representatives, based on a survey of congressional staffers. Take a look at the graph on the next page.[6]

As you can see, in-person visits from constituents are the *most effective way* to influence your representatives and public officials—and this shouldn't come as a shock. When we're face-to-face, we're much more persuasive. A recent study published in *Harvard Business Review* found that in-person requests are *34 times more likely* to be successful than requests made by email.[7] We overestimate our ability to be influential and charming in a virtual world, and we underestimate those abilities in person. It's why showing up at a town hall to ask a question or bring up an issue affecting your community is an effective tactic for engaging with your representative, too.

Frances Perkins, the first woman ever appointed to a US president's cabinet, as secretary of labor (read: badass), deeply understood the most effective tactics for influence. Before she was appointed by President Franklin

"If your Member/Senator has not already arrived at a firm decision on an issue, how much influence might the following advocacy strategies have on his/her decision?"

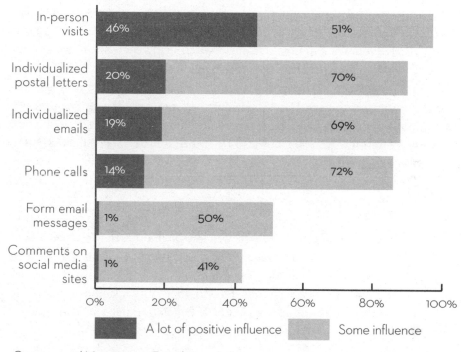

| | A lot of positive influence | Some influence |

Congressional Management Foundation, 2016

Delano Roosevelt to lead the Department of Labor, she was an advocate for the working poor in New York City. She was incredibly effective at it, because she knew how to change people's perspectives. She would take state senators on tours of working factories so they could see with their own eyes the conditions in which factory workers operated. Among other things, the senators could see for themselves that, in the event of a fire, there was no hope of escape. She knew that when you put abstract problems in terms of real people, change is often accelerated.[8]

In the wake of the 2016 election, a series of tweets by Emily Ellsworth (former staffer for now-retired Utah congressman Jason Chaffetz) went viral. In those tweets, she reaffirmed that letters, emails, and phone calls all get attention; in fact, congressional staffers are often assigned to tracking and responding to constituent outreach. Less effective? Petitions, as well as posting on Twitter or Facebook, unless those posts go viral or the constituency of the people signing or posting can be determined.[9]

To sum up: The best channels to influence your members of Congress (or representatives at any level of government) are in-person meetings, personalized letters (whether delivered via snail mail or email), and phone calls. However, what you include or do when using each of these advocacy tactics—what you write in your letter, what you say on your call, what you do in a meeting—can make you a whole heck of a lot more or less effective. To put this in perspective, consider that members of Congress receive millions of communications from constituents every year. Your goal is not just to communicate *more*, but also to communicate more effectively and more persuasively.

Here are a few things that hugely increase your effectiveness when you incorporate them into your message:

- **Your personal story and why you support/oppose the issue.** Why does this issue matter to you? Why is it one of your priority issues? Here, reflect back on the questions you answered in Chapter 5 about why this issue is important to you. Why, specifically, do you support or oppose this issue? If legislation has already been proposed, why is the bill a good or bad idea?

- **Information on your district/state.** How does this issue affect your community? Again, be specific! Use data if it's available. Would the impact just be on you, or are others affected? Who are they and how would it affect their lives? Are already vulnerable or underrepresented groups disproportionately impacted?

- **Your ask or request.** What do you actually want your representative to do about your concern? (*Note*: A specific request also requires knowing what tools are at your representative's disposal and what they actually *can* do—which, thanks to the earlier chapters of this book, you do! It also means knowing what's happening on that issue—for example, has legislation on this issue already been introduced?)

Stories are psychologically proven to be powerful influencers—but numbers are also important, especially when it comes to communicating how an issue or bill impacts the broader community in your state/district. Your story may be moving, but it's always helpful to have done your research, so your representative will know that your issue is bigger than you. It makes it easier for them to take action quickly and justify to the rest of the community why it's a priority. Helping your representative understand how your issue affects a group (or groups) of constituents will not only help them make it a priority for their offices, but also give them the compelling information they need to help convince colleagues.

Another way to share your story is by giving testimony at a committee hearing. While you need to be invited to do so on the federal level, state and local committee hearings are often fairly accessible. In New Hampshire, for example, every single bill introduced receives a public hearing—and the hearing information must be made public 72 hours in advance (as you learned in Part I). If you want to speak at a New Hampshire State House or state senate hearing, you can just show up at the committee room and sign up to speak, or just register your opinion.

Wendy Davis, former state senator in Texas, recounted the following about the impact constituents can have when telling their stories during committee hearings:

> One of the most memorable moments that I've had as a state senator listening to hours upon hours of testimony from people who came before us in committee hearings was that of a young woman who was there articulating support for the continued funding for the alternative high school program we have in the state of Texas.
>
> She probably was 16 or 17; she was already a mother, she had dropped out of high school when she had her baby, and she described her despair, as feeling as though she was never going to get a high school diploma. A particular school reached out to her, one of the alternative schools in our state, and they encouraged her to believe in her ability to get back on the path of education and to get her high school diploma. She talked about what her day-to-day experience was, rising every morning very early, getting her baby ready and herself ready, getting on the bus with a baby, a stroller, a backpack, taking her infant son to childcare where she would then get on a second bus

to go to school, and then the kind of support that she received when she was there. And how, on the days when things got so hard that she decided to give up, the school just wouldn't let her. If she didn't show up for a few days, they would reach out to her and encourage and support her and she would get back on track.

As she ended her testimony, all of us were so moved by it and understood that the impact of what we were doing as legislators was one that had a potential tremendous benefit to young people just like her and of course it encouraged all of us to feel as though we wanted to be a part of helping to solve her problem and to support the continued funding of our alternative high schools in Texas.[10]

Professional advocates also affirm how valuable storytelling is for advocacy work. Ebony Tucker, former advocacy director for the National Alliance to End Sexual Violence, where she worked on policy and advocacy issues important to survivors of sexual violence, says: "As a person who does federal advocacy I can ... talk about the big picture, how things look in a lot of different areas, but that member of Congress wants to know what is happening in their own home district. For you to meet with their staffers or meet with them personally in their office and say 'I live here. I'm your constituent. This is how federal funding is helping us, these are the issues we're having, this is what we need,' all of those things are really significant."[11]

Libby Wuller, a self-described "government nerd," grew up in Oklahoma and moved to Washington, DC, for college and to pursue a career in politics. During college, she interned for Senator Jim Inhofe (R-OK) and at the YMCA working with their advocacy team. She then got a call from a friend who knew some people who were starting public affairs software company Quorum. Wuller describes their product as a "moneyball for Congress": software that helps people understand what's going on in Congress (e.g., the broader patterns and behavior of elected officials, and how to be smarter with advocacy strategy). During her five years at Quorum, Libby worked with nonprofits, corporations, trade organizations, and individual advocates on utilizing technology to better move the needle on issues they care about. These experiences gave her up-close knowledge of what really works from a grassroots-advocacy and member-engagement perspective. Her advice echoed Tucker's and others': "Personal is always best." The most effective campaigns *always* include the personal.

Wuller gave the example of the ALS Association, which in 2014 introduced the "ice bucket challenge." For those who remember the campaign, it went viral and raised $115 million for the organization—but it also did much, much more than that. Wuller says, "[The ALS Association] was able to gain momentum but also utilized that social media campaign to collect a lot of advocate stories. Now, when they do Capitol Hill visits, they take advocates from districts of members, who are able to talk about the disease that impacted their lives. So even though they're known for the big, flashy campaign that was run five years ago, and still is something that is buzzy . . . the organization has done a fantastic job . . . putting the people behind the campaign."[12]

Unfortunately, many current constituent messages often do not include the elements to make their advocacy as effective as it could be (your personal story, why you oppose/support the issue/bill, information about the issue/bill's impact, and a specific ask). Check out CMF data on how helpful it is for constituent messages to include that info versus how often it's actually included:

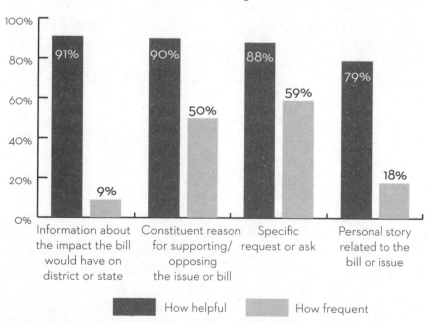

"How helpful is it for messages [from constituents] to include the following? How frequently do messages include the following?"

Congressional Management Foundation, 2016

These are big gaps. The good news? Now that you know what's important to include, your outreach will have all these things; you'll stand out from the crowd. When you're writing a letter or email, remember that it doesn't need to be pages and pages long (in fact, it shouldn't be!). It can be two to three paragraphs, as long as it includes the elements that will make it effective. As one congressional staffer told the OpenGov Foundation in their 2017 research, "If you want to be heard, use your own voice."[13]

It's also important to note that all of the outreach tactics we've talked about—emails, letters, etc.—become part of the public record. If you've watched C-SPAN, or a presidential debate, you'll have heard candidates tell stories. These stories are from their constituents who have come forward and whose experiences have left an impression.

I *totally* understand that all of this can feel intimidating or overwhelming. There's no quick fix when it comes to changing policy; engaging thoughtfully and advocating effectively for the issues you care about takes time and preparation. If you really care about an issue, you need to be prepared to do more than make one phone call or write one email. I promise that it *does* become less intimidating the more that you do it, but it can be really scary at first to use our voices in a public way. This is why it's so important to be able to tap into your passion for your priority issue or issues. It keeps you moving forward, especially when it feels risky to do so. Write down why you think your issue or issues are important enough to give your time and energy to and put it somewhere you can see it all the time. Find others who feel the same way you do and lean on each other when it gets hard (remember, this stuff does not change overnight). There is power in your passion and in your persistence.

It can also help to remember that your representative wants to hear from constituents like you so they can be more effective. They want to engage in more thoughtful, high-quality ways with the people they represent. If you're willing to put in the time and energy, and you use the tools that are proven to make your communications more effective, you'll see results.

I spoke with Minnesota lieutenant governor Peggy Flanagan, the highest-ranking Native woman elected to statewide executive office in the country (*learn more about Lieutenant Governor Flanagan in her Advocate in Action profile on page 178*), who told me, "[T]o do any of these [advocacy] jobs well, it requires that you really know who you are and embrace your experience and life, and then bring that perspective into [your representative's] office . . . To be honest, I think it is the only thing that is required [to be an effective advocate] is to really know your personal story, who you are, where you come from, and why you care about the things you care about. Leadership doesn't look one way."[14]

Following are specific tactics for employing some of these advocacy strategies.

HOW TO CALL YOUR REPRESENTATIVE

- **Be polite!** Typically, it will be an intern or junior staff member who's answering the phone; they may be as nervous as you are.

- **Identify yourself as a constituent** (share your name and zip code); remember that elected officials want to hear from people that *they* represent.

- **State your "call to action."** This should be regarding the specific issue you're calling about, which most often will be one of three things:
   ◊ voting a certain way on an upcoming bill
   ◊ co-sponsoring/introducing a bill (remember to do your homework beforehand and see if any bills have previously been introduced on this topic!)
   ◊ making a statement

- **Allow them to respond:**
   ◊ If they're already doing what you want them to, thank them.
   ◊ If not, explain why this is important to you (your story) in 30 seconds or less, the expertise/experience you bring to this issue, and how this is affecting your district more broadly.

- **Ask them to confirm that your opinion is being recorded.**

- **Say thank you and hang up!**

- **Save their contact information.** Afterward, save the representative's local and DC office numbers in your cell phone. If there's a big vote or bill, you may not be able to get through to their

DC office; their local office is less likely to have the same amount of phone traffic. Plus, the staffers there are also more likely to be based locally and may potentially be more sympathetic to the issue you're bringing up.

- **Follow up.** Feel free to follow up a couple weeks later, if nothing's happened, to check in on the status of your issue (or even schedule time to come and meet your elected official in person!).

HOW TO WRITE A LETTER/EMAIL TO AN ELECTED OFFICIAL

- **Address the letter appropriately.** Whether you're writing a physical letter or an email, use your official's proper title (e.g., senator, council member, etc.). Also, include your return address and contact information so the elected official can respond.

- **Keep it short!** One page is really all you need to get your point across (about 500 words if you're writing an email), and, again, focus on one specific issue (don't make it a laundry list of complaints).

- **Include the fact that you are a constituent.** Similar to a phone call, tell your story—how this issue affects you and others in your district—and state your call to action (again, be as specific as possible).

- **Share your personal relationship with the elected official, if any.** Did you vote for this person? Contribute to their campaign? Volunteer? Meet with them? Reference it. For example: "I voted for you in 2016, but have been disappointed in your lack of action on X."

- **Take into consideration the urgency of your issue** when deciding which mode of communication—physical letter or email—to use. If it's especially urgent, write an email; physical letters go through a more vigorous screening process.

Here's a sample letter template to get you started (but remember to make it your own!):

Date
Your name
Your address
Your email
Your phone number

The Honorable *proper title and name*
Legislative body (e.g., United States Senate)
Office address

Dear (*proper title and name, e.g., Senator Murray*),

As a constituent who lives in (*town or city*), I'm writing to ask that you (*specific request*).

 This is an important issue to me personally, as well as to our community. It's important to me because (*brief summary of your personal experience with this issue*).

 It's important to our community and your district more broadly because (*brief summary of how it impacts the district; cite any data or evidence, if available*).

 Thank you.

Best,
Your name

HOW TO SCHEDULE AND RUN A MEETING WITH A REPRESENTATIVE

Scheduling the meeting

- Look at the legislative calendar of the elected official you're trying to meet with, if it's available; remember that elected officials will often split their time between the Capitol and their district offices (and officials will be solely in the district when legislatures are in recess). Are you able to travel to Washington, DC, or your state capitol? If not, you'll need to specifically ask a scheduler or staff member the next time the official plans to be in the district.

- Submit a meeting request. Many times, elected officials will have forms you can submit through their websites to request meetings. If there isn't an online form, there may be contact information listed for a staff member responsible for the official's schedule. If there's none of that, call the office directly and ask who is responsible and for their contact information! Your meeting request should include info about you and what you'd like to meet about, as well as a requested meeting date. Make sure you do this well in advance of when you want to meet—ideally about a month ahead of time.

- Follow up with a phone call. If you submitted a meeting request or sent an email to a scheduler and haven't heard back, follow up by phone a day or two later. But remember that staffers are incredibly busy, so be kind! They're not ignoring you. When you do get in touch with a member of the staff, be as flexible as you can about the date and time of your meeting. Your elected official has a lot of competing things going on.

- Confirm the date and time the day prior. Schedules of elected officials change all the time, so call ahead or email the staff member you've been in touch with to make sure the time will still work.

Running the meeting
- Be on time and be polite!

- Stay focused on the one issue you're there to discuss, as you would for a phone call or letter or email. Make sure you've prepared the story you want to tell about how this issue affects you and your fellow constituents. You might only have 15 minutes, so be as succinct and clear as possible, particularly around what you want your official to *do* about this particular issue.

- Don't be upset if you end up meeting with a staffer instead of your elected official. Chances are, that staffer may actually be more knowledgeable about that particular issue than your official and will be critical in shaping your official's response to that issue. This is also a great opportunity to begin building a long-term relationship with a member of your representative's staff.

- Share materials (one to two pages) that capture the core messages or information you want to deliver, particularly any background data or additional detail about the issue you were there to discuss. You don't need to go through this during the meeting, but it's helpful as a leave-behind!

Following up after the meeting
- Send a note to the staffer or representative, thanking them for their time (if you send an email, attach a PDF of your leave-behind materials, so they have them easily accessible digitally as well).

- Keep the conversation going! You can follow up afterward with one of the official's staffers about the issue or cause you met to discuss, or, longer term, with invitations for your elected official to a relevant event, or even with an article or new development about the issue you're advocating for. Again, this is a great way to build a relationship with their office—you'll be the person top of mind for them when they need information or expertise on this issue in the future.

If you're trying to meet with a local representative (not a member of Congress), there's a good chance you'll be able to get together with them and/or their staff in person. The first time someone told me that was a possibility, I'll be honest, I didn't believe it. But I made it my New Year's resolution one year to reach out to my then-city council member, Helen Rosenthal, to try to schedule an in-person meeting. I emailed her scheduler (whose contact info I got from her website) and said, "I have an event coming up that I'd love for the councilwoman to join. There will be about 30 women there, all live in NYC, a few are constituents, and they're all incredibly eager to better understand how local government works and operates. Would the councilwoman be willing to meet them and do a Q&A with the group?" The scheduler's response could have knocked me over with a feather: "Sure, what day and time? Let's get it on the calendar." I'm not a CEO or a member of Congress, but I did have access to a community of women who were engaged and wanted to learn, and a few weeks later, we had an awesome meeting with the councilwoman.

Meeting with a representative can be especially important if you want to bring attention to an issue that you think may not be on their radar, or if there isn't current legislation on the floor. As former state senator Wendy Davis explained:

> If you're concerned about an issue where there's not yet been a bill filed . . . one of the first things you'll want to do is meet with your representative . . . to talk with them about your idea. As a state senator, some of the very best ideas I had came from constituents who met with me either in my district office or my office in the state capitol and helped me understand a problem that needed a solution. One example I can think of was someone who came in to share with me their concern about the potential backlog of rape kits in our state. That turned into me filing a bill requiring an accounting from all law enforcement agencies to disclose what their backlog was. It revealed that we were looking at somewhere in the range of 20,000 untested rape kits in our state and that resulted then in some very proactive legislation to address that backlog. So don't ever worry that your thought or idea is one that will be dismissed because I can assure you that many legislators . . . are very eager to hear from constituents about problems that need solving and ways that we can be helpful in that regard.[15]

If you can't meet directly with your representative, don't sweat it. Former Quorum employee Libby Wuller has the following advice for you: "Get to know the staff. That legislator has dozens of meetings a day across a variety of policy topics; especially if they're in the House and have a smaller staff, they're running a hundred miles an hour. [They have] a few areas where they have a depth of knowledge, most likely related to the committees they sit on, but if you're going in to talk about an issue that's *not* related to one of their committees, that topic can fall onto one of those staffers . . . Meeting with a staffer is frequently thought of as a step down but it's probably your best strategic opportunity."[16]

And don't just get in touch: *stay* in touch. As Wuller says, once you meet with the staff, "Keep their contact information. Send them an email every couple of months. Find the person in the office whose job it is to pay attention to that issue area and when you have news (for example, if you're holding a fundraising walk to solicit money for your issue), make sure the staffer knows it's happening. You're never going to get that correspondence back and forth from a legislator, but if you can get that staffer in your corner and you can be top of mind, be the name and face that staffer thinks of when they think of that issue, that is your golden ticket."[17] Your news doesn't have to be as big as arranging a major event, either. It could be new research on the issue, a development at the local level, a new organization you or a group you're involved with are partnering with—just keep them informed!

Keep in mind that, when it comes to contacting your representative—whether you're calling their office or arranging to meet them—you don't have to do all of the heavy lifting yourself. Sherry Leiwant, cofounder and co-president of A Better Balance (*whose Advocate in Action profile begins on page 161*), recommends seeking out and working with nonprofit and advocacy organizations that align with your areas of priority if you want to lobby your elected officials, as they are most likely already doing this kind of work. "Whenever there are issues that are before the legislature, there will be groups that are going to spend resources . . . to bring people to the state capitol, for example, or more locally to city hall to talk to their legislators,"[18] Leiwant says. Those organized trips are typically called "lobby days."

"Normally what happens in a lobby day is that the organizations that are responsible for putting those days together will schedule the meetings with the legislators and . . . bring people, hire the buses, or give people information how to get to city hall and then divide people into groups so that they can meet with as many legislators as possible to talk about the issue or issues that are most important to them," Leiwant explains. Not only are lobby days an opportunity to engage with your representative face-to-face, they're also just effective—Leiwant shared that bringing people who really cared about the issues made a big difference in being able to pass bills addressing sick days and paid family leave. Finally, Leiwant says, "It's also empowering to be able to talk to people who are making decisions about your life. So I think that it's a great opportunity for people to do that."

If there are organizations that are fighting for the issues that *you* care about, join their mailing lists or start volunteering; both are great ways to learn when lobby days are happening and how to get involved.

Outside of issue-focused organizations, also consider working with corporations to make progress on the issues you care about. As Rachna Choudhry, cofounder of POPVOX (*see her Advocate in Action Profile on page 24*), told me, "One of the biggest changes in advocacy I've seen . . . is that, before, companies weren't so vocal about specific legislation. They often relied on their trade associations to speak on their behalf or the chamber of commerce. But now you see so many companies speaking out on current affairs, especially around social issues like the bathroom bill debates in North Carolina or stronger gun control legislation. It helps to think about how businesses, small or large, might relate to your issue. Is there a company in your area that might be interested in learning more about how they could get involved? It's worth asking and building a relationship."[19]

Here's a quick summary of the Dos and Don'ts we've discussed for lobbying your representatives for change if you want to make a big impact.

DON'T:

- . . . expect online petitions and form emails alone to influence your representative's point of view; they're impersonal and often don't allow representatives to confirm that you are a constituent. Petitions are essentially a way for organizations to build their membership lists; they're not always the most effective when it comes to influencing your elected officials. And as former state senator Wendy Davis warned AIT members about form emails, "An email can oftentimes be something that you just copy, paste, and send, and what's left out of it usually is that personal connection, which makes it less resonant than it could be: a personal letter, story, and narrative. As a legislator, oftentimes letters [with a personal story] were put directly in front of me to read . . . because [my staff] felt they were ones that would really be important for me to see."[20]

- . . . use scripts for phone calls and emails. In other words, don't use other people's voices as a substitute for your own (though using some statistics or data pulled from scripts is fine). Using a script to call is better than not reaching out at all, but relying on it means you're not nearly as effective as you could be. Don't forget to share why the issue matters to you in *your* voice, even if you do use a script as a starting point.

- ... call representatives or political officials who don't represent you. Again, representatives don't care as much about constituents they don't represent, because only their constituents can rehire or fire them. There are exceptions, like the Speaker of the House, who may care about the national pulse on an issue. But for the most part, you should be focusing on your own representatives, especially locally, on the state and municipal levels.

- ... use social media as your only advocacy tool. Again, social media can be important for community and campaign building, particularly when it comes to raising awareness of an issue, but it is not especially persuasive if you're trying to influence your representatives, unless your post or hashtag goes viral.

DO:

- ... engage in tactics that allow your representatives to get to know you. Make phone calls, write individualized emails and letters, and meet with them in person. Use your own voice around your own issues. Make it personal! Why does this issue matter to you?

- ... be specific. Include information on this issue as it relates to your community, district, or state, and share specific details of how it affects your community and what exactly you're asking your elected official to *do* in response. Ask your representative for a specific outcome, whether it's voting a certain way on a bill or introducing new legislation.

- ... be professional. This means being both polite and prepared (for example, creating the fact sheets or one- to two-page leave-behinds that allow your representatives or their staffers to refer back to the key data or information about your request).

- ... sync up and work with other organizations to identify moments of urgency and opportunities to meaningfully engage. Research and support organizations that are active on your issue. Sign up for their mailing lists and/or reach out to their employees or volunteers. Take advantage of their work and organizing so you're not starting from scratch!

ENGAGE IN INDIRECT INFLUENCE

You've done your research, you're engaging your representatives ... but there are also other, *indirect* ways to influence policy decisions. These are ways that you can contribute to or change the public discourse on a given topic, perhaps making it a priority issue for your community or convincing others it's a cause they should participate in as well.

In some ways, tactics that involve engaging or mobilizing the community can be the scariest because of the public nature of the action. They are the most visible, and therefore the most vulnerable to criticism. I once attended a seminar with **The OpEd Project** in New York City, which trains attendees on how to write (and publish) op-eds. I'll never forget what my facilitator said: "When you say things of consequence, there may be consequences. The alternative is to be inconsequential."

One way you can engage in public discourse is by writing a letter to the editor or an op-ed, either for a print or online publication. What's the difference between the two? Let's break it down. A letter to the editor is typically a response to something the publication has already printed (this could be an article or column). Letters to the editor are typically pretty short (around 250 words) and are printed in the editorial section of the publication. An op-ed (the term comes from their original location printed "opposite the editorial page") is a longer piece, around 700 words, and is typically commentary or opinion. It's easier to get a letter to the editor published than an op-ed, but both are important ways to share your perspective.

Publicly sharing your views and experiences can be very impactful because it can raise awareness of an issue in your community, but it can also influence the actions of your representatives. Your representatives (or their staffs at the very least) are constantly reading op-eds and letters to the editor of local papers to keep a finger on the pulse of constituent opinion, especially if those letters specifically refer to the action (or inaction) of that representative.

If you're excited about the idea of writing an op-ed, definitely check out **The OpEd Project** as your go-to resource. Their website has a whole section dedicated to incredibly useful tips and tricks for op-eds, from writing to submission. It even includes a guide for submitting to the top online and print publications in the country that lays out all the rules and requirements (e.g., word limits, submission contact information) for op-eds and letters to the editor for each publication, from the *New York Times* to the *Cincinnati Enquirer*. **AAUW** (the American Association of University Women) also has great, step-by-step advice for how to write a letter to the editor or an op-ed.

And if this is intimidating to you, remember that you don't have to go it alone! Consider coauthoring with a friend. Not only will this take some of the pressure off, but being signed by multiple people could also signal to your representative or community that there's more weight behind your point of view. In fact, with regard to any of the advocacy tactics we've talked about, the more the merrier!

These tactics are going to help you make progress on the issues you care about, and, in addition, your participation will help close critical gender gaps in public discourse. In 2019, PhD candidate Kimberly Probolus wrote her own *New York Times* letter to the editor lamenting the lack of women's voices in the letter to the editor section of the paper. She wrote: "As I scan through various national newspapers, day after day, year after year, I find myself hoping that someday, *eventually*, women will be represented proportionally. I am always disappointed; they always skew male."[21] This was especially troubling to Probolus given that, "unlike an Op-Ed—where the writer presumably has some expertise in the subject matter—anybody can submit a letter to the editor. It is, I'd argue, the most democratic section of the paper." Writing (and submitting) letters to the editor, Probolus argued in her letter, is "asserting that your ideas and words deserve an audience in a world that has historically devalued them."

Not only did the *New York Times* publish her letter, they responded to it. They shared that only a third of letter-to-the-editor submissions tend to come from women, and they committed to a goal of gender parity. As of February 2020, they shared that, while 43 percent of their published letters to the editor were now written by women, the percentage of submissions from women was still hovering between 25 and 30 percent.[22]

This gap isn't unique to letters to the editor, either. Foreign Policy Interrupted (FPI), an organization that aims to address the gender disparities in foreign policy experts represented in media, looked at four of the most widely circulated newspapers in the country (the *New York Times*, *Washington Post*,

LA Times, and the *Wall Street Journal*) to understand what percentage of women were contributing op-eds on the topic of foreign policy and national security. They found, on average, that in 2016, men still accounted for 81 percent of total op-ed writers on those topics.[23]

You should consider writing in and sharing your perspective, whether in a letter to the editor or op-ed, on whatever issue you care about. But there are actions you can take to ensure women's voices are equally represented in public discourse even when you're not the one speaking, by helping to create demand on the system. If you're at an event and there are all-male panels, write a note to the organizer; you can share it with a volunteer and ask them to pass it along. The same goes for the news; on talk shows, TV, or radio, raise your hand if the gender ratio seems skewed. Help be part of the solution by using apps like **GenderAvenger**, which collects information about the gender and race of participants in public dialogue. The app also allows you to time how long women spend talking versus how long men are talking. Creating greater gender equality in public discourse means creating space for more women's voices in general. Encourage men to do the same; some high-profile men have refused to speak on panels unless there are women on the panel as well. We need more of that. We certainly have an incredible supply of talented, extraordinary, inspiring women—let's make sure they're heard.

. . . .

Before we wrap up this chapter on advocacy, a brief note on an important topic we haven't touched on yet: protests. Protests and marches can serve *incredibly* important functions, most important among them building a powerful community, bringing visibility to an issue, and showing solidarity on that issue (especially important when the policy or issue being protested affects groups that are marginalized or have limited voice or power in the situation). However, like petitions, it's difficult for public officials to know whether *their* constituents are participating in a protest, and that means it is often difficult for those officials to know how to act or respond, particularly if there isn't a clear set of demands.

Sometimes protests aren't very well organized, either; there's a lot of passion for the issue, but not a lot of clarity on exactly what participants are hoping to achieve by protesting. Is it helping to bring awareness to the issue? Is it trying to change a particular policy? If you're joining a protest, make sure the issue or issues that are motivating you to be there are also ones you're advocating for in more *direct* ways as well (for example, through visits or calls to the offices of relevant legislators). Push to make sure that the organizers and other participants are being clear on the explicit outcomes they're hoping to achieve through the protests.

That said, there is much to be learned from the protests and demonstrations that *are* successful. Take, for example, the student-led March for Our Lives demonstration. Organized by survivors of the shooting at Marjory Stoneman Douglas High School in Parkland, Florida, in 2018 (in which 17 students tragically were killed and 17 more injured), the protest was one of the largest in US history. Some estimate that nearly 800,000 people participated in the march in Washington, DC[24]—and this doesn't include the thousands more who joined over 830 similar demonstrations across the world.[25] But the Parkland teens' work didn't stop there; they also met with members of Congress, organized a group of 100 students to go to the Florida state capitol to meet with lawmakers, and traveled across the state to register voters for the midterms. The march helped launch a movement, but was just the beginning. To date, 137 laws to prevent gun violence have been passed since the Parkland shooting.[26]

Or take the incredible example of the Black Lives Matter movement: In the first half of 2020, an estimated 15 to 26 *million* people in the US participated in protests, outraged over the murder of George Floyd, Breonna Taylor, Ahmaud Arbery, and too many others.[27] As of mid-2020, this mass mobilization had already led to concrete changes, from the removal of Confederate statues from the US Capitol and several state capitols, to commitments to reimagine police departments in cities across the country.

But none of this would have been possible if the movement's infrastructure hadn't already been built over the prior seven years. Black Lives Matter was cofounded in 2013 by three Black women: Patrisse Cullors, Alicia Garza, and Opal Tometi. Because of the robust infrastructure, relationship building, and strategic decision-making they worked on over the course of nearly a decade, thousands of organizations and activists were ready—ready to organize protests and mobilize protestors, and ready to push for specific local, state, and federal policy changes.[28] Protests are powerful, but what we often see in impactful protests is just the tip of the iceberg.

At the end of the day, advocacy is a careful balance of analysis and action. You want to make sure you have enough information about your issue that you feel confident and prepared, but don't let not knowing *every-thing* prevent you from acting. Remember: Your experience is what makes you an expert. And you'll only learn more about how the political process works through the trial and error of navigating it. Your representative or their staffer is not going to debate you! They're there to listen and take your perspectives into consideration as they shape policy. Your voice is valuable, important, and necessary.

Advocate in Action: Sherry Leiwant, Cofounder and Co-President, A Better Balance*

Sherry Leiwant in 2005 cofounded A Better Balance, whose mission is to promote equality and expand choices for men and women at all income levels so they can care for their families without risking their economic security. Prior to founding A Better Balance, Leiwant was a senior staff attorney at NOW Legal Defense and Education Fund, where she ran the State Advocacy Project, and worked on issues intersecting women's rights and poverty, including reproductive health, violence, and childcare. Leiwant graduated summa cum laude and Phi Beta Kappa from Princeton University and from Columbia Law School, Columbia University.

On turning personal passion into a national advocacy organization:

I was very interested both in the rights of low-wage workers and also women who did not have economic security, especially single mothers or women living in poverty. My father died when I was very young, so I had a single mother who struggled because of wage inequality and closed opportunities. Those issues are where my heart is. I worked for the Welfare Law Center, which was a welfare policy and litigation law office, and then I worked for the NOW Legal Defense and Education Fund, a women's rights organization that grew out of the National Organization for Women. I started and ran their Women in Poverty Project and worked on issues of childcare discrimination, and particularly on the new welfare programs and reproductive rights issues in those programs, and domestic violence.

During those years I had three children, and the lack of support for working mothers in terms of public policy really hit hard for me. There were five of us at NOW Legal Defense who wanted to work on paid family medical leave and childcare from the perspective of women who didn't have access to it, so a group of us just decided that we would found our own organization. Around the same time, there was a lot of talk about the opt-out revolution. Women in the workforce are choosing to give up very good jobs because we just can't balance work and family. Our feeling was, if it's that hard for people who are professionals, how much harder is it for women who don't have the same resources? We advocated around these issues—legislation, litigation, and direct representation—because we felt like you shouldn't be doing policy work without some grounding in what's actually going on in people's lives.

---

* Sherry Leiwant, interview with the author, October 11, 2019 (adapted for clarity).

On leading women-centric advocacy:

We take cases to court that we think are going to make a difference. And we have had a lot of success partially because we take people's stories into account. In our pregnancy discrimination work, we were getting calls from women who were refused extra water at their workplace. Women in retail who were denied extra bathroom breaks. Women in construction, in heavy lift situations, who were not assigned lighter work for those few months. We were able to pass laws all over the country that protect women by giving them specific and reasonable accommodations when they're pregnant, and now we're working at the federal level on laws that will help all American women: the Pregnant Workers Fairness Act, a national pregnancy-accommodation law, the Healthy Families Act, a national sick-time law, and a federal paid family-leave law.

On influencing others by meeting them where they are, and helping them take action:

All people, first and foremost, think about themselves and their families. That's to be expected. So relating issues to people's real lives is the most important thing you can do. For example, even if you're somebody who has paid sick time, there are still public health issues involved: people without sick days are going to work when they're sick and riding the subway with you, or sending their kids to school with your children. That speaks to people. And also, having stories of people who were like, "I'm a mom, I have kids, my daughter had to go to the emergency room. I called my bank employer, and they said it was OK. But then when I came in, they fired me." These stories speak to our humanity.

It's also important to give people a road map as to what they can do if you're trying to pass legislation. Getting them to learn about the issue and then speak to their representatives or write something for their local paper. Together we can all get the word out.

CHAPTER 8

. . . .

CAMPAIGNING

It's true. I no longer have highly trained, professional campaign man-
agers. So what? Are most murders committed by highly trained, pro-
fessional assassins? No, they're committed by friends and coworkers!
—Leslie Knope, Parks and Recreation

When you see the word "campaign," you might assume I'm sug-
gesting you run for office—and I am, if you're interested! But
you can also campaign on behalf of others, by volunteering your
time or expertise, and by contributing financially—both for candidates and
for issue-based organizations. Supporting individuals and organizations that
are committed to the issues you care about can be an incredibly effective
way to make progress.

CONTRIBUTE FINANCIALLY

A quick flashback: It's July 2017 in New York City. Weaving through
crowded midtown sidewalks, clumsily jumping over rapidly forming pud-
dles as I clutch a newly purchased umbrella, all I can think is: *I hope the rain*
doesn't keep people away. I turn the corner and see my destination: an Irish

pub on West 42nd Street. Noting the chalkboard sign out in front of the bar—"Senator Gillibrand fundraising event on the 2nd floor"—I walk in and begin to climb the stairs.

I shouldn't have worried. The room is full and buzzing. A crowd of twenty- and thirty-somethings excitedly chat over beer and wine, eager for the event to begin. I immediately see a number of friendly faces, girlfriends I had invited to be there, as well as a member of the senator's fundraising team whom I'd met the month before. I head over to a table with name tags and spot mine amid those of my fellow Host Committee members. I grab it and squeeze into the crowd of animated guests. I immediately bump into one of the senator's NYC staffers, and we chat about the kinds of citizen engagement we're both seeing since Trump's win, and, before I know it, the event is underway.

That night, Connie Britton, star of *Nashville* and *Friday Night Lights*, took the stage (!) for a planned Q&A with New York senator Kirsten Gillibrand. While Britton was live onstage, Sen. Gillibrand joined by videoconference due to a delayed vote that kept her in Washington, DC. Their conversation was dynamic and wide-ranging: from the recent travel ban to how citizens can use their voices for impact, to how Connie and the senator met (answer: during a semester abroad in China while they were undergrads at Dartmouth). The senator fielded question after question from the crowd patiently, her answers insightful and specific. For many guests in the room, this was the first chance they had ever had to engage with one of their representatives in real time and in a relatively intimate environment. The space was packed and standing room only. I was so riveted by the conversation that, at the end of the night, I left the pub to a dry sky and completely forgot the overpriced, newly purchased umbrella I had stuffed into a corner earlier (not the first umbrella I've lost to a midtown bar, nor the last).

Before starting AIT, I had never made a donation to a political candidate, but I believe in the importance and power of campaign contributions today, *especially* in local races, where small amounts can make a big difference for candidates. Yes, money in politics is a *big* problem (more on that in Part III)—but the reality is that it costs money to run for office, regardless of whether a candidate is running at the federal, state, or local level. In 2012, the average winning US Senate candidate spent $10.4 million on their campaign, and the average winning US House candidate spent $1.3 million.[1] At the local level, in the 2013 NYC city council elections, my former city council member Helen Rosenthal spent $265,922.[2] As you can see, there are big differences in campaign spending based on the seat candidates are running for (as well as how competitive they are), but they all cost something.

Oklahoman Libby Wuller (whom we met in the previous chapter) is passionate about electing more women to political office, and she is deeply involved in organizations like the RightNOW Women PAC, which works to elect more Republican women (Libby serves as the youngest member of the PAC). As Libby says: "Whether or not anyone feels like there should be more or less money involved in politics, it is the world we operate in right now. If it's the system we're operating in, then women need to know and be empowered to have a voice in that system . . . The system exists as it does today, and women aren't participating. Until we change the system, we need more women to participate."[3]

However, participating in the system (even as it is) doesn't necessarily mean spending a lot. Wuller says: "Something I think people don't understand is how little money it takes to give to a candidate to get that campaign to pay attention. Of course, it's different for different levels of government, but if you were to give $15, $25, or $50 to your state representative and then also get your friends to contribute the same amount, then have people come over for coffee or wine night—the candidate would come. They would show up; they would be there; they would listen to your issues; they would engage in dialogue . . . They believe they're the person that can represent your community and they believe they have ideas that best represent or reflect the change the community needs, and in order to do that, they need to be able to win. And they need money to be able to do that."[4]

If you *are* able to contribute larger amounts, for better or for worse, this is how you get access to candidates today. By contributing $100, and sharing the invitation with friends, I was able to be in a room with a relatively small number of other people listening to a senator and a famous actor talking about issues that were important to me, and getting a better sense of my then senator's priorities. To me, that was worth it.

Your political giving doesn't just increase your access; it can also help create a more diverse candidate pool—in this way, you're able to "vote with your purse" (meaning you help candidates get in and stay in the race through your financial support) for the kind of candidate you want to see in office. Unfortunately, not all types of candidates get equal financial support: research from the Center for Responsive Politics, Common Cause Education Fund, and RepresentWomen found that women of color receive the least in political contributions from donors. In 2014, the average amount received from donors giving more than $200 was lower for candidates of color, especially women—and this wasn't just from men. Men *and* women donors, on average, contributed more to white women than to women of color. Take a look at the table below.

Average total individual donations to congressional candidates, by race and gender of candidates, 2014 (donors giving $200+)[5]

	Average from women donors	Average from men donors
White men candidates	$161,060	$533,816
White women candidates	$234,912	$457,461
POC men candidates	$109,599	$339,029
POC women candidates	$109,836	$223,123

We can do so much better than this! Supporting candidates financially, particularly women of color, can help create a more level playing field for those running and bring more diversity to politics. Furthermore, research shows that women, like men, give the *least* in campaign contributions to challengers and give the *most* to incumbents, which may contribute to incumbent advantage (and perpetuate overrepresentation of white men in elected office, given that they make up the vast majority of incumbents today).[6] Ensuring that contributions support a diverse set of candidates, particularly women of color, ultimately will create more competitive races as well as, hopefully, more diverse representation at all levels of government.

Donating to campaigns is yet another way in which women are under-participating politically compared to men. In 2016, not only were 62.9 percent of total donors men, but men gave *more* of the total contributed to candidates as well; 70.4 percent of all contributions came from men. Men were also nearly twice as likely as women to give more than $200, and exactly twice as likely to give more than $2,700.[7] In short: Men are giving more, and more often. Part of this may be because women are not being *asked* to give. As GOP fundraiser Lisa Spies told *The Atlantic*, "I had women all over the country tell me, 'You know what? Nobody ever asks me. They call and ask for my husband.'"[8]

Let's not ignore, of course, that men are likely to earn more than women: you're probably familiar with the phenomenon of the gender pay gap. Overall, women in the US are paid 80 cents for every dollar paid to men, and the disparity is significantly worse for women of color.[9] Black women, for example, earn 61 cents for each dollar earned by white men,[10] and Latinas earn 53 cents.[11] The National Partnership for Women & Families found the wage gap constitutes up to $900 billion in lost earnings for American women every year.[12] This is obviously a huge problem with many implications, one of which may be that it hinders women's ability to contribute financially to political campaigns.

Women may also want to give to causes that have more *direct*, tangible benefits: giving money to a candidate who may not win can feel like gambling. Plus, aren't there better ways to spend money? For example, giving to a charity or investing money in your family might feel like more urgent priorities.

Still, I think there is a significant benefit of contributing to candidates, even if it's only five dollars, creating a counterweight to special-interest dollars.

As we talked about a little bit in Part I, there are typically limits to how much one person can donate to political campaigns. For local and state candidates, these will vary across municipalities and states. There are 11 states in the US that have *no* contribution limits for individuals at the state level: Alabama, Indiana, Iowa, Mississippi, Nebraska, North Dakota, Oregon, Pennsylvania, Texas, Utah, and Virginia.[13] For the remaining 39 states, contribution limits vary wildly: check out the table below for the highest and lowest caps to illustrate the differences (they're pretty shocking).[14]

	Governor	State senator	State representative
Highest limit on individual contributions	$47,100 (New York)	$13,292 (Ohio)	$13,292 (Ohio)
Lowest limit on individual contributions	$500 (Alaska)	$180 (Montana)	$180 (Montana)

In other words, it's important to look at your state to understand your campaign contribution caps. And they can vary across primary and general elections, as well. The **National Conference of State Legislatures** is a great resource to find out contribution limits in your state.

At the federal level, contribution limits are a little more straightforward. For individuals giving to federal candidates, the limit is $2,800 per person per election.[15]

So, if you want to support a candidate financially, what can you do?

- **Contribute to campaigns you care about.** Give whatever you can afford, whether it's $1 or $100 or $1,000. Check to see if there are public matching programs in your city or state; contributing to campaigns in places with a public finance option will make your dollar go a lot further. In New York City, any donation I made to a city council candidate was matched eight to one. This made me feel really good about what I was able to give and the benefit it would have for local candidates. We'll talk more about public financing in Part III.

- **Host a fundraiser!** This is a great way to get to know a candidate in a more intimate setting, and help others learn more about them as well. (You could also use this opportunity to learn more about the issues or how the government works—candidates are happy to answer those questions, too!) Another benefit is being able to build relationships with your candidate and their staff. Especially for state and local candidates, this is actually a lot easier than you think. If you're not sure yet which candidate you want to support, start talking! Engage in a dialogue with your friends and your neighbors. Once you've selected a candidate, find out who is in charge of their fundraising (you can look them up on the candidate's website or go through the state or local party) and reach out to them.

- **Confirm with the candidate's campaign that fundraising is the most helpful thing you can do.** As Libby Wuller advises, ask the campaign: *What do you need?* "Because maybe it's not money," she says. "Maybe they have a lot of money coming in but they don't have anyone to put yard signs out." If their needs are monetary, Wuller says, "[W]omen are so good about asking for money for causes and we don't always think about that translating to candidates. Go talk to people, ask if they're interested [in supporting a particular candidate], and, if they are, find a way to get them into a room."[16] (We'll talk more about volunteering for campaigns in the next section.)

Political donations are also a good way to engage if you have limited time. When I've been too busy with work to volunteer for a campaign, or to spend time advocating for an issue that I care about, I've used campaign donations to support candidates. Remember, donations are necessary to help create the kind of races you want to see—ones that enable the best and the brightest to run for office, bring more diversity to our government, and ultimately lead to a more democratic, representative system.

VOLUNTEER YOUR TIME

Building on the idea of asking campaigns what they need, there are ways to support a campaign beyond monetary contributions. Yes, all campaigns need money, but they also need people to help get the word out about their platforms and candidacy by making phone calls and knocking on doors. They need people to help mail out flyers and other campaign materials. They need people to help organize and clean campaign offices, or maintain databases of donors and volunteers, or run social media. Regardless of how much time you're able to give to a campaign, there is a role for you. They often need all the help they can get! Even in my busiest jobs, I've always found a few hours on the weekend during election season to help candidates and issue-based organizations I'm passionate about support-ing (even if that's making phone calls to potential voters—called "phone banking"—from my apartment!).

Volunteering for a campaign benefits both the candidate *and* you. From the candidate's perspective, they're getting much needed womanpower to help build awareness of their campaign and the issues they stand for, and to keep things organized and running smoothly. The benefits to you are equally important: you'll gain firsthand knowledge of the inner workings of a campaign—something many people don't know too much about. By volunteering for a campaign, you'll also learn a lot more about the candi-date you're supporting, including their nuanced views on all kinds of issues (including, of course, the issues that are most important to you).

The first day you show up as a volunteer can be a little intimidating—how are you supposed to help represent a candidate's platform and what they stand and hope for, for your community, when it's all new to you? Never fear. All volunteers were once in your shoes. Everyone has to start somewhere! Campaigns are usually very good about creating and distributing ready-to-go materials and talking points to support newbies (and of course to make sure everyone is giving a consistent pitch and message). You'll be surprised how quickly you pick things up just by hearing others give their pitch! Plus, the more time you spend volunteering, the more well versed and confident you'll become.

The type of work you'll do as a volunteer on a campaign will depend a lot on the amount of time you have, what the campaign needs most, and the unique skills you bring to the table. Great with numbers or Excel? Maybe you can help keep donor databases or expense records up to date. Savvy on social media? Perhaps you can work with the communications team on social media content or keeping their accounts consistent and updated. Have a background in coding or web development? Maybe you can help maintain or update the campaign website. The list goes on. There are so many things happening behind the scenes on a campaign that would benefit from your skill set and expertise, from experience in event planning to accounting to writing. And if you're already doing a lot of advocacy on an issue (say you have a local event coming up in support of that issue), you can work with the campaign team to see if that candidate would be interested in joining the event to show support. If so, you can help coordinate with the campaign to make that happen and make sure things run smoothly. The opportunities are nearly endless!

If you really love campaign work, you might decide it's worth pursuing full time—as a career. Lots of volunteers build relationships with the professional campaign team, and those relationships can lead to real job opportunities as new roles are created or open up on the team. And *if* the candidate wins, the campaign job could potentially lead to a career in local, state, or federal government. People who work on campaigns are some of the most hardworking, driven, idealistic people I've ever encountered. They care enough about a candidate's vision to make it their full-time job to help them win. Full-time staffers work *incredibly* hard to help make their candidate's visions for their community a reality; campaigns are notorious for the 24/7 nature of the work.

For Minnesota's lieutenant governor Peggy Flanagan, volunteering for a senate campaign was how she got her start in electoral politics. "It certainly wasn't my plan," the lieutenant governor told me. "I wasn't the little girl who dreamed about being the second most powerful person in the state of Minnesota." After majoring in child psychology and American Indian studies at the University of Minnesota, her plan was to work in the community after graduation, then ultimately go back to grad school to become an early childhood special education teacher—but the universe had other plans:

> My senior year of college [in 2002], I was driving by the Wellstone for Senate office and I just stopped. I said, "You know what, I really like Senator Wellstone, so I'm just going to check out what's happening in the office," and I walked into the office and about seven different people enthusiastically welcomed me and asked if I was there to volunteer and I said, "I guess so!" So I sat down with complete strangers and stuffed envelopes for two hours and talked to folks from all different walks of life and communities at that table, and we all had a shared value . . . that we all do better when we all do better. And I got bit by the bug.
>
> At that point I never thought I'd run for office, but [felt it was] critically important that our voices—"our voices," meaning of the Native community—are part of the electoral politics in this state and that our issues are addressed, so [I decided] to keep working on campaigns. Through the process, I met a lot of really amazing people . . . who took me under their wing and gave me lots of opportunities . . . It was really helpful for me to see that electoral politics was not the be-all and end-all but was a tool in our toolbox to make change.[17]

There are so many great, impactful ways to support a candidate you feel passionately about that go beyond campaign donations. Here's some advice for doing just that:

- **Update your resume.** It's always best practice to bring an up-to-date resume with you when you're looking to volunteer. You have probably already done this, but be sure to identify on that resume any particular strengths you have, or programs/software you're comfortable using, like Excel or Adobe Acrobat, for example. Not only will you come off as serious and more professional, but a campaign will hopefully be able to find an opportunity for you that closely aligns with your skill set. This will ensure that you're able to add the most value possible with your time, however limited it may be! Plus, you'll feel even better and more motivated because you're able to contribute something that you excel at. Playing to your strengths and passions is also important when it comes to making your engagement sustainable (more on that in Chapter 9!). If there isn't a role or activity right away that matches your skill set, don't despair; the needs of a campaign change all the time, and they'll be grateful for you being a team player and helping however you can at the outset.

- **Get in touch with a campaign.** There are a couple ways to go about this. First, you can find a local campaign office for the candidate you want to support (this information is almost always on the candidate's campaign website). Go there and bring your resume! Express that you're interested in volunteering, and leave your resume with the team (make sure it has your contact information on it!). They may have an opportunity for you right away, or may get in touch later, as the campaign heats up.

  If there's no campaign office listed or it's inconvenient for you to get to, there are usually volunteer forms on the campaign website. You'll be able to express the kinds of opportunities you're most interested in (canvassing, phone banking, fundraising, delivering yard signs, etc.). You'll also likely be added to a newsletter that will notify you and other volunteers of upcoming opportunities to support the candidate. These mailings will keep you apprised of live events that you can show up to and support the candidate with your presence as well.

  For presidential elections, even if you live somewhere that you think of as a "safe" state (maybe you're a Democrat in a blue state or a Republican in a red state), campaigns help organize and direct volunteers to where they can be most useful. For example, although I lived in New York City in 2016 while volunteering for the Clinton campaign, I did phone banking that involved calling voters in Florida. In addition, the campaign had organized buses to bring New Yorkers to Pennsylvania for in-person canvassing and get out the vote (GOTV) efforts. Given that Florida and

Pennsylvania are both swing states, this made me feel that, even being a Democrat in a city that was most likely going to vote for a Democrat, I was helping to get out the vote in places that would make a difference.

- **Bring others with you!** This is another way to make giving back more fun and more social. Find opportunities to volunteer with a group—maybe your friends or neighbors who also support the same candidate. If you're in college, Democrat or Republican clubs or even issue-based organizations are likely already organizing campaign volunteer opportunities during elections. So if you're currently a student, these groups are great places to start. If these groups *don't* exist on your campus, start them!

- **Be professional.** This likely goes without saying, but when you volunteer for a campaign, you're representing that candidate publicly. Be polite when you're engaging with potential voters, regardless of whether you agree with them. This can be hard! Obviously, you care passionately about your candidate. However, this isn't the forum to rant and rave (although there are times and places for that). Your objective is to represent the candidate as well as you possibly can, especially when you're engaging directly with voters. In all likelihood, you'll be so energized by getting to work alongside others who are like-minded and passionate about the issues you're passionate about, and by helping to support someone you believe in, that you'll be able to brush off those who don't. Expect to engage with people who disagree, and be prepared for it.

One note here: When a candidate agrees with you on every issue, wanting to mobilize and support them is easy. In all likelihood, though, most candidates will have some perspectives on issues that differ from yours. If, in a crowded election field, a particular candidate is the best option for your community (even if you disagree with them on *some* things), consider volunteering for them anyway. Or donating to their campaign. In battleground states or districts, candidates often have to make tough choices on issues—and these are the campaigns that often need the *most* resources or support. Food for thought!

RUN FOR OFFICE

If you have lots of great ideas for your community, running for office is something you should seriously consider. We won't spend much time on this section because there are a lot of great resources and organizations out there already, especially for women (**Running Start, She Should Run, Vote Run Lead, The Campaign School at Yale**, and **IGNITE,** just to name a few!), which I encourage you to check out if you're considering running. But here's some advice from County Commissioner Angela Conley in case you're looking to take the next step and run for office yourself:

> I want women not to doubt themselves. I'm a Black woman who'd never been in the political realm but [ran against] a twenty-eight-year incumbent who was a white man . . . There's going to be some self-doubt, but if this is something that's in your gut to do, do it.
>
> Seek out your "ride or dies": your best friend, your cousin, people who believe in you. Tell them, "I want to run for this seat and here's why." Then start reaching out to [elected officials]. Start reaching out to people you want to run against. Get to know them. Ask what it was like running for office or being in this position. Start taking notes and finding that out. Even if you hear, "Don't do it," keep taking notes. When people would say, "I'm not going to support you right now," I'd be like, "That's fine. I would just love your take on some things [the incumbent] has done." Find out who your base is—who are those three friends—and write down all of your elected officials and meet with them and have coffee. Training was helpful for me, too; you might find [classes or training programs] in your communities and take them. I would also say, go to your local caucus. Become a delegate there. Start getting involved and start seeing those inside, behind-the-scenes things that the typical person doesn't know about. Start prepping yourself to run and run as hard as you possibly can.
>
> I lost a lot of time with my family; there will be nights when you don't sleep, when you break down and cry. It's not easy running for office, and people know that. From the beginning, the day you launch, no matter who your incumbent is, don't ever go into running for office thinking you have it in the bag or that you're going to lose. Fight for this no matter what. Keeping that motivation going is what other people can feel and will naturally gravitate to. We can do it.[18]

If you win, you'll have an extraordinary platform from which to improve the lives of those who live in your community. And if you lose, just running and sharing your ideas can seriously shake things up. Challengers often change the discourse of the campaign, and they even shape the party's platform on a whole bunch of issues. Take, for example, the campaign of Liuba Grechen Shirley, who ran for election to the US House to represent New York's 2nd District. She lost her race but still made history. As a candidate, she lobbied the Federal Election Commission (FEC) to allow congressional candidates to use campaign contributions for childcare (this was previously not allowed). She won that battle with the FEC and managed to change the system by challenging it, even without winning the election. In the process, she's made things better for the women and men who will come after her, and she inspired others to make the same demands at the state level.

As Grechen Shirley told Vox in an interview before her 2018 election: "It's really, really difficult to take a year off of your life with no salary and somehow manage to pay your school loans and your mortgage and your taxes. That's the very real reason why we have so many millionaires in Congress. Almost half of our representatives are millionaires. Only one in ten of them even owe school loans. We need to make sure that we have a government that's actually reflective of our society."[19]

Or consider the example of Nabilah Islam, who ran in 2020 to represent Georgia's 7th District in the House of Representatives. Inspired by Grechen Shirley, she petitioned the FEC to use campaign funds to pay for health insurance. As she told *ELLE* magazine, "The average net worth of a Congressperson is $500,000, and that doesn't reflect America today. Instead of feeling ashamed of the fact that I wasn't a rich person, I was just like, 'This is a problem.' This is why government isn't for us—because it's not by us. I just leaned into it. It's really vulnerable to talk about the fact that I don't have healthcare or that I put my college loans into forbearance or the fact that I'm eating ramen on an everyday basis."[20] While the FEC closed her request when Islam lost her primary, it's another great example of candidates identifying barriers and putting pressure on the system to make public service possible for more people.

In this way, it's pretty simple: the best way to change the demographics of those who represent us is to support a diverse set of candidates. This means volunteering for their campaigns, donating so that they're able to run, running yourself, and even changing the system so that it's easier for everyone else to run, too (more on this in Part III). As Grechen Shirley and Islam show, we all have a lot more power and control than we think to help put in place a government that better reflects the people it serves.

Key Takeaways on Tools for Influence

- **Do your research and set the stage to keep learning and acting upon what you've learned.** Make it easy to contact and keep track of your political officials and representatives. Follow them on social media; save their phone numbers in your cell. When elections come around, look at the organizations that have endorsed them: Do they share your values and views? This is a helpful way to sift through the noise. Make sure you've prepped and planned for everything on your upcoming ballot—from candidates at *all* levels of government to propositions. Propositions can be tricky, so it's incredibly important to put in the work up front and in advance of heading to your polling place. Remember the who-what-when-where-how-why of voting!

- **Hold your representatives accountable by advocating for your issues and lobbying their offices directly (as well as indirectly!).** Put aside time to engage if this doesn't come naturally or isn't yet a habit. I don't know about you, but if something is not on my calendar, it doesn't exist for me. Schedule 30 minutes every other week and commit to it, whether it's to research an issue you care about, learn about your reps, or make a phone call. Put this time aside the way you would for a dinner with friends, a meeting, a workout class—and remember to engage in activities that make the most of your time. If you're doing outreach to a representative, always include the things that will make your outreach more effective! Start local. Attend a local public hearing. Make a phone call to your local representative about an issue you think could be improved. Build relationships with your local officials. Bring attention to your issues and help shape public opinion by sharing your story publicly, or demonstrate public support for a cause and put pressure on your elected officials by organizing or participating in a sit-in or protest.

- **Help candidates you care about win.** Volunteer for their campaigns. Donate to their campaigns, or hold a fundraiser! There's so much you can do to support a candidate running for office (even if it's just helping to build awareness of that candidate by doing your research and sharing what you've learned with your friends or on social media). If you don't believe any candidate has the vision you think is needed for your community to reach its full potential, consider running for office yourself. There are so many wonderful resources and organizations out there helping women run for office! Check them out, or consider donating to them to help other women run for office as well.

Advocate in Action: Peggy Flanagan, Lieutenant Governor of Minnesota*

Peggy Flanagan is Minnesota's fiftieth lieutenant governor Elected in 2018, she's the highest-ranking Native woman in executive office in the country. She worked for nearly a decade at Wellstone Action, the organization founded to carry on the work of the late senator Paul Wellstone. As one of the original trainers of Wellstone Action's signature program, Camp Wellstone, she has trained thousands of progressive activists, community and campaign organizers, and elected officials and candidates. Following her work at Wellstone Action, Peggy served as the executive director of Children's Defense Fund Minnesota, where she helped lead a coalition that advocated for (and won) an increase to the state's minimum wage in 2014. In 2015, she was elected to the Minnesota House of Representatives. While in office, Peggy served as the DFL lead on the Subcommittee on Child Care Access and Affordability and a founding member of the POCI (People of Color and Indigenous) caucus. She graduated in 2002 from the University of Minnesota with a bachelor's degree in American Indian studies and child psychology. She is the mom of a smart and funny seven-year-old kiddo. Peggy is an enrolled member of the Minnesota Chippewa Tribe and a citizen of the White Earth Nation.

On the importance of authentic leadership:

As a Native woman, one thing I find important to remember is that Native women have been leaders since time immemorial. All that's new is the rest of society is catching up to what we've always known. That is critical for us to carry and own. Women are leaders; we are problem solvers and we are fixers.

Sometimes there are people—usually men—who like to comment on what I'm wearing. It's hilarious because I'm usually wearing a dress or a ribbon skirt, which is a skirt that Native women wear, with a blazer. They just have an assumption about what a "real leader" looks like. It's certainly not a woman or a woman of color or an Indigenous woman. Every day we're changing the definition of what it means to be a leader—and you can really embrace it and make it your own. When I see successful legislators or advocates at the capitol, that is what they do. They make it their own and bring their full selves into the position.

Democracy functions best when it accurately reflects the community; I think we see these changes happening all across the country with more women, women of color, Indigenous women who are serving in office, and I think we are starting to see the results of that leadership.

---

* Peggy Flanagan, interview with the author, November 25, 2019 (adapted for clarity).

On addressing imposter syndrome:

I have a serious case of imposter syndrome. But I'm not afraid to talk about it because too often what happens is that we say, "Here's my trajectory and here's what I've done over the course of my career, and it was really great and wonderful and now I'm in this position and everything's fine," and that's really a disservice to ourselves and other women. There is strength in vulnerability, in talking about things that make you nervous or afraid and how you push through those things and find your circle of people who will love you no matter what, who will help you take care of yourself and each other.

Because here's the deal: there are plenty of people who will try to make you small when you walk into a room. You should not do it to yourself. That is something that I think about every single day. You are representing the women who came before you, your ancestors, and all the people who deserve to have a seat at that table but haven't yet been invited to take one. So I think our job is to pull up enough chairs and also to bring the table to communities. There are a lot of folks who don't even know that the table exists in the first place.

On finding (and using) your superpowers to drive change:

Women need to get involved in electoral politics. That doesn't mean every woman should run for office, but you can join in at the ground level of a campaign. Figure out what you like to do. I love canvassing. I love talking to people in the community about things that bring them hope and pride. That, for me, is one of my superpowers. Folks need to figure out what their superpower is. Maybe it's that you're a good storyteller and connector. Some of the most successful people I see in leadership are folks who are naturally curious and ask a lot of questions—one of the most important questions being, "Why is it this way?"

Another important thing I would encourage people to do is to try to break out of trying to talk about issues and policies, and really get to the values behind them. That's where your conviction should lie and where you can build a really solid foundation.

One of the last things I would say is to be kind: be kind to yourself as you're figuring out what the next steps are and be kind to each other. As women we can lift each other up in a way that is positive and nurturing and will make us all collectively stronger.

CHAPTER 9

. . . .

SUSTAINABLE ENGAGEMENT

Success is its own reward, but failure is a great teacher too, and not to be feared.

—Sonia Sotomayor, from her memoir *My Beloved World* (2013)

Politics can be *stressful*. In fact, a 2019 study found that nearly 40 percent of Americans say politics causes them stress; nearly 20 percent say that they've lost sleep over politics.[1] And while stress alone is bad enough already, it's also harmful if feeling stressed about politics makes us tune out or stop engaging—in particular because political change still takes time. It doesn't happen overnight. Political engagement, as we've discussed, is a marathon, not a sprint. One of the most critical things that you can do as an advocate is to engage and advocate to advance your issue consistently and continuously. Engagement requires perseverance and patience. You have to be in it for the long haul and be prepared to continue fighting for your issues even when you face challenges and setbacks. And to be able to do that, it's critical to make your political advocacy feel as sustainable and stress free as possible—to deploy tools and tactics that allow you to recharge and keep fighting.

I know this can be tough to do. After all, the issues that make us want to engage can often be scary and frustrating—emotions that certainly don't make us feel good. So, in this chapter, we'll talk about some strategies and actions that make smart, sustainable political engagement possible over the long haul—specifically, making engagement feel good, focusing on learning from the process as much as you focus on the outcomes you want to achieve, and creating plans and habits that help keep you accountable.

MAKE ENGAGEMENT FEEL GOOD

Making engagement feel "good" may at first seem counterintuitive, as we've discussed. The issues that compel us to act—the ones that make us feel afraid or angry or upset—often *don't* make us feel good. But making the work you're doing to address those issues feel as good as possible, despite those potentially negative emotions, means engaging in ways that you enjoy, celebrating wins, bringing others along, and, finally, taking care of yourself. A 2011 study found that, when engaging in a new health behavior (e.g., meditation), experiencing positive emotions during that behavior was the *only* predictor of whether that behavior would become a regular habit over a year later.[2] Feeling good isn't just a "nice to have"; it's crucial to you in order to continue the important advocacy work you're doing.

As we covered in the previous chapter, there are a lot of ways you can directly and indirectly influence your elected officials (as well as shape public opinion)—so do what you enjoy as much as you can. In addition to prioritizing the issues you want to engage on, spend time thinking about what you really *love* to do. Do you like talking to people? Consider canvassing on behalf of a candidate or issue campaign, or phone banking. If you feel stressed out about the idea of talking to strangers, pick another option—organizing fundraisers, doing research on the issues you care about, writing letters to your representatives or op-eds to local papers, contributing financially, having one-on-one meetings with your elected officials . . . the list goes on. This doesn't mean you shouldn't push yourself out of your comfort zone from time to time; it just means you should make purposeful decisions about how you engage so you don't burn yourself out by doing things you just don't like doing.

Celebrating wins, no matter how small, also makes engagement feel good. If you've ever worked on a team of any kind, then you've seen the importance of celebration firsthand as a way to boost morale and build motivation. Did you get a meeting with a member of your city council on the calendar to discuss your issues? Celebrate it! Did your letter to the editor appear in your local paper? Celebrate it! Did you help even one other person get to the polls on Election Day? Celebrate it! Celebration is an inherently social activity—whether you share your wins on social media, or with your mom, or with a group of advocates you're working with, just find a way to celebrate them, however large or small, with other people. Again, change takes time, so, as one congresswoman once told me: "Learn to delight in the incremental."

Third, engagement feels better when we bring others along. There's no question that, when we collaborate and build coalitions, we can be way more effective in creating the kind of change that we want to see regarding the issues that we care about. But it also just feels so much *better* to do this work when we do it with others who share our values and vision for the world.

Bringing others along has benefits beyond just making your own engagement feel better, too. Once you're in possession of knowledge that others can benefit from, it's important to find opportunities to pass along that knowledge and information, especially to those who may not have had the same privileges or opportunities as you. Host a civics workshop in your neighborhood or in partnership with a local nonprofit. Mentor younger people or students and talk to them about the importance of their voices, perspectives, and participation in our democracy. Heck, lend this book to a friend and talk about the tactics you want to deploy to create change in your local community. The possibilities are endless.

Finally, remember to take care of yourself. When you're fighting for your issues, you're often doing so on behalf of an entire community—which is commendable. However, you can't do this effectively if you're not prioritizing your own well-being—you have to "put on your own oxygen mask before assisting others," just as the airline safety videos say. What do you need to do to make sure you have gas in your tank to keep working toward the change you want to see? Whether it's taking the time to catch up with a friend, going to a workout class or on a walk, picking up an old hobby (I've recently started reteaching myself to sew), or watching Netflix while wearing a sheet mask and eating ice cream, do what you need in order to recharge.

FOCUS ON LEARNING—
NOT JUST OUTCOMES

We've already talked extensively about not needing to be an "expert" on an issue or in politics to be qualified to start engaging on matters you care about. And you don't. But, as you begin advocating for your issues, keep in mind that, even if you don't start out as an expert, you can certainly become one over time. It can be all too tempting to focus just on the outcomes of your advocacy (e.g., have I achieved my goals?) instead of what that advocacy has taught you—about your issues, how the political process works, and what strategies are most effective. Both the outcomes *and* the learning are hugely critical!

One way to think about this attitude is to have a "growth mindset." According to Carol Dweck, professor of psychology at Stanford University, individuals who have growth mindsets "believe their talents can be developed (through hard work, good strategies, and input from others) . . . They tend to achieve more than those with a more fixed mindset (those who believe their talents are innate gifts)."[3] Having a growth mindset, in politics and in life, puts you at an advantage over having a fixed mindset.

But research shows that, in general, women may be less likely to demonstrate a growth mindset than men. Harvard economics professor Claudia Goldin found that women who received a B in introductory economics were half as likely as women who received an A to major in the subject, whereas men who received Bs were as likely as those who received As to stick with it.[4] We have to be willing to participate, even if we're not sure we know the answer, or even if it's possible we'll fail (it's likely we won't). We can't let fear of being wrong, or not getting the A, force us to the sidelines. Failing and making mistakes is how we learn.

In doing the work of advocacy, you are *certainly* not going to win all the time. There will be losses that feel personal. The key, when we lose or fail, is to take a step back and evaluate what we've *learned* from that experience, rather than what we lost. In consulting, my teams would often facilitate what's called a "postmortem" (a little morbid, I know) following a big project. Together as a team, we would discuss what went well, what didn't go so well, and what we could do differently next time that would help us avoid making similar mistakes. Do the same with your advocacy. Talk to others about their perspectives on what could have been done differently and carry those lessons forward in your next attempt. Because of the ever-changing nature of politics (and who's in charge politically), there's almost always an opportunity to try again.

Another way we learn is by engaging with others—and not just with people who already agree with us. It's easy to become entrenched and deeply committed to our own positions. Is the dress gold and white, or black and blue? Is the robot saying "laurel" or "yahnee"? The debates rage on. As you enter the world of politics, you will definitely encounter people who disagree with you. When you do, try your best to move from certainty to curiosity, and remember that your lived experience is not everyone else's lived experience. Rational people can disagree. Be curious about other people's views and perspectives.

As human beings, it's all too tempting to seek out information that validates what we already think (remember confirmation bias from Chapter 7?). Instead, we need to continuously push ourselves to learn more, understand more, and listen more, particularly when it comes to people who don't share our views. This is not at odds with your being a strong, forceful advocate; you can fight fiercely and ferociously for the things you care about while also being open to dialogue and learning. In fact, having a more comprehensive view of the issues you care about—and understanding *all* sides of an issue—will make you a better advocate.

Here are a few practical tips for when you encounter someone who has a different perspective or opinion than you:

- **Become a professional listener.** Genuinely listen to what the other person is saying, and ask open-ended questions (answers that you can't answer with yes or no—for example, "What did you think of that movie?" instead of "Did you like the movie?"). Open-ended questions are much more conducive to conversation.

- **Play back what someone says before you respond: "So what I hear you saying is . . ."** Make sure the person you're talking to feels heard before you jump in to share your own perspective. Not only will they feel that they're truly being listened to (something that, frankly, everyone appreciates), but it will also ensure that you really *do* understand what they're saying, and that your response addresses their point! It's a win-win.

- **Stick to the issue at hand.** Don't bring in other topics or baggage. You won't gain any points in a conversation about a specific policy by all of a sudden launching into a tirade about, say, why you dislike a particular politician; it could make the other person defensive and derail the entire conversation. If you really want to debate or better understand the issue at hand, keep the discussion specific.

- **Bring your social media conversations offline.** Remember: In-person is always better! It makes the entire conversation more personal and more human; online interactions can often feel anonymous. We also communicate not just by what we say but also *how* we say it, so speaking in person reduces the chances for misunderstanding.

All of this comes with an important caveat: it is not entirely up to you to make sure the conversation is civil. Being able to have discussions with people you disagree with—listening, empathizing, striving to understand—is an important tool in your toolbox, but a conversation takes two. Too often women are expected to be the ones who compromise and find common ground. That's an awfully heavy burden to carry. And politics can be deeply personal. Sometimes decisions or policies are made that go against our most strongly held convictions, values, and beliefs. And when that happens, when you are enraged, impassioned, in despair, don't hold back—part of using your voice is knowing not just when to listen, but when to talk, and when to shout.

As Soraya Chemaly writes in her book, *Rage Becomes Her*, "Anger has a bad rap, but it is actually one of our most helpful and forward thinking of all our emotions. It begets transformation, manifesting our passion *and* keeping us interested in the world. It is a rational *and* an emotional response to trespass, violation, and moral disorder. It bridges the divide between 'what is' and what 'ought' to be, between a difficult past and an implied possibility. Anger warns us viscerally of violation, threat, and insult." Get angry even if it makes people uncomfortable; the "real danger of our anger," writes Chemaly, is that "[i]t makes it clear that we take ourselves seriously . . . [B]y effectively severing anger from 'good womanhood,' we choose to sever girls and women from the emotion that best protects us against danger and injustice." She continues: "We are so busy teaching girls to be likable that we often forget to teach them, as we do boys, that they should be respected."[5] Anger can be a critical tool in your advocacy toolbox—just as critical as thoughtful listening and civil civics.

When we advocate for the things we care about, we will inevitably see failures and successes. We can listen and engage and be empathetic to the experiences of others, but also rage against their positions when we disagree. We don't have to be one thing. And we don't have to do any of it perfectly. What's important is that we try—and keep trying. Through this, you'll continue learning, too. Your advocacy will be more effective for it.

CREATE A PLAN

If political engagement is relatively new for you, yet something you want to do more of and really commit to, think of how you get stuff done in every other aspect of your life. At work, do you keep a calendar so you know when you have meetings? Do you make a to-do list? Establish goals for yourself? Reward yourself if you've successfully completed a task? All of these things translate to your political engagement, too. Here are a few tips for creating a plan—and sticking to it.

- **Start small—and set specific, reasonable goals.** The more specific you can be about exactly *what* you want to do as you get started, the better. Maybe your first goal is just to understand your issue better. If that's the case, perhaps your action plan could be to research your issue for 20 to 30 minutes every day for the next month. Or maybe your goal is to get more up to speed on political goings-on. In that case, consider listening to a daily political podcast or subscribing to an email newsletter that shows up in your inbox each morning. Your goal really could be anything—figuring out when your next city council public hearing is and attending, completing the worksheet sections of this book and putting them up on your fridge as a reminder—but whatever it is, set a near-term goal and then the specific actions you'll take to get there.

    As much as possible, too, try to be realistic about how much time you have to commit to achieving your goals. Better to start small and grow from there than to set unrealistic goals and feel discouraged about not following through! You can use the workbook in Part II to do this, but start brainstorming now what that might look like for you.

- **Schedule your engagement(s).** We've touched on this before: consider setting specific time aside (daily, weekly, monthly—whatever makes sense for your goals) and set a reminder using whatever system you like best (e.g., calendar appointments). Even if you end up moving it, it'll be a more conscious decision, and you'll be reminded to reschedule it.

  I'd also recommend taking a look at your town or city meeting schedule. Many local government meetings in small towns are open to the public; even in New York City, there are numerous public hearings taking place *daily*. If the subject of one piques your interest, put that in your calendar, too!

- **Create a system of accountability.** As we talked about earlier in this chapter, working with others on your advocacy efforts makes engagement in general feel better. But it can also help create a system of accountability. Inviting a friend to meet me at the gym or workout class makes me way more likely to work out. Being part of a book club where I'm expected to have read the book makes me more likely to finish it. Use the same approach to help hold you accountable to your political engagement goals as well! Buddy up with a friend who also wants to do more politically (or even start a civics club!). Share your goals and have an agreed-upon check-in to discuss the progress you're making, challenges you've encountered, or successes you've had.

Meaningful political engagement can be hard work—no question. Increasing your effectiveness means knowing how the system works. It means knowing which strategies you can deploy that will help you move the needle on your issues. But being effective *also* means taking care of yourself—making your engagement feel as good as possible and setting yourself up to stay engaged for the long haul.

Advocate in Action: Tonya Williams, Former Director of Legislative Affairs for Vice President Joe Biden*

Born in North Carolina, Williams has worked across multiple levels of government, from serving as general counsel to Senator Marc Basnight of the North Carolina Senate to chief of staff for Congressman G. K. Butterfield at the US House of Representatives to director of legislative affairs for Vice President Joe Biden in the Obama White House. She currently serves as the director of government affairs for Softbank Group. She graduated from the University of North Carolina at Chapel Hill and University of North Carolina School of Law. Williams is a senior advisor to the All In Together Campaign.

On the differences in how the system works across different levels of government:

At the local level, you're right there; it's your community and people's immediate needs. As a policy maker, it's in your immediate control and it's very practical: plowing snow, or trash collection, or school issues—all of which can be emotionally charged. You see the people you serve every day, and often experience the issues and concerns they bring you in your capacity as a leader; they're your neighbors and friends.

With state government, you can have a similar ability to fix things. Most issues and problems are common enough across the state, so you can figure out all the parts and pieces relatively quickly, which allows you to effectively analyze the problem, negotiate deals, and craft meaningful solutions. I found that to be very satisfying.

What was surprising to me at the federal level is that for the most part, you develop the parameters, you get the money, and then you send it home to your state for rulemaking and distribution. There's very little nuance at the federal level. The programs are big, and you have to consider and negotiate the needs of your constituents with someone from as far away as Alaska, whose constituents may have very different needs and priorities. Experience with process and relevant players in office is extremely helpful at this level because over the years you get to know what somebody's district is like, you've heard their issues, and you get to know their priorities, which informs how to approach them. You also have to remember that effective legislating is not just about the fight today—you have to play the long game; it's a journey.

---

* Tonya Williams, interview with the author, October 18, 2019 (adapted for clarity).

On influencing policy outcomes:

An elected official's time and priorities in office are often directed by what they're hearing and who they are hearing from. Even if it's not a "big" problem, if they're hearing it a lot, it can become a problem—perception is important. The other thing to remember is that no one wants to address a problem that has no answer. World peace? We all want it, but how do we get there? You have to chop it up into bite-sized pieces. So, when you are talking to policy makers, it is more effective to speak up about issues that are relevant and suggest your ideas or proposals for realistic solutions. Public officials and staff will get creative if your asks are specific. Additionally, each representative has a reason they ran for office, and at every level they serve on some panel or committee with defined jurisdiction and policy priorities. It is important to dig down and understand those dynamics so that your goals align as much as possible with the person you are trying to persuade.

Another effective approach is to speak directly to their interests. There's a little bit of strategy to this. Does the issue you are discussing matter to them? If so, why does it matter? Is it in the interest of their district? Do you have a personal story that can explain and enliven your points and position? If you can evoke emotion and make it memorable, you're halfway there. Unfortunately, for the most part, this type of strategy seems to be lost in modern-day influence campaigns. People opt for quantity over quality and it's simply not as impactful. It's the reason tactics such as robocalls and mass form letters don't really matter in most cases.

On staying engaged in the long term:

Advocacy isn't a one-off. The thing that has kept me going is if we're not doing it, how's it getting done? Working in politics is really tough and much less satisfying these days, and the partisan divide has grown in deep and ugly ways that I could never have imagined when I started out in this line of work. The easy thing to do is to wash your hands of it. The hard thing to do is to stay engaged and to remember that you are in fact making a difference. Consistency really pays off; relationships and longevity matter. Also, in some cases, your mere presence can be consequential. When you're sitting in a committee room and you look around and realize that you're the only person of color, the only woman . . . the lack of diversity when major policy and funding decisions are being made is frightening. If you're not in the game, you are turning it over to someone else who has their own goals or visions of what America is or should be.

PART II WORKBOOK

As we've discussed, there's no one way to engage in advocacy; there are a lot of tools and tactics at your disposal. It *is* important, however, to get specific about your issues and on the change you want to see, and ultimately decide which tools will be most effective in helping you achieve your goals, particularly as you participate in the electoral process and hold your elected officials accountable. Use this section to articulate *your* prioritized issues, and how you want to engage on behalf of them.

DEFINE YOUR ISSUES

Start by defining your top one or two issues. Fill out each of the buckets on the next page, using the question prompts as a guide.

Category	Question prompts
Experience/expertise	*Personal experience:* What issues have personally affected you? Your family? Your community? What have their impacts or outcomes been? *Expertise:* On what matters do you have professional expertise or knowledge? Maybe you've studied an issue in depth in school or worked in a specific field for years.
Passion	What are your main voting issues? In other words, what issue, if a candidate didn't support it, would make you consider not voting for them? What kinds of charities do you donate your time or money to? What gets you fired up? *Note:* It's okay if your passion for this issue is linked to your experience; for many, it certainly will be. We're often most passionate about the experiences that have affected us personally.
Timeliness	Of the issues you care about most, which need to be acted on *now* instead of *later*? Which is the most urgent? For example: Is there a bill coming up for a vote? Is something currently affecting you and/or your community that needs to be addressed now? Is this issue timely for a different reason (e.g., an important anniversary for this issue is coming up, or there seems to be a groundswell of interest on this issue)?

Your answers

Time for a quick analysis: Where do these answers intersect for you? Are there one or two common themes that jump out? Do any of the themes align with something you already thought might be one of your priority issues? Does anything that came up surprise you?

Include your thoughts to the above questions in the space below:

Remember, it's okay if your passion—the thing that really drives you—does not line up with your experience or expertise. As we discussed, it just means your action plan will be a little different; your first step may be building your knowledge base by talking to experts in your community, reading, and speaking to other constituents. Similarly, if there is an issue that feels particularly urgent now, lead with that—and take the time to define why this issue matters to you (in your own words) as well as to learn as much as possible to ensure your position is informed.

IDENTIFY YOUR TOOLS
FOR INFLUENCE

Now that you have a sense of the one or two issues you really want to advocate for, let's drill deeper into the tactics you can use and the plan you can put into place in order to have influence on those issues.

The first piece, as we talked about in Chapter 6, is **voting**. Fill out the table below to make sure you're prepared and have all the pieces in place to be able to vote for the candidates who support your issues and who you believe in.

Category	Information needed	Your specifics
When	Date of the **next election** in your district **Note:** Include dates for **early voting** as well, if available in your state.	
	Deadline to **register** for the election (if you're not already registered)	
	Deadline to **vote absentee** (if planning on voting absentee)	

Category	Information needed	Your specifics
What	**Seats** up for election (include federal, state, and local positions)	
	Propositions on the ballot (if applicable)	
Who	**Candidates** who are running for available seats (who is running for what?)	
Where	**Polling place** location and hours	
How	**Voting options** available to you (e.g., early voting, absentee voting, etc.) and any relevant deadlines for each	

If it's too early to know exactly what will be on the ballot, set a reminder or calendar alert for yourself to check back in plenty of time before the election.

Resources to help fill out this information include:

- **Ballotpedia**
- **League of Women Voters**
- **Vote.org**
- **When We All Vote**

The next critical step is creating your strategy for how to **advocate** for your issues. First, recap the issues that you prioritized on the previous pages:

Your issues:

1._____

_____

_____

_____

2._____

_____

_____

_____

Core to any advocacy efforts, as you heard from the experts, is staying *focused*. So staying grounded in your issues, and in the things that really matter to you, is critical. Learn as much as you can on your priority issue or issues. Be sure to read viewpoints on both sides of your priority issues (part of being an effective advocate is knowing where the other side is going to push). Talk to others in your community to understand how your issue or issues affect them and do your best to stay neutral in those conversations. They're not debates; you're seeking to understand as much as you possibly can.

Then it's time to research what the landscape of each of your issues looks like, at each level of government. (The form on the following pages has space for one issue; if you have multiple issues you want to dig into, just use the same prompts on a separate piece of paper!)

	What's happening with this issue If your issue is specific to one level of government, this may not be relevant for the others.
Federal	
State	
Local	

The stance (if any) of your elected officials on this issue If they haven't indicated a stance, call their office and ask.	Elected officials with personal experience in or passion for this issue Is there someone in office who could help spearhead change?

Next, you'll want to sync up your interest and focus with the work already being done by others. Are there any organizations or groups that are focused on your priority issues? List them below, as well as if they have an office or presence near where you live.

Organization/ group name	Local office/presence? If yes, include location and local leadership.	Opportunity to volunteer or otherwise support ongoing advocacy efforts?

Remember, even if there aren't any immediate opportunities to volunteer or support a particular organization, there is almost certainly a mailing list that you can join. This is also a good way to stay apprised of any developments and mobilization opportunities in your priority issue, as we heard from some of our Advocates in Action.

If there *isn't* a group that is already advocating for the issue you care about (and shares your values), consider creating one. As you'll hear later on from activist and executive director of The People, Katie Fahey, who led a movement to end partisan gerrymandering in Michigan (*see her Advocate in Action profile on page 235*), incredibly effective movements can be started with just a Facebook post! If you know people who already care about this issue, start there. Movement happens on issues when people work together and coordinate. With your group, brainstorm the best way to engage your elected officials—given what you care about, and the political environment, is it best to write letters and make phone calls? To schedule a meeting with your representative? To write an op-ed to educate the community or public? To attend (or even testify at) a public hearing?

Whatever your approach, make sure you are including in your advocacy the elements research shows are most persuasive to public officials.

Element to include in advocacy/ outreach to your representative	What that looks like for your issue or issues
Personal story and why you support/ oppose the issue	
Information/data on the impact of this issue on your district	
Your specific ask or request regarding the issue or issues	
Any other important information (e.g., specific expertise, groups you're involved with, interactions with the elected official in the past, etc.)	

Finally, plan for how you can **campaign**—whether that's your support of a candidate running for office that you believe in or running for office yourself. Is there a candidate running for the next election that you're particularly excited about? This could be for any seat—federal, state, or local. Take a few minutes to do a little research on that candidate and what you might be able to contribute in terms of support—whether that's volunteering your time, making a campaign contribution, hosting a fundraiser, etc.

Candidate name and position *(e.g., state senator, city council member, county commissioner)*	
Campaign headquarters location	
Local campaign office? *If yes, include location.*	
Campaign website and volunteer contact information (if any)	
Next campaign event near you *Include date/time/location.*	
In what way could you support this candidate? *Think about how much you would be comfortable contributing financially, or how much time you could volunteer and what skill you think might be relevant for the campaign (e.g., social media experience, fundraising, etc.). Once you've listed all the ways you might offer support, circle the activities that sound most exciting and interesting to you.*	

If you're considering running for office yourself, that's amazing! And the good news is that there are *tons* of incredible organizations and resources out there to support you already. Here are a few to explore (all nonpartisan):

- **She Should Run**
- **The Campaign School at Yale**
- **Vote Run Lead**
- PLUS: resources and organizations specifically for young women:
    - ◊ **IGNITE**
    - ◊ **Running Start**

MAKE A PLAN FOR SUSTAINABLE ENGAGEMENT

Core to making advocacy sustainable is having a plan and being accountable to that plan. So, for the last section of this Part II Workbook, write out your specific commitments to engage on your priority issue or issues, and think about whom you might ask to join you. Advocacy is more fun—and way more effective—when we engage as a group or as a community (not just as individuals). Be as specific as you can be—in terms of the actions you will take, your deadlines, and how you'll hold yourself or your group accountable to actually completing it. I've included an example on the following page for some brainstorming—but really make this your own!

To take action on the issue I care about, I commit to:	I will complete this action:
Example: scheduling a meeting with my city council member (or staff) to help them understand the safety issues in my neighborhood	*Example: in the next month (before my birthday!)*

I will hold myself accountable by:	I can include others by:
Example: putting a reminder on my calendar to look up my city council member and reach out by phone (email if I can't reach them)	*Example: asking a friend interested in this issue to join me in my meeting and helping with research/prep*

PART III

STRENGTHENING OUR DEMOCRACY

CHAPTER 10

. . . .

CAMPAIGN FINANCING

The good we secure for ourselves is precarious and uncertain, is floating in mid-air, until it is secured for all of us and incorporated into our common life.
—Jane Addams, *Philanthropy and Social Progress* (1893)

Let's take quick stock of where we are. In Part I, we reviewed Civics 101: some basic structures of our democracy, what elected officials *really* do, and how legislation is introduced and enacted at all levels of government (local, state, and federal). In Part II, we went through Advocacy 101: how to prioritize the issues that *you* really want to take action on, and the tools that will enable you to have real influence on them, from how to vote smarter, to how to engage your representatives most effectively, to how to support campaigns, and even what it would mean to consider running for office yourself. Through it all, you've heard from women leading change across the country—from professional advocates, elected officials, and citizens who care. You've also gotten insight into making all of this feel sustainable (or, at the very least, a little more doable!).

But all of the work of advocacy carries much more weight when our democracy is functioning properly—and that's often not the case. It's always surprising to me how many books lay out how to be a credible and impactful political advocate without discussing the structural barriers that currently hobble our system. In this part, we'll cover three fundamental issues that undermine our ability as citizens to have our voices heard: money in politics (specifically, campaign financing), lack of representativeness in our democracy (this spans a range of issues, from gerrymandering to a lack of diversity), and barriers to voter participation and voter access. Each of these topics could be the subject of a book in and of itself; in this section we'll just walk through the basics along with some potential solutions proposed by experts.

American democracy has a long history of being ... well, undemocratic. Women didn't get the constitutional right to vote until 1920, and in practice, only white women enjoyed this right at first. Voting rights weren't established for Native American women until 1924 with the Indian Citizenship Act, and they weren't really secured for Black women in many parts of the country until *1965*—almost half a century later—with the passage of the Voting Rights Act. As Cynthia Terrell, founder and executive director of RepresentWomen and an advocate for reforms to advance women's representation and leadership in the United States, told me, "So many reform organizations are always talking 'reclaiming' democracy or 'reforming' or 'reigniting' something, as if there's some date in history that we want to go back to instead of saying, 'Wow. We need to create something that hasn't happened.'"[1] Creating a democracy that reaches its full potential and promise—one that works for everyone—is an ongoing project.

The topics we'll cover in the next three chapters, while not an exhaustive list of dangers to American democracy, are among those that are most damaging, and, left unchecked, will continue to enable a government that is not by the people and for the people, but rather is governed by a small minority (for the record, that minority looks awfully white, extraordinarily wealthy, and male). Our government shouldn't work that way, and it doesn't have to.

The following chapters can also serve as food for thought as you ponder the issues you really want to focus on (maybe in addition to the one or two you prioritized in Part II). Part II helped you identify and develop the tools to propel your own advocacy efforts; Part III will help you understand challenges we face collectively. These structural issues are often "unsexy" (and complicated!), but they are critically important. They're nonpartisan in the sense that they impact every single one of us, regardless of party, and our ability to have our interests represented politically. If part of being an engaged, informed citizen is understanding how the system works, then it's equally important that we understand where the system *doesn't* work and that we demand the breakdowns be addressed.

Our system of government was *designed* to change—just take a look at the 27 constitutional amendments that have been ratified since the US Constitution was enacted. These include *major* change, from freedom of speech to abolishing slavery to establishing voting rights. Anyone who thinks big change is impossible should take a closer look at the lessons of American history, as well as the intention set out by the Founding Fathers to create a system that *could* be changed. Let's look at what we can do to make that system work better for everyone—starting with campaign financing.

American elections are expensive—*really* expensive. According to the nonpartisan, nonprofit Center for Responsive Politics and its website, **OpenSecrets.org**, which tracks money in US politics, the 2016 presidential and congressional elections combined cost approximately $6.5 *billion*.[2] For the same amount of money, the US could increase federal aid to K–12 schools by over 40 percent.[3] Unlike many countries around the world, the US imposes no limits on how much candidates can spend on their campaigns. In Great Britain, political parties can only spend up to $29.5 million in the year before an election, and televised campaign advertisements are banned.[4] In the US, however, spending money to promote a political message has been established as akin to speech by the Supreme Court, and therefore is protected under the First Amendment.[5]

According to an October 2017 *Washington Post* and University of Maryland poll, 96 percent of Americans blame money for creating dysfunction in the political system.[6] And according to a 2018 Pew survey, 77 percent say there should be limits on the amount of money individuals and organizations can spend on campaigns.[7] In other words, most Americans already believe that the amount of money in politics is a problem for our democracy. In this section, we'll discuss *why* and *how* this has become such an issue, and what we can do to fix it.

So, where did that $6.5 billion spent on federal elections in 2016 come from? Unfortunately, there is no simple answer to that question; tracking where the money comes from and where it goes is a complicated undertaking. A candidate's campaign can accept money directly from a number of different sources. These include:

- **Individual donors like you or me.**

- **National, state, and local political parties.** For Republicans, at the national level, this would be the Republican National Committee (RNC); for Democrats, at the national level, this would be the Democratic National Committee (DNC).

- **Political Action Committees (also known as "PACs").** These are political committees "organized for the purpose of raising and spending money to elect and defeat candidates."[8] They can be organized around business or ideological interests, and typically contribute to candidates based on policies they support or oppose. One example is WUFPAC (Women Under Forty PAC), which raises money to support women under the age of 40 running for office at the state and federal levels.[9] But there are PACs related to almost every interest and industry you could name—from animal welfare (Humane USA PAC) to the environment (Sierra Club Political Committee) to dermatology (SkinPAC). Companies can also create their own PACs, which their employees can contribute to—more on that in a minute.

- **Other federal campaigns.** Yes, federal campaigns can also accept donations from other federal campaigns—so, for example, a presidential candidate could receive money from a senatorial candidate's campaign.

Any money that is donated directly to a candidate's campaign is known as "hard money." There are a lot of rules around how that money can be donated and what it can be used for, and each direct donation must be reported. For example, there are strict limits on how much money an individual or group can donate directly to a particular campaign. Campaigns must also disclose to the Federal Election Commission (FEC) their lists of donors and how much each donated. For the 2019–2020 federal elections, individual donors were capped at $2,800 per federal candidate (although there's no limit to how many candidates you can give money to), and PACs were capped at contributing $5,000 per federal candidate.[10]

There are also groups that *aren't* allowed to donate directly to a campaign; these include corporations, labor organizations, national banks, foreign nationals, federal government contractors, churches, and charitable organizations (however, as briefly mentioned above, corporations and labor groups *can* form PACs that employees or members contribute to, which can then donate to candidates).

Then there's what's known as "soft money," which describes a fuzzy category of money that's used to benefit candidates but isn't given directly to their campaigns. Let's walk through an example of what one of these "indirect" contributions could look like. An individual could donate to a political committee like the DNC—not directly to a campaign. While that donor's information is still disclosed to the FEC, and there are limits on their contributions ($35,500 to a national party committee during the 2019–2020 elections),[11] the DNC has a *lot* more leeway on how they spend that money, as long as they aren't doing it in coordination with a candidate. For example, the DNC could, in addition to contributing some of that money directly to a candidate's campaign (subject to limitations), also spend additional money on "party building activities," like voter registration efforts or ads focused on specific issues important to the party. And those efforts would still end up benefiting candidates—perhaps as much as (or more than) a direct contribution would.

The same is true for PACs. While there are limitations on how much an individual can donate to a PAC ($5,000 during the 2019–2020 elections) and how much that PAC can in turn give to a candidate, PACs have the flexibility to take the money they receive and spend it in ways that indirectly benefit campaigns.

The distinction between hard money and soft money is important, because soft money donors don't have to follow many of the rules that restrict direct campaign contributions. The influence of soft money in elections was dramatically amplified by the landmark 2010 Supreme Court case *Citizens United v. FEC*. With its holding in *Citizens United*, the Supreme Court overturned a ban on corporate and union involvement in federal elections that had been in effect since the 1990s. Two months later, another federal court held that, in light of *Citizens United*, organizations making only "soft money" expenditures to influence elections could receive donations in *unlimited* amounts.[12] These two cases paved the way for the "independent expenditure-only political action committee"—also known as the "Super PAC."

A Super PAC can raise and spend as much as it wants to support or oppose a candidate as long as it does not directly give to the candidate or coordinate directly with their campaign. And while corporations and labor organizations aren't allowed to contribute to a campaign from their treasuries, they *can* contribute directly to Super PACs.

There is *some* transparency required: Super PACs must disclose to the FEC who they get their donations from on a monthly or semi-annual basis (they get to choose which). But here's where it gets tricky: certain kinds of nonprofit organizations, which cannot contribute to campaigns but *can* contribute to Super PACs, *are themselves not required by law to disclose their donors*.

Here's what all this means in practice (and where it gets scary). A wealthy person or group with strong political preferences could donate millions of dollars to a nonprofit, which in turn could donate those millions of dollars to a Super PAC; the Super PAC would be required to disclose the contribution from the nonprofit, but the nonprofit would not be required to disclose the donor or donors who contributed the millions of dollars in the first place.

When the source of political money isn't known, it's called "dark money." Nonprofit groups are a major source of dark-money spending.[13] And while nonprofits can't have politics as their "primary purpose," a nonprofit could still, in practice, spend up to 49 percent of its funds on political activities, including advertisements for candidates or particular issues. In addition, nonprofit organizations are overseen by the IRS, not the FEC, and don't have the same restrictions in terms of accepting funds from foreign nationals (who, as you may recall, are forbidden by the FEC from donating to candidates and campaigns directly).

There's also the issue of how—and whether—those rules are enforced. Responsibility for regulation and enforcement falls to the FEC, which is made up of three Democrats and three Republicans. It takes four votes for a ruling to go into effect, and ties along party lines happen regularly, as you might imagine.

The loosening of campaign finance laws (most clearly symbolized for many by the *Citizens United* ruling) plus weak enforcement of those laws has enabled a massive surge of money into politics, particularly from ultrawealthy donors. In 2016, the wealthiest donors provided a much larger share of total donations compared with 2012: according to **OpenSecrets**, the top 0.01 percent of donors in 2012 gave $1.6 billion, compared to $2.3 billion in 2016—a 45 percent difference (despite the size of the group increasing only 3 percent). And most of that increase was in the form of soft money, which more than doubled in that same time period.[14]

It hasn't always been like this. From 1976 to 1996, public financing was actually the norm in presidential elections; elections weren't run on major donations from ultrawealthy individuals. In the wake of Watergate, there was an enormous effort to reform campaign financing, and part of that effort included the public financing of presidential elections, with funds collected voluntarily from voters. In practice, this worked by adding an option on people's tax returns to allocate small amounts of money to the public-finance campaign fund; the option is actually still on the tax return forms we use today! Essentially, it's a "vote" for allocating a small amount of your tax money to the fund; it doesn't cost you anything extra. Of course, there are rules for candidates who accept public funds: to even be eligible for public funding, presidential candidates, for example, must raise a minimum of $100,000 in the primary, including at least $5,000 in small donations from at least 20 different states. Once candidates meet those eligibility requirements, they are then also limited in how much they spend in total during the primaries in each state, based on the size of the voting-age population (a disadvantage in critical but low-population primary states like New Hampshire and Iowa). Also, during the general election, major party candidates who accept public funding are not able to take or spend any additional private contributions (except for $50,000 of their own money).

Election funding completely changed in 2008 when Barack Obama became the first major-party candidate to reject public funds for the general election, relying instead on private donations.[15] And while public financing is still available to candidates (Democratic presidential candidate Martin O'Malley used public financing for his campaign in 2016), relying on private contributions has since become the norm. Today, candidates can raise and spend a lot more money by themselves if they forgo public financing. In 2008, Barack Obama was, as a general election nominee, eligible to receive approximately $84.1 million in public funds from the Treasury—but his campaign spent $745 million. Obama outspent his opponent, John McCain, who did accept public money and use public funds, four to one.[16] Additionally, fewer and fewer taxpayers check the box on their taxes to fund the public campaign–financing program (only 6 percent in 2013 versus 27.5 percent in 1976).[17]

Since 2008, campaign financing has become a bit of an arms race. Candidates tend to reject public financing because they know they can raise more money through private contributions, and because it is what they expect their opponents to do—making campaigns enormously expensive.

And, in today's world, it would be tough to compete in a presidential election with public financing alone. At this point, a candidate relying on the public-finance option couldn't viably compete against candidates with private funders, especially in small states. In theory, if all candidates agreed to accept only public financing, that could help level the playing field. But even if all candidates made such a promise, it's difficult to imagine going back to the system of publicly financed elections: because of soft money (and especially dark money), a ton of private funding would still be influencing the outcomes—that influence would just be less visible. Without reforming campaign finance broadly, it's difficult to imagine a return to public financing, particularly in presidential elections.

WHY THIS MATTERS

We've gone over some of the key terms and biggest changes to campaign finance over the past several years. Why does this matter? How does it make our system less democratic?

- **The very wealthy (individuals and special interest groups) have outsized influence.** Money equals access, and access equals power and influence. As Laura Friedenbach of Every Voice, a nonprofit advocating for campaign finance reform, has said, "When you see that the bulk of money is coming from a few very wealthy donors—who, by the way, tend to be male, white, and older—it's worrying. It gives the impression that the government is not working for the rest of us."[18] When you have a tiny group of people controlling so much money and influence, politicians are beholden to a very narrow set of interests, rather than the interests of a broad range of constituents.

- **Without transparency, we can't have accountability.** If we don't know the sources of political giving, it's incredibly difficult to understand the motivation and meaning behind those donations. Without contribution transparency, we cannot hold organizations, leaders, or citizens accountable for their positions, or understand where there are possible conflicts of interest. Think of all the food companies, for example, that fund studies touting the health benefits of their products; knowing who funds those studies helps us know how skeptical we should be of their findings.[19]

- **There are (much) better uses of money—and time.** Election spending is out of control and there is *so* much (alternate) good that could be done with that money. This isn't to say that electing qualified, competent representatives isn't important—as we've established, it absolutely is. It just doesn't have to cost this much.

  And the massive effort of fundraising isn't confined to "election season" as we think of it, either. Members of Congress are *constantly* fundraising, for hours a day (remember that there are no term limits for senators and representatives—and representatives are up for election every two years). Certainly, there are better ways for politicians to spend their time.

- **Races may be less competitive and less diverse.** Research from the Brennan Center at New York University suggests that limiting campaigns to public financing could increase the diversity of candidates running for office across racial, socioeconomic, and gender identity lines.[20] The Center for Governmental Studies also found that, of all candidates running under public financing, minority candidates made up 30 percent (compared to 16 percent of non-publicly financed candidates) and women made up 39 percent (compared to 31 percent of non-publicly financed candidates).[21] We know correlation doesn't equal causation, but it's worth noting that five of the six states with public funding for legislative elections—Arizona, Connecticut, Hawaii, Maine, and Minnesota—all have higher levels of female representation in their state legislative bodies than the national average.[22]

- **Contributions can also impact legislative outcomes.** Cynthia Terrell, executive director of RepresentWomen, points out that campaign finance reform can also influence legislative outcomes. "Campaign finance reform," says Terrell, "is super important [with regard to] policy outcomes. The fact that members of Congress are beholden to the NRA to win seats completely impacts whether they're willing to take on gun reform legislation, which the majority of suburban voters, many of whom are moderate and progressive women, feel passionately about. It's a classic example where the polling is phenomenal on support for gun safety legislation . . . but the NRA has effectively lobbied members of Congress to say 'we'll actively oppose you if you take us on.' So legislatively, the lack of campaign finance reform has huge impact."[23]

POTENTIAL SOLUTIONS

The outsized influence of money in politics is a major issue. So how do we fix it? The good news is that there are some very innovative initiatives happening at the local level that are worth watching (and perhaps replicating across the country at all levels of government). Remember, local government often provides opportunities to test out creative ideas before implementing them state- or even nationwide.

Take New York City, for example. Public financing of city campaigns was introduced in 1988 to combat the increasing cost of running for office, reduce reliance on wealthy donors, and encourage candidates to focus more on small donations from average New Yorkers. Today, NYC uses what's called a multiple match ratio; for every small donation (up to $175 for borough president or city council candidates and up to $250 for mayor, public advocate, or comptroller candidates), the city matches the donation eight to one with public funds. In other words, if someone donates $10 to a candidate, that candidate would actually receive $90 ($10 from the individual and $80 from the city). There are restrictions to this matching, of course, like limits to how much the city will match in total; for a city council candidate, that limit was $168,888 for citywide elections in 2021.[24]

The impact of NYC's donation matching has been encouraging. In 2013, more than 90 percent of funds raised came from *individual* contributions (not special-interest groups). That year also saw the largest number of contributors in NYC ever, two-thirds of whom made small donations ($175 or less). Compare that to New York State, which does not have a public financing program, and where 70 cents of every dollar contributed to campaigns comes from special interests (corporations, PACs, unions, or party committees).[25]

Beyond NYC, other cities and states are also experimenting with public financing programs. Seattle, for example, recently introduced a "democracy voucher" system. Each voter receives four $25 vouchers that can be given to the candidate or candidates of their choice in city elections.[26] These vouchers are great from a participation perspective; after all, you're more likely to pay attention to a race you've contributed to. However, vouchers may not do much to balance out the huge amounts of money being poured into the most competitive campaigns.

Those who oppose public financing of campaigns say that money is better used to pay for other programs or services. Many states seem to agree; as of 2019, only 14 states have some form of public financing of campaigns at the state level.[27] But public financing of campaigns isn't prohibitively expensive; a study by the nonpartisan Campaign Finance Institute found that implementing it at the state level would cost approximately two dollars per taxpayer, at least in New York State.[28] In my opinion, that's a small price to pay for a better, more diverse, more responsive government—in particular, one that's less beholden to a small group of mega donors.

FINAL THOUGHTS ON CAMPAIGN FINANCING

We've discussed a lot of challenges in this chapter, but thankfully, money isn't everything. Your votes are what count. Yes, money can buy ads and lots of airtime (just ask former New York City mayor Michael Bloomberg, who spent over *$500 million* in political ads during his short-lived 2020 presidential campaign).[29] And once that candidate is in office, money can buy access and attention to the biggest donors' issues and priorities. But if we do our homework, and equip ourselves with the tools and information we need to get involved, we can negate some of the impact of that money—as well as demand changes to the system itself. When it comes to how campaigns are financed, our candidates (who is able to run, and who can win) and our legislation (the policies they enact once in office) are at stake. Unless we fix these problems, it will be hard to fix anything else.

Advocate in Action: Rina Shah—
Political Advisor and Businesswoman*

Rina Shah is a political maven, reformer, and social entrepreneur based in Washington, DC. Prior to forming consulting firm Loom Global Partners, she was a senior staffer to representatives Scott Garrett (NJ-5) and Jeff Miller (FL-1). Rina was elected as a delegate to the 2016 Republican National Convention before becoming chief spokesperson for 2016 independent presidential candidate Evan McMullin. Rina serves on the boards of Republican Women for Progress, RepresentWomen, Vote Run Lead, and Running Start. She is cofounder and emeritus board member of Women's Public Leadership Network. Rina is a regular guest on MSNBC, PBS, and Al Jazeera.

On growing up civic-minded:

I was raised to believe that our democracy demands my participation in the public square just as much as anyone else. Being born and raised in a rural West Virginia coal-mining town, most people would not guess that I spent my mornings listening to NPR and evenings watching PBS. I found it just as interesting to read and watch local news as I did to browse the many national magazines my parents subscribed to. But my civic engagement was also motivated by my family story. My father and his family were expelled overnight from Uganda, which they had called home since the 1800s, solely because of our Indian ancestry. Learning that a dictator at the helm of a big, oppressive government was responsible for my family losing everything they had acquired over three generations made me deeply concerned and more passionate about participating in activities related to government at all levels.

We all walk through life with diverse attitudes, goals, and expectations. As Americans, we have an inherent right to demand a better government for ourselves. That is what our nation's founders really wanted: a more perfect union. We must all work together and strive toward that goal. Our government can and should always be accessible to all of us, and it's incumbent upon each one of us to take steps to create a better society for our and future generations.

---

*   Rina Shah, interview with the author, October 23, 2019 (adapted for clarity).

On the benefits (and limitations) of social media:

Even if resources are limited, social media platforms allow advocates to move the needle in ways that traditional activism cannot. In the #MeToo movement era, we saw women of all ages, socioeconomic statuses, and ethnicities lift each other's voices and lead us toward positive change. This is the beauty of democracy: each American is responsible for working toward a better America for all of us—not just for some of us. In response, lawmakers across the political spectrum have come together to enact meaningful legislation that strikes the sexual harassment problem at the jugular while laying the foundation for long-term systemic change.

But too often, many of our fellow citizens decide to hide behind their screens and are simply keyboard warriors. You could be riffing on Facebook every day, but if you are not also getting out there and exercising your right to vote, then what you are really doing is a disservice to yourself and ultimately your country. If talk online is not translated to a walk offline, then your cause risks being rendered meaningless. It's crucial that your online and offline advocacy efforts work in tandem.

On using tried-and-true advocacy tactics to drive change:

None of us leave our homes each morning without encountering a law or government policy that impacts our lives and livelihoods. It is my genuine belief that whether you're 24 or 84, it's never too late to get involved in your government.

The effort it takes to vote or engage in civic discourse is minimal compared to what America loses if we do not express our opinions. We must not forget that tried-and-true older tactics still work and can not only complement but can also enhance online activism. There are numerous hyperlocal ways to be an activist: making signs to put up in public places, attending city council meetings, writing a letter to the editor, sharing your heartfelt story with your local TV station's newsroom assignment desk as well as with your elected representatives, staging a sit-in or organizing a rally, volunteering with action-oriented nonprofit groups, or even educating and empowering others by having conversations with friends and family about an issue that affects your community.

On ensuring "women's issues" are everyone's issues:

Women often wonder why we, as women, are held to an impossible double standard each time we enter the public sphere. Since the passage of the 19th Amendment over 100 years ago, we have been sold the lie that women's issues are not everyone's issues. Women's issues are everyone's issues—they belong to all of us. The irrefutable fact is any issue that impacts a woman, however small, in turn, impacts society.

I do not believe, however, in excluding men from conversations focused on women.

As a millennial mother, I am accustomed to advertisers and change-makers targeting me with messages of, "You're a Girl Boss" or "Girls Rule the World." But those girl-power messages marketed in cursive, feminine font scrawled on everything from wineglasses to tote bags have no chance of becoming the norm—at least not until we have most American men believing those messages, too. So, truly we are all in this fight together, women and men.

CHAPTER 11

· ·

REPRESENTATIVE
REPRESENTATION

Remember the Ladies, and be more generous and favourable to them than your ancestors. Do not put such unlimited power into the hands of the Husbands. Remember all Men would be tyrants if they could. If perticuliar care and attention is not paid to the Laidies we are determined to foment a Rebelion, and will not hold ourselves bound by any Laws in which we have no voice, or Representation.

—Abigail Adams, in a letter to her husband, John Adams (1776)

A merican democracy works best when people participate, and when our government is responsive to that participation. At the federal level, the House of Representatives, as we discussed in Part I, is explicitly designed to represent public opinion most closely. The same goes for legislative bodies at the state and local levels. Unfortunately, there's a problem: our system is not as representative as it could (or should) be.

At the time of our country's founding, only white, property-owning men had the right to vote. We've come a long way with regard to bringing more citizens into the process, but we still have *a lot* of work to do. In this chapter, we'll cover some challenges that make our government not super representative: the size and scale of our democracy (and the related challenges that inhibit representative diversity) and extreme partisan redistricting (also known as partisan gerrymandering). Again, these are not new issues, but modern developments pose new challenges that require new solutions.

John Adams said Congress should be a "miniature, an exact portrait" of the public as a whole.[1] Let's see how we're doing, shall we?

SIZE, SCALE, AND DIVERSITY

You may remember from Part I that we have 435 representatives from 50 states in the House of Representatives (441 including nonvoting delegates from Washington, DC, and US territories like Puerto Rico). These representatives are distributed according to population size, but for our country's first 150 years, this total number of representatives was far from constant. In the First Congress, there were 65 representatives; based on an estimated population of 3.7 million, this meant there was one representative for every 57,169 people.[2] The number of representatives grew along with the country's population until 1911, when it was increased to 435 members; the size of the House was then officially capped at this number with the Permanent Apportionment Act of 1929.[3] Of course, the population of the United States has not stopped growing!

As a result, today we have, on average, one US House of Representatives voting member for every 750,000 people.[4] Yikes. Can one person really claim to represent the interests of three-quarters of a million people? Of course, that's just the average; the actual ratio varies considerably from state to state. For example, as of 2018, one House member represented Montana's 1,050,493 people, while a representative from Rhode Island represented nearly half as many (529,820 people).[5]

This is, *by far*, the highest ratio of representatives to citizens in any modern democracy. To put it in perspective, Canada has one representative for every 101,624 people, and the UK has one representative for every 99,124. The country with the second highest ratio is Pakistan, with one representative for every 590,630 people.[6]

The current cap on the size of the House presents some challenges. First is the simple feasibility of one official representing that many people. But here's another problem: because the Constitution mandates that every state have at least one representative, and the total number of representatives has been capped, low-population states are, in a sense, *over*represented in the House. Let's continue with the example of Rhode Island, which as of the 2010 census had a population of 1,052,567. In total, Rhode Island has four representatives (two members of the House of Representatives, and two senators). California, according to the 2010 census, had a population of 37,253,956 and, in total, has 55 representatives (53 members of the House of Representatives, and two senators). Rhode Island's population is just under 3 percent of California's, so you might expect that Rhode Island's congressional delegation would also be 3 percent the size of California's—but it's actually 7 percent. So while California has more influence outright given the number of members, Rhode Island has *outsized* influence for its population size. And this outsized influence extends beyond voting on legislation. The number of representatives in each state also determines how many Electoral College members (called "electors") each state has: every state is assigned a number of electors that is equal to its two senators plus the number of House members (Washington, DC, which does not have federal representation, gets three electors). Because the president is elected not by direct vote but by the Electoral College, low-population states have disproportionate influence in presidential elections.

There's also the issue of *descriptive* representation, or how much those in our government reflect the characteristics (like gender, race/ethnicity, age, sexual orientation) of the broader population. In 2006, according to the World Economic Forum, the US ranked sixty-sixth in the world when it came to political gender equality (a ranking mostly informed by the balance between women and men in governmental leadership positions).[7] In 2020, as we discussed in Part I, the US ranked eighty-sixth.[8] In other words, we're moving in the wrong direction. A record number of women served in Congress in 2018—yet women still only make up 23.7 percent of its 535 members.[9] Record breaking, perhaps, but also a far cry from equal. Moreover, while women of color make up approximately 19 percent of all Americans, they made up only 8.8 percent of the 116th Congress.[10] And of the 10,363 members who have ever served in the House of Representatives, only 75 have been women of color.[11]

Diversity in who represents us matters for a bunch of reasons. For example, research shows that people are more likely to vote if there's a candidate in an election that looks like them, and that members of Congress who belong to underrepresented groups are more likely to advocate for those groups in their dealings with federal agencies.[12]

The body that is supposed to most closely resemble and represent the US population (remember that "miniature portrait" of the public Adams mentioned?) doesn't look very representative, does it? We've been talking about this at the federal level, but leadership gender gaps abound in state and local government, as well.

Here are some fast facts:

- **State legislatures:** At the beginning of 2020, 29.1 percent of state legislators were women. Nevada had the highest percentage of women legislators (52 percent—the first state *ever* to see women outnumber men in a state legislature), while in West Virginia, only 13.4 percent of state legislators are women.[13]

- **State and local executive positions:** In state and local executive offices, too, the numbers of women leaders are quite low. Only 18 percent of governors (as of early 2020) are women, and only 22 percent of mayors in cities with over 30,000 people are women.[14]

A bonus federal representation fun fact: In 2012, New Hampshire became the first state ever to send an all-female delegation to Congress. Both senators were women, as were the state's two representatives—not to mention Governor Maggie Hassan (who is now serving as one of New Hampshire's senators).

POTENTIAL SOLUTIONS

The good news is that there are a lot of great ideas out there for how we can address the challenges of size, scale, and diversity. Even better, many states are already seizing the opportunity to experiment with new strategies and examining the impact they have (remember that states are laboratories of innovation!). This is far from an exhaustive list of solutions and ideas for reform. Instead, I'm focusing on two ideas that I find particularly compelling: the first is increasing the size of the House of Representatives, and the second is introducing ranked-choice voting.

The first idea: change the structure of "the People's House" by increasing its size. In 2018, the *New York Times* published a series of opinion pieces by its editorial board arguing for a larger House of Representatives, in addition to other reforms. As the *Times* wrote, "The bottom line is that the House today is far too small, and that poses a big danger to American democracy."[15]

So, what to do? Should we bring back the ratio of the founders (one representative to approximately every 30,000 citizens)? This would bring the size of the House to approximately 11,000 representatives—which would likely hamper effective decision and policy making (wrangling a group of that size would be a huge challenge). Some experts have argued that we should make the size of the House proportionate to other mature democracies, where the size of the national legislature is approximately the *cube root* of the country's population.[16] The University of Virginia Demographics Research Group's *Stat Chat* blog points out that, using this cube root rule, the size of the US House of Representatives should be 687 representatives (the *New York Times* recommended 593 in their editorial). If we increased the House to 687 members, the ratio of representatives to people would not match what it was in 1911 (the last time the size of the House was increased), but it would be a lot closer (roughly matching the ratio of representatives to constituents in 1970).[17]

It's probably obvious by now, but I agree that the size of the House should be increased. As the *Times* stated in an editorial, "[E]xpanding the House would mean not just a government with more representatives, but one that is literally more representative—including more people from perennially underrepresented groups, like women and minorities, and making for a fuller and richer legislative debate."[18]

The second idea: introduce ranked-choice voting (RCV). What is RCV and how does it work? Here's a quick explanation. The way most of us vote today is by casting our vote for the *one* candidate that we like best (or maybe dislike least!). With RCV, however, you rank as many—or as few—of the candidates that are running for office as you like. So, if there were four candidates running for office in a primary, you could rank all four in the order of your preference. All first-choice votes are then counted, and the candidate with the *fewest* first-choice votes gets eliminated. The second-choice votes on those ballots then get counted and added to the total number of votes for each candidate. This process is repeated until one candidate gets the majority of votes (50 percent plus one vote).

RCV may sound like a big change, but it's currently being used by more than a dozen US cities for their municipal elections, including San Francisco, Cambridge, Minneapolis, and Santa Fe (with New York City set to start using RCV for primary and special elections in 2021). Maine introduced ranked-choice voting for the 2018 gubernatorial and Senate elections and, as of 2020, is the only state to use RCV for statewide elections.

There are many proven benefits to RCV. To begin with, it encourages campaigns to be more civil, since candidates need to appeal even to voters who might support their opponents in order to capture second- and third-choice votes.[19] I'm not sure about you, but I don't know anyone who doesn't wish politics were more civil, especially in today's polarized environment. It also encourages voters to really get to know each candidate, since you have to rank them all in order of your preference rather than just voting for your party's candidate. It also eliminates the spoiler effect (i.e., we can stop shaming voters who vote for third-party candidates for "stealing" the vote of major-party candidates), as the winner is determined by who receives the majority share of votes. And when it comes to diversity? Encouragingly, research shows that adopting RCV is associated with an increase in the percentage of women, people of color, and women of color running for and winning local office.[20]

Let's take a real-world election that used RCV as an example. In 2010, during the Oakland mayoral election, Don Perata, a white man, was the heavy favorite. He also spent more money than any other candidate on his campaign. Jean Quan, another mayoral candidate, spent her time engaging voters directly, and explicitly reached out to folks to ask for their second- or third-choice vote. Her strategy paid off: she became the first Asian American woman to be elected mayor of a major American city.[21] And, in 2018, under a RCV system, London Breed made history when she became the first African American woman mayor of San Francisco. At the time, she was also the only female mayor in the largest 15 US cities.

There are downsides to RCV as well. It can take money and resources to bring in new voting equipment to accommodate new ballot types. It also requires voter education and outreach to ensure that folks understand the new ballots. But these downsides seem minimal compared to the possible benefits, and a 2018 report from FairVote found that voter turnout in RCV districts surpassed expectations, implementation was smooth and inexpensive, and voters made few errors.[22]

Now let's dive into another barrier to more representative representation: partisan gerrymandering. Voters are supposed to choose their representatives, but today, representatives in many critical states are choosing their voters.

AN OVERVIEW OF PARTISAN REDISTRICTING ("GERRYMANDERING")

Whether you first heard the term "gerrymandering" when it came up earlier in the book or you're already familiar with the concept, it's worth starting with a rundown of what it is and how it works.

Every voter belongs to a specific voting district (or legislative district), determined by where they live. House members today each represent a single district, and they are elected by the voters that live within that district. The lines that determine the shape of each district are not static; they can be redrawn every ten years, informed largely by what the census says about how populations have shifted over the past decade (some states take other data into account, as well).

Partisan gerrymandering is what happens when district lines are intentionally drawn in a way that benefits a specific party. This is done through techniques called "cracking" and "packing" groups of voters within the districts. Packing is when you draw lines to create districts with majority numbers of the opposite party; because its members are "packed" into a small number of districts, where they will win by wide margins, their influence is limited. Cracking is when you spread out the remaining members of the opposite party in such a way that your party represents the majority within other districts, if just barely.

Here's an example. Say you have five districts in your state, and your state is 40 percent Democrats and 60 percent Republicans. Through cracking and packing, it's possible to draw lines such that, in an election, Democrats would take three districts and Republicans would only take two, despite Republicans being in the majority.

If each of the five districts had 100 percent Republicans or 100 percent Democrats, this is what the party breakdown of the districts would look like:

District 1 (100% Dems)	District 2 (100% Dems)	District 3 (100% Reps)	District 4 (100% Reps)	District 5 (100% Reps)

But you could also divide your state into five districts a different way that would make it so that, although the Democrats only make up 40 percent of the state overall, *three* of the districts would have Democratic majorities:

District 1 (67% Dems, 33% Reps)				
District 2 (67% Dems, 33% Reps)			District 4 (100% Reps)	District 5 (100% Reps)
District 3 (67% Dems, 33% Reps)				

The composition of the voters' parties stays the same at the state level, but not at the district level. This could lead to very different election outcomes. In the first example, it's likely that the state would have three Republican elected officials and two Democratic officials; in the second, the reverse is likely (three Democratic officials and two Republican). You'll notice, however, that while Democrats do have a majority in Districts 1, 2, and 3 in the second example, it wouldn't be *impossible* for Republicans to win, especially if there was low turnout among Democrats. This is the risky part of gerrymandering; when a minority party aims to win by redistributing the opposition party as much as possible, they need to create margins that are slim (especially if the number of minority party voters is even less than the 40 percent used in this example), but not *so* slim that their party is at risk of losing.

Gerrymandering can take many forms—for instance, opposing parties may collude to draw districts such that they'll protect incumbents. Lines can be drawn in racially discriminatory ways, as well. And while racial gerrymandering, where district lines are drawn in order to diminish the voice and influence of people of color, is illegal, it remains a problem in part because of the difficulty of proving the intent was to draw districts along racial and not simply partisan lines.

The term "gerrymander" originated way back in 1812, over 200 years ago, when then governor of Massachusetts Elbridge Gerry signed into law a bill that allowed his party to redraw state senate districts to its advantage. It resulted in some pretty strange shapes. A cartoonist from the *Boston Globe* noticed that the shape of one district resembled a salamander and called it a "Gerry-mander."[23] Needless to say, the name stuck—and the practice of gerrymandering continues to this day.

So, who is responsible for drawing district lines? New district maps are generally drawn and passed by the state legislature, then signed into law by the governor. When a single party has control of the state legislature and the governorship, that party can essentially choose what all the voting districts in the state look like. Unsurprisingly, the party in control often gives itself an unfair advantage.

Districts are redrawn at the start of each decade after a new census. They will be reevaluated and redrawn in 2021, and then again in 2031. The year following the census is a critical time to stay vigilant as to what's taking place at the state level with regard to redistricting. As activist Katie Fahey, who led an enormously successful campaign to put an end to partisan gerrymandering in Michigan, says, you "have a group of people drawing maps for their benefit that will impact millions of people for ten years, if it happens."[24] Ten years!

Not all states trust their legislatures to draw district lines (although the majority do); increasingly, bipartisan commissions, citizen commissions, or panels of civil servants are being made responsible for redistricting instead, which could help curb harmful partisan gerrymandering (but more on solutions later in this chapter).

For some states, gerrymandering isn't an issue (at least in terms of drawing congressional districts), because they're single-district states. In other words, some states have only one representative because of their comparatively low populations. These single congressional district states include Alaska, Delaware, Montana, North Dakota, South Dakota, Vermont, and Wyoming. But even if you live in one of those states, there are still commissions or groups drawing district lines for state legislatures—so you're not off the hook!

Or maybe your state is currently gerrymandered to favor your party. Well, you might say, the current system benefits me—why would I want it to change? But you don't need to be a political buff to know that nothing about politics is a guarantee. In the next election, you might find yourself on the opposite side, without a government that represents you—where *you* are part of the group that those in leadership are trying to disadvantage.

It's probably pretty obvious at this point, but if your goal is a truly representative, democratic government, then gerrymandering is always a bad thing. Ideally, the goal for drawing districts should be what experts call "responsiveness." In a highly responsive map, you would see one party increase its proportion of seats as it increases its share of the vote. In other words, if one party made up 40 percent of the population, you would see that party in approximately 40 percent of elected positions.

Unfortunately, this is not the case today. FairVote, a nonpartisan organization, found that, in 2010, only 70 of 435 US House districts had what they deemed a "competitive partisan" balance. This is already quite low, but after redistricting in 2011, this number fell to 53—just over 10 percent of House seats.

Ultimately, an electorate will be more engaged when its members trust that their government represents their interests—a worthwhile goal, in my opinion. But engagement aside, gerrymandering is tremendously problematic for a democracy; it skews political outcomes in ways that don't necessarily reflect the will of the people, but rather the will of a party. Doesn't sound very democratic to me.

POTENTIAL SOLUTIONS

First, to create more responsive, representative districts, it's important to have accurate census data. As we talked about in Part I, most states use census data as the primary input to the redistricting processes. Ensuring that all people living in the US participate in the census—and feel safe doing so—is crucial.

Next, the process of *how* redistricting happens is important. If state legislatures are responsible for drawing district lines, it's all too easy for the majority party to draw district lines in ways that favor their party. And while gerrymandering is not a new practice, as we've discussed, modern software and an abundance of data have enabled legislatures to create gerrymandered districts with new, surgical precision.

So what to do? In 2019, the Supreme Court ruled that the question of partisan gerrymandering was a political one—not one for courts to decide.[25] This means that partisan gerrymandering, while a harmful practice, is not *illegal.* Given that it seems the courts are unlikely, at this time, to intervene on this issue, experts are pushing to make redistricting a more independent process, specifically by giving responsibility of drawing voting districts to an independent commission, rather than leaving it up to the state legislature.

Today, a number of states use independent or bipartisan commissions to draw district lines, including Alaska, Arizona, California, Colorado, Hawaii, Idaho, Iowa, Michigan, Missouri, Montana, New Jersey, New York, Ohio, Pennsylvania, Utah, Vermont, and Washington.[26] But as experts at the Brennan Center, a nonpartisan law and policy institute, point out, all commissions are not equally effective, and that the most effective and independent commissions share the following attributes:[27]

- geographical, political, and demographic diversity of commissioners

- clear criteria for drawing maps, including a ban on drawing maps in such a way that favors a political party

- an independent selection process for selecting commissioners, including screening for potential conflicts of interest

- transparency requirements and encouragement of public input

- sufficient time and funding

- rules that incentivize compromise in map approvals (e.g., requiring at least some support from every major political party to pass)

Understanding what the redistricting process looks like in *your* state, and advocating for change if that process is not as independent or transparent as it should be, is critical. Just ask Katie Fahey, who led the movement to transform the redistricting process in Michigan—an Advocate in Action you'll hear from right after this chapter.

FINAL THOUGHTS ON REPRESENTATIVE REPRESENTATION

In combination, the solutions we've talked through in this chapter could make our representation, well, more representative, from bringing more diversity to government to making it harder to gerrymander districts to advantage one party over another. Of course, these policies all need more testing. A larger number of states and cities need to try them out, to see what works and what challenges still need to be addressed. But making changes that allow more people to be better represented seems worth at least trying. As the *New York Times* editorial board eloquently stated: "When citizens feel that their voice is being heard by government, they'll be more eager to participate, more likely to vote, and more politically engaged overall. That's what a democracy should look like and, in the long run, it's the only way a democracy can survive."[28]

This seems like an outcome worth fighting for.

Advocate in Action: Katie Fahey, Activist and Executive Director of The People*

Katie Fahey is an activist who led a successful grassroots campaign to end partisan gerrymandering in Michigan. As the founder of Voters Not Politicians, she helped organize thousands of volunteers who collected over 425,000 voter signatures for Proposal 2, a ballot initiative amending the state constitution to create an independent redistricting commission. Fahey now serves as executive director of The People, a national nonpartisan democracy reform organization.

On starting a movement with a Facebook post:

In 2016, I was growing increasingly concerned with the state of politics in general and in Michigan specifically. In Michigan, we had the Flint water crisis; it was horrifying to see an entire city being poisoned by their water and to watch our government try to cover that up for several months! But the Flint crisis was tied to a political decision called the Emergency Manager Law, which people felt was targeting minority communities and taking away their direct decision-making power when it came to their financial assets. In Michigan, we have a "citizen veto" for any law; the Emergency Manager Law was put on the ballot and the voters repealed it. But the first act of the legislature, after being elected to office through gerrymandering, was to find a loophole in the repeal process and reinstate the Emergency Manager Law. And that law is the reason the decision was made to switch where Flint's water came from.

I was so mad and just reached a breaking point where I couldn't *not* do something! I made a Facebook post that said: "I want to end gerrymandering in Michigan. If you want to help, let me know." The post was shared with a couple of Facebook groups, and suddenly I had a lot of people I didn't know sending me messages saying, "Love what you're doing, can't wait to help, let me know what to do." I felt a lot of responsibility and excitement about that. Seeing such a quick response, I knew we were on to something.

On creating a strengths-based movement:

I made a Google Sheet where people interested in helping could state who they were, their background, why they were volunteering, what they were hoping to get out of the experience, and how much time they had. We had these amazing people: a woman who was executive director of the Renaissance fair, retired vice presidents from Ford, a stay-at-home-

---

*   Katie Fahey, interview with the author, September 27, 2019 (adapted for clarity).

mom-slash-Jazzercise-instructor who was also a woodcarver. My previous professional experience dealt a lot with project management. Once we understood everyone's skills and background, we could build a plan and get to work. And by understanding what people were trying to get out of the experience, and where they were already comfortable, we had a lot of success.

On leading change without being an "expert":

If we had gone in thinking we knew the exact right answer and the exact right way to end gerrymandering, we would have failed. There were plenty of policy experts who thought they knew exactly what Michigan needed, but that wasn't a participatory process. By actually talking to people with different lived experiences, we created a much more robust policy that we could stand behind.

There's also a lot of power in being there due to your own conviction. The urgency that you feel that's making you want to participate is such a big driver. The fact that I wasn't being paid to be there allowed me to be bold and unafraid to take chances, and unafraid to fail.

Chapter 12

....

VOTER ACCESS
AND PARTICIPATION

Democracy only works when we work for it. When we fight for it.
When we demand it.

—Stacey Abrams, in a campaign speech as the
Democratic candidate for Georgia governor (2018)

So far, we've established that our representatives don't always look very representative, and that even though the system should enable voters to choose those representatives, gerrymandering flips that dynamic on its head, enabling representatives to choose their voters. What's more, the way campaign finance currently works means a small group of wealthy citizens have outsized influence on who actually gets to run. But even if we address all of the issues we've talked about so far in Part III, there's still one more critical challenge to electing people who properly represent us: encouraging citizens to vote, and ensuring everyone has equal access and opportunity to exercise this right.

Many people today just ... don't vote. Nearly one-third of eligible American voters are not even registered. Only 56 percent of eligible American voters cast ballots in the 2016 presidential election.[1] And while women are more likely to vote than men, as we've discussed, there are significant gaps *between* groups of women—for example, in the 2016 election, of eligible voters, 66.8 percent of white, non-Hispanic women voted; 63.7 percent of Black women voted; 50 percent of Hispanic women voted; and 48.4 percent of Asian/Pacific Islander women voted.[2] We need more women (and men) participating in electoral politics.

Of course, historically, voting (or not voting) hasn't always been a matter of choice. The US has a complex, troubling history when it comes to who has the right to vote. And having the legal right to vote hasn't always translated into the practical ability to do so. For example, while Black men gained the right to vote in 1867, the Jim Crow laws of the early twentieth century hugely limited these rights in practice, as we discussed in Part II, from grandfather clauses to poll taxes to outright intimidation and violence. Literacy tests, for example, were required for voter registration in many districts. Yet for Black citizens, even passing one of these literacy tests was not a guarantee of getting to vote: Rosa Parks, an organizer and leader in the civil rights movement, was required to take a literacy test to vote. She passed and was told she would receive her voting card in the mail—but it never came. When she retook the test, she was told she failed (and was denied the opportunity to see her results). The third time she took the test, she passed, and finally received her voting card—but when she went to vote, she was told that she needed to pay the $1.50 poll tax . . . *for every year she had been eligible to vote* (she was 32 at the time).[3] She paid, and was finally able to vote, but only through sheer determination and overcoming obstacles that should never have existed in the first place—and that certainly did not exist for her white neighbors.

These types of laws and discriminatory actions had a huge impact on Black voter registration and turnout; with the adoption of the 1901 Alabama State Constitution, for example, the number of Black males registered to vote in Alabama fell from 820,000 to just 4,000.[4] It took the Voting Rights Act of 1965 to put a stop to these discriminatory laws and policies and to re-enfranchise Black voters. Fundamental to the VRA was the placement of federal observers at polling places, and the requirement that states with the worst histories of voter discrimination get any changes to voting or elections cleared by the Department of Justice.

And yet, threats to voting rights continue today. Some states have begun to introduce a wave of new voter laws and requirements, specifically around voter ID. The primary justification offered by supporters of these

ID requirements is that they are necessary to prevent fraud. Of course, no one wants voter fraud—we want our elections to be free and fair. But there is broad consensus among experts that claims of voter fraud are overblown. In North Carolina, for example, an investigation found that there were only two cases of voter impersonation between 2000 and 2012 out of 21 million votes cast.[5]

Opponents of voter ID requirements claim that those restrictions will reduce turnout. While a new study shows that voter ID laws don't have a negative impact on voter registration or turnout overall for any group (defined by race, age, sex, or party affiliation),[6] this emerging research deserves to be closely monitored. As Dan Hopkins of the website **FiveThirtyEight** writes: "It's certainly not a consensus, but the weight of recent research suggests that even if voter ID laws have limited effects on which party wins specific elections, they still affect tens of thousands of voters in larger states, particularly Black, Latino, Democratic, and elderly voters. And importantly, these laws' long-term impacts may well differ from their immediate effects upon implementation. So as politicians, lawyers, and social scientists continue to debate these laws, the very effects themselves are likely to change beneath our feet."[7] If a law doesn't do much to fix a problem and also has the potential to put an undue burden on voters of color,* or young voters, or women voters†—as voter ID laws appear to do—we ought to really examine whether that law does more harm than good. It's also hard to argue that these restrictions are not purely political, when experts have noted that three factors lead a state to introducing stricter voter laws: (1) Republican takeover

---

* The 2016 Survey of the Performance of American Elections found that while only 7 percent of white Americans didn't have an ID, 17 percent of Black Americans and 9 percent of Hispanic Americans did not have one—showing that there could be a clear impact along racial lines and undue burden carried by voters of color compared to white Americans (Charles Stewart, *2016 Survey of the Performance of American Elections*, Harvard Dataverse, April 14, 2017, https://doi.org/10.7910/DVN/Y38VIQ).

† Women could also be disproportionately affected. I chose to keep my maiden name when I got married, but many women (roughly 80 percent of American women, in fact, based on a 2015 survey) change their names when they get married (Claire Cain Miller and Derek Willis, "Maiden Names, On the Rise Again," *New York Times*, June 27, 2015, www.nytimes.com/2015/06/28/upshot/maiden-names-on-the-rise-again.html?smid =tw-nytimes&abt=0002&abg=0&_r=0). As a result, they often don't have multiple IDs that match—or maybe they registered to vote with their new name, but their ID doesn't match, or vice versa. If you've changed your name, you know how complicated that process can be—and it can take a long time, which can conflict with an election cycle. I'm not saying that we should be mapping our personal decisions to the political system, just that the system is working in a way that makes it harder for a whole bunch of people.

of state government after years of Democratic control, (2) being a political "battleground state," and (3) being racially heterogeneous.[8]

That's not to say the outlook is all bleak. Over the last 50 years, there have been a lot of good changes to both federal *and* state voting laws, too: increases in opportunities to vote absentee, making it possible to register closer to election day, reductions in residency requirements, and measures permitting people to register to vote while applying for a driver's license, to name a few. But it can still feel like the barriers to voting, whether those barriers are personal, like lack of time, or systemic and state-imposed, like voter roll purging and the closing of polling stations, are ever-growing and overwhelming.

I remember the first time I voted: it was the New Hampshire primary, and I was registered as an independent. I walked into my polling place, registered as a Democrat, voted, unregistered (so I went back to being an independent), and walked out. Easy as pie, and it took all of ten minutes to do. Given that this was one of my formative voting experiences, I've never accepted that voter registration needs to be overly complex and bureaucratic. And now, living in Seattle, I vote by mail. But my experience is far from the norm in many states. At the end of the day, we should make voting as burden free as possible (of course, keeping security and administrative resources in mind), and pay particular attention to the ways this right can be chipped away at, especially for communities that have historically been marginalized and disenfranchised.

These decisions about the mechanics of voting are also about what kind of country we are. How a country votes and who is able to do so speaks volumes about what that country values. And putting restrictions in place to fight a bogeyman that doesn't exist, *especially* when those restrictions can affect voter confidence and voter turnout, doesn't align with the aspirational values we have for our democracy.

POTENTIAL SOLUTIONS

When it comes to motivating people to vote, the unfortunate reality is that a lot of the traditional get out the vote (GOTV) efforts, like mailings, calls, or volunteer visits, have proven marginally effective at best.[9] So what *can* we do? Don't despair—there are plenty of measures to try.

First, we can make voter registration easier. Many proponents advocate for same-day registration, which would mean citizens could register at their polling places on Election Day. Research shows that this increases turnout by five to seven percentage points.[10] Today, 10 states and Washington, DC, allow same-day voter registration (including New Hampshire, where I registered to vote for the first time).[11] It may not be a coincidence that four of the five states with the highest voter turnout allow same-day registration.[12] Indeed, MIT Election Data + Science Lab found that same-day registration is the one reform most *consistently correlated* with higher voter turnout.* More long term, we can also move toward Automatic Voter Registration (AVR). AVR would mean that any time eligible citizens interact with a participating government agency (for example, the DMV), they would be automatically registered to vote, or their voter registration information would be updated. In 2015, Oregon pioneered an AVR program in which citizens who applied for or renewed their driver's license at the DMV were automatically registered to vote, unless they opted out. Oregon voter demographics in 2016 saw increased diversity in income, age, and race; first-time voter participation was also up.[13] Today, 16 states plus Washington, DC, have implemented AVR.[14] Bonus: AVR submits voter registration information to election officials electronically, so it is also a greener process.[15]

Adopting by-mail voting is another way to increase voter participation (as well as ensure voter safety during a public health crisis; as you likely remember, vote by mail was debated and discussed at length leading up to the 2020 presidential election due to COVID-19 concerns). Where I live, in Washington State, *all* elections are vote by mail. I love it because it gives me a chance to easily review the ballot in advance (it shows up in my mailbox a few weeks before ballots are due), do my research, and make informed decisions before filling it out and sending it in. Although data on voter participation using vote by mail has been mixed, the MIT Election Data + Science Lab writes that "the safest conclusion . . . is that extending VBM options increases turnout modestly in presidential elections but may increase turnout more in primaries, local elections, and special elections." We need more participation in all elections anyway! And as of the 2020 election, 17 states require voters to provide an excuse (e.g., physical disabilities,

---

* However, it's important to note that it's unclear whether this is correlation or causation; it also may be true that states with higher turnout in general are more likely to pass Election Day registration laws (it's likely a mix of both).

absence from the country) to be able to vote by mail (28 states offer no-excuse absentee voting, and 5 states, like Washington, have elections held by mail-in ballots). Adopting no-excuse absentee ballots in all states, at the very least, could help voter turnout.

Others have suggested making Election Day a national holiday to give people time to get to the polls or having Election Day take place on a weekend—but evidence of these reforms' effectiveness is mixed. First of all, making Election Day a national holiday would likely mean that many service employees would still be working (think folks who work in retail or at restaurants, grocery stores, or pharmacies, or in health care)—just as they are on other national holidays. Weekday school closures could also exacerbate childcare challenges for people in those jobs. Plus, it may not actually be that effective for anyone else either: one study that looked at whether giving state employees a holiday to vote led to higher turnout for those employees found that it didn't.[16]

That's not to say that these types of initiatives aren't worth doing at all; it could be important to signal the value of elections and, perhaps at the very least, take away an excuse for many people not to vote! And it's not just governments that have the power to try out initiatives to support voting; as we've seen, companies are also increasingly introducing initiatives that help get people to the polls. For example, Lyft has offered discounted rides to the polls on Election Day to reduce the mobility barrier for voters who may have transportation challenges.

Of course, for many voters, it may not be issues of convenience or time that keep them from the polls. Some may be intimidated or feel they don't have enough information to make an informed choice. So there's more we can—and must—do. We need to ensure that information is getting to all voters—not just the ones who are *already* the most engaged. Professors Jan Leighley and Jonathan Nagler, in their book *Who Votes Now?*, suggest that the most effective way to increase turnout and improve the representativeness of voters might be to increase the information they have about candidates' policy positions. Looking at evidence from presidential elections between 1972 and 2008, voters who perceived differences in policy and ideology between the Republican and Democratic candidates were more likely to vote than those who did not perceive any such differences.[17]

Another way to increase voter turnout is by helping people understand that their vote is crucial. Some people report skipping voting because they feel their vote doesn't matter. In 2016, voter turnout in the 11 states where the presidential margin of victory was five points or less was 67 percent, compared to 56 percent in the seven states where the margin of victory was greater than 31 points.[18] Voters know when their votes are likely to be swamped by their state's partisan demographics. This is where reforms like ranked-choice voting, campaign finance reform, and a larger House might also have the added benefit of getting more people to the polls—after all, you're more likely to feel like your interests are represented when the system feels—and looks—more representative.

There are also actions that you can take right now to improve voter participation! Social pressure, as we discussed in Part II, can be really impactful; make sure you're all set to vote, and ask your friends what their voting plans are. Help them understand why their vote matters, particularly when it comes to midterm and local elections. If you're on social media, share that you voted with others!

FINAL THOUGHTS ON VOTER ACCESS AND PARTICIPATION

To quickly recap: there's compelling evidence that we can improve turnout by making registration easier (particularly, by implementing AVR or same-day registration), implementing vote-by-mail options, and helping people understand the policy positions of candidates running for office, as well as *why* their vote matters. Making voting accessible also means fighting against voter suppression (whether that consists of burdensome ID requirements or other nefarious or misguided actions like unlawful voter roll purges)—so it's important to pay attention to what's happening with regard to voting rights within your state. Remember that state law largely defines how voters get registered and how voting takes place—so understanding what's happening in *your* state is critical.

. . . .

At this point you might be thinking: *Why engage politically if the system is so stacked against us? Why do anything at all?* It's true that these are big, thorny problems that will limit our ability to have real voice and influence in our democracy until they are resolved. But that's why they need to be addressed. And, again, the issues we've discussed are only some of the challenges to our democracy. I'd encourage you to talk to others in your community about the barriers *they* feel are most daunting or repressive when it comes to their voices being heard. These aren't the sexiest or most glamorous topics, and they get far less airtime than others that dominate our news cycles, so it's on each of us to make sure we're informed—that we know what's working in our democracy, what's not, and how we might change the latter.

The challenges in our system today don't make it impossible to influence that system. You can, and women have done so—women are doing so right now! But it's why we have to prioritize major reform in addition to our other big issues.

Three important things to remember:

1. **We can create change—even in a less-than-perfect system.** We can work within the system as it stands, even if it's hard. The way our government works seems set in stone, but it's not. Remember that voters did not always directly elect senators. And the voting age used to be 21. Changing these things may have once seemed impossible as well, but, due to the determination and commitment of dedicated citizens, they *did* change. Our way of government is more flexible than we think; it was designed to change, to evolve based on the needs of its citizens.

2. **We need to stay vigilant about threats to our democracy.** It can be really hard to keep tabs on the structural aspects of our democracy when there is so much else happening that feels more urgent in our day-to-day. But imagine the change we could create if we had a system that worked better for all of us. Ultimately, this vision should be what inspires us to do more. We won't be able to see the change we want—we won't be able to create a government that fully realizes our democratic values—unless we stay engaged on these issues. There are lots of organizations that are drawing attention to these issues—from the Brennan Center to the Center for Responsive Politics to Common Cause and many, many others. Follow them or sign up for their newsletters to make it easy to stay on top of what's happening.

3. **It's important to start local!** I'm probably starting to sound like a broken record, but lots of the reforms and changes highlighted in this part of the book started at the state or even the city level.

If we can get things working there, if we can drive change there, we can either replicate those changes at the federal level or use them as a way of introducing legislation that gets picked up at the federal level.

The voice of every citizen matters—and we only get closer to making that a reality by focusing on the hard, often unglamorous work of making our democracy work for everyone.

PART III WORKBOOK

This workbook section will be a little different from the previous two. This one is all about exploring what these systemic issues we've talked about in Part III look like in your state or district and reflecting on whether there are any other issues you think are preventing people from fully engaging in our democracy. Because every state is so different, some states have proactively worked to address these issues, while others are quite far behind. By understanding where your state and local government falls on that spectrum, you'll be able to decide if our country's structural challenges are something you also want to work to address as part of your advocacy efforts or—if your state is doing pretty well—if there's something to celebrate!

THE INFLUENCE OF MONEY IN POLITICS

What rules are in place in your state and/or municipality around campaign finance?

_____

_____

_____

_____

_____

_____

_____

_____

_____

Are there any public financing efforts available to support candidates? Do candidates use those programs?

_____

_____

_____

_____

_____

_____

_____

_____

_____

What groups have contributed the most (financially) to your elected officials? How might this have affected their legislative priorities?

_____

_____

_____

_____

_____

_____

_____

_____

_____

_____

REPRESENTATION

How does your state draw district lines? Who is involved in making those decisions?

_____

_____

_____

_____

_____

_____

_____

_____

_____

_____

How many people do your representatives represent (at the state, federal, and local level)? How does this compare, generally, to other states (remembering that the average ratio at the federal level is one to 750,000)?

_____

_____

_____

_____

_____

_____

_____

_____

What percentage of your federal, state, and local officials are women? People of color? Other dimensions of diversity? How does this compare to the state population overall? What might any gaps indicate about the "representativeness" of your district?

_____

_____

_____

_____

_____

_____

_____

_____

_____

_____

_____

Has your state or municipal government done any experiments with new or different ways of voting (e.g., ranked-choice voting)? What was the reaction or outcome?

_____

_____

_____

_____

_____

_____

_____

_____

_____

_____

What are your state's voter ID laws? What are voters required to present when they show up at the polls?

_____

_____

_____

_____

_____

_____

_____

_____

_____

_____

_____

What initiatives exist in your state to increase voter turnout (e.g., mail-in ballots, early voting), if any?

_____

_____

_____

_____

_____

_____

_____

_____

_____

_____

What others issues have come up in your state with regard to voter access (e.g., limited number of polling places, purging of voter rolls, etc.)? What organizations are working to solve them?

_____

_____

_____

_____

_____

_____

_____

_____

_____

_____

What else do you see as a barrier in your district to fuller, more equal political participation of all citizens?

_____

_____

_____

_____

_____

_____

_____

_____

_____

_____

_____

CONCLUSION

························

A CALL TO ACTION

I 've long been a *major* fan of The Chicks (formerly known as the Dixie Chicks). I remember being in our family van with my sisters, belting out "Goodbye Earl" and "Wide Open Spaces." To me, many of their songs spoke to the unleashing of voice and power, of independence and integrity. Even today, their refrains play in my head: When I moved from the East to the West Coast? *It takes the shape of a place out west/but what it holds for her, she hasn't yet guessed* ("Wide Open Spaces"). When I feel I'm not being heard or taken seriously? *You don't like the sound of the truth/coming from my mouth* ("Truth No. 2"). I could go on. Needless to say, their messages and musicianship were (and continue to be) inspiring to me.

But while their music encouraged me to use my voice, they were punished for using theirs. In 2003, during a live concert, they criticized then president George W. Bush. The backlash was immediate. They received death threats, people burned their CDs, and news anchors talked about their career-ending stand. I was sixteen at the time and remember being confused about the discrepancy between the world they created in my headphones and the reality unfolding in the headlines.

You don't have to look too hard to see similar events in politics today, either. In July 2019, President Trump, referring to Congresswomen Ilhan Omar, Alexandria Ocasio-Cortez, Rashida Tlaib, and Ayanna Pressley, tweeted that they should "go back and help fix the totally broken and crime infested places from which they came,"[1] a reaction prompted by their criticism of his border security policies. (All four are American citizens—and all except Omar were born in the US.) As a woman, using your voice can be a risky proposition (something that can be especially true for women of color).

Maybe the world is starting to change; after all, there are a record number of women serving in Congress. And, as we found out in late 2020, just before this book went to press, Kamala Harris made history when she was elected as the first-ever female vice president, not to mention the first-ever Black vice president and first-ever Indian American vice president. Of course, Vice President Harris was not alone in her history-making win during the 2020 election: for example, LGBTQ+ advocate Sarah McBride became the first-ever openly transgender woman to serve as state senator, and organizer, pastor, and nurse Cori Bush became the first Black woman to represent Missouri in Congress. More women are running for, and winning, political office than ever before. And progress hasn't just been made in the halls of Congress or state legislatures. The #MeToo movement, thanks to the bravery of survivors sharing their experiences, led to a twenty-three-year prison sentence for one of the most prominent offenders identified by the movement, movie producer Harvey Weinstein. Millions of women have marched in protest and spoken out against sexism and misogyny.

In fact, the world is changing *because* of women. Stacey Abrams, former Democratic leader in Georgia's state legislature—along with activists and organizers across the state—was instrumental in registering approximately *800,000 voters in Georgia* between 2018 and 2020.[2] And you don't have to look further than the pages of this book to be inspired by the extraordinary impact of other women, from Katie Fahey's success at ending partisan gerrymandering in Michigan, to New Hampshire state senator Safiya Wazir's legislation to allow women running for state office in New Hampshire to use campaign funding for childcare, to my friend Ameneh showing up at JFK to provide legal assistance to immigrants arriving to what must have been an overwhelming and terrifying situation. Heck, even The Chicks released a new album in 2020 to major acclaim. This is all progress worth celebrating, and reason to hope there is more progress to come.

These women, and their stories, remind us that we are not alone. That we all start somewhere—no one is born knowing how our system of government works, or how to influence it. That incredible change is possible if we take it one step at a time.

Democracy, if it's to reflect our priorities and preferences, requires persistent participation. And when I say participation, I mean *real* participation. Not just voting (although that's certainly important). Not just following politics as we would a sports team or reality show, and trading headlines with our friends.

Eitan Hersh, associate professor of political science at Tufts University and author of *Politics Is for Power*, describes this kind of behavior as "political hobbyism." People who treat politics as a hobby, he writes in an article for *The Atlantic*, "follow the news . . . and debate the latest development on social media. They might sign an online petition or throw a $5 online donation to a presidential candidate. Mostly, they consume political information as a way of satisfying their own emotional and intellectual needs." He contrasts these hobbyists with people who use politics to empower themselves and their communities, engaging in "the methodical pursuit of power to influence how the government operates." Hersh highlights the example of Querys Matias, a sixty-three-year-old immigrant from the Dominican Republic living in Haverhill, Massachusetts (a small city of approximately 64,000 people[3]):

> In her day job, Matias is a bus monitor for a special-needs school. In her evenings, she amasses power. Matias is a leader of a group called the Latino Coalition in Haverhill, bringing together the Dominicans, Puerto Ricans, and Central Americans who together make up about 20 percent of the residents of the city. The coalition gets out the vote during elections, but it does much more than that. It has met with its member of Congress and asked for regular, Spanish-speaking office hours for its community. It advocates for policies such as immigration reform for "Dreamers" and federal assistance in affordable housing. On local issues, the demands are more concrete. Dozens of the group's members have met with the mayor, the school superintendent, and the police department. They want more Latinos in city jobs and serving on city boards. They want the schools to have staff available who can speak with parents in Spanish. They want to know exactly how the city interacts with U.S. Immigration and Customs Enforcement.[4]

Matias is an example of how to create real change: by understanding how our system works, understanding the tools of influence at our disposal, and engaging with our elected officials at all levels, as well as mobilizing members of our own communities. We also need to be aware of the structural challenges that can act as headwinds to the change we want to enact. Hopefully, by now, you know a little bit more about all these things. But, at the end of the day, none of these tools matter if you don't actually *do* something with them.

Yes, political engagement can be hard, and thankless, and risky. But I hope you feel, after reading this book, that it's still worth doing. That it's worth the risk. After all, the stakes are high; our democracy—and our world—depends on it. What you do after you vote has the power to change lives.

In moments of doubt, I look to the words of one of my role models: Senator Elizabeth Warren. As she suspended her race in the 2020 presidential election, Senator Warren shared the following words with her supporters: "So if you leave with only one thing, it must be this: choose to fight only righteous fights, because then when things get tough—and they will—you will know that there is only one option ahead of you: nevertheless, you must persist."

Change is possible, but only if we *truly* engage, courageously and continuously. Only if we fight when things get tough. Our voices are powerful, but only if we speak up.

And that part is up to us.

RESOURCES
FOR IMPACT

Here's a list of resources and organizations that will help amp up your political advocacy and engagement, whether you're looking to learn more about your government officials, lobby your representatives, or run for office yourself!

All In Together Campaign (AIT)
About: AIT encourages, equips, educates, and empowers voting-age women to participate fully in America's civic and political life.
Tools/resources: Use the AIT Action Center to learn who represents you at the state and federal levels. Plus, check out recordings of past webinars with elected officials and activists across the country to learn how government really works.
URL: www.aitogether.org

American Association of University Women (AAUW)
About: AAUW is a nonprofit organization that advances equity for women and girls through advocacy, education, and research.
Tools/resources: Learn more about issues from the gender pay gap to implicit bias, as well as access their advocacy toolkit, which includes how-tos on activities from writing an op-ed or letter to the editor to hosting a candidate forum.
URL: www.aauw.org

Ballotpedia

About: The digital encyclopedia of American politics and elections; their goal is to inform people about politics by providing accurate and objective information about politics at all levels of government.

Tools/resources: Tons of detailed information about federal, state, and local government, as well as a tool to learn who represents you at each level of government. Also includes an option to sign up for a regular newsletter (helping information come to you about political goings-on). Use the elections calendar to know what's upcoming, as well as what will be on *your* ballot so you can do your research to make sure you're prepared well in advance.

URL: www.ballotpedia.org

BallotReady

About: BallotReady aggregates content from candidates' websites, social media, press, endorsers, and board of elections for comprehensive, nonpartisan information about the candidates and referendums on your ballot.

Tools/resources: Get information on the background of every candidate and referendum (or proposition) on your ballot, and compare candidates based on their stances, biographies, and endorsements.

URL: www.ballotready.org

Center for American Women and Politics (CAWP)

About: CAWP, a unit of the Eagleton Institute of Politics at Rutgers, the State University of New Jersey, is nationally recognized as the leading source of scholarly research and current data about women's political participation in the United States. Its mission is to promote greater knowledge and understanding about the role of women in American politics, enhance women's influence in public life, and expand the diversity of women in politics and government.

Tools/resources: CAWP offers programs for women interested in running for office, as well as robust research and scholarly articles on topics from women voting to the current representation of women in elected office (at state and federal levels).

URL: www.cawp.rutgers.edu

Civics 101

About: *Civics 101* is the podcast refresher course on the basics of how our democracy works.

Tools/resources: Each episode of the podcast provides an overview of a different topic, ranging from the Electoral College to the Bill of Rights to the emergency powers of a governor. Use this to continuously brush up on your knowledge of the fundamentals.

URL: www.civics101podcast.org

Common Cause

About: A nonpartisan, grassroots organization dedicated to upholding the core values of American democracy, they work to create open, honest, and accountable government that serves the public interest; promote equal rights, opportunity, and representation for all; and empower all people to make their voices heard in the political process.

Tools/resources: Like Ballotpedia, Common Cause has a tool to help you find out who represents you at the federal and state levels (including contact information and links to your elected officials' websites, as well as official social media profiles).

URL: www.commoncause.org

Congress.gov

About: Congress.gov is the official website for US federal legislative information. The site provides access to accurate, timely, and complete legislative information for members of Congress, legislative agencies, and the public.

Tools/resources: Use this to learn about your members of Congress— for example, committees they serve on, their congressional voting records—or even check in on the status of a particular bill or issue.

URL: www.congress.gov

GenderAvenger

About: A community that ensures women are represented in the public dialogue.

Tools/resources: The GA Tally allows you to tally and count who is present and speaking (from a gender equity perspective) and share it instantly on social media. You can also sign up for the GA newsletter, which provides other ways to take action regarding gender balance in the public dialogue.

URL: www.genderavenger.com

GovTrack

About: GovTrack.us tracks the United States Congress and helps Americans participate in their national legislature.

Tools/resources: Learn about congressional procedures, members of Congress, committees, as well as ongoing investigations. You can also track when your members of Congress vote or introduce new legislation and check out their voting records.

URL: www.govtrack.us

Higher Heights for America

About: Higher Heights is the only national organization providing Black women with a political home exclusively dedicated to harnessing their power to expand Black women's elected representation and voting participation and advance progressive policies.

Tools/resources: Higher Heights offers numerous research reports on their website as well as online training for women considering running for office, featuring women leaders like Stacey Abrams.

URL: www.higherheightsforamerica.org

IGNITE

About: IGNITE is a movement of young women who are ready and eager to become the next generation of political leaders.

Tools/resources: IGNITE facilitates K–12 and college programming, as well as online workshops on topics from voting accessibility to digital advocacy. You can also apply to be an IGNITE fellow if you're in or just out of college.

URL: www.ignitenational.org

League of Women Voters (LWV)

About: The League of Women Voters of the United States encourages informed and active participation in government, works to increase understanding of major public policy issues, and influences public policy through education and advocacy.

Tools/resources: LWV offers a ton of civic resources, from ways to look up who represents you (from the president to your chief of police) to how to support voter registration (including volunteer opportunities to help register others). They also offer resources to address partisan redistricting, money in politics, and voter suppression. You can sign up to receive alerts, and join a local LWV office for local resources and community.

URL: www.lwv.org

MIT Election Data + Science Lab

About: The MIT Election Data + Science Lab supports advances in election science by collecting, analyzing, and sharing core data and findings. They also aim to build relationships with election officials and others to help apply new scientific research to the practice of democracy in the United States.

Tools/resources: Access data on voting in the US—from voter turnout to voter registration and confidence—and evidence-based research on how to increase voter participation.

URL: http://electionlab.mit.edu

National Conference of State Legislatures (NCSL)

About: Founded in 1975, NCSL represents the legislatures in the states, territories, and commonwealths of the US. Its mission is to advance the effectiveness, independence, and integrity of legislatures and to foster interstate cooperation and facilitate the exchange of information among legislatures.

Tools/resources: Access tons of information about state legislatures— from legislative calendars to the legislative process (e.g., how a bill becomes a law) to legislator compensation and benefits—for all 50 states.

URL: www.ncsl.org

National League of Cities (NLC)

About: NLC is a resource and advocate for the nation's cities and their leaders.

Tools/resources: NLC offers more information about how municipal governments operate, as well as highlights examples of how cities across the country are addressing different kinds of challenges, from infrastructure to public safety.

URL: www.nlc.org

OpenSecrets

About: OpenSecrets.org is the most comprehensive resource for federal campaign contributions, lobbying data, and analysis available anywhere. It's a project of the Center for Responsive Politics, the nation's premier research group tracking money in US politics and its effect on elections and public policy.

Tools/resources: Who's contributing to your members of Congress? Look up your congressional representatives to see top industries and donors contributing to their campaigns to understand which groups may be influencing your representatives.

URL: www.opensecrets.org

POPVOX

About: POPVOX is a neutral, nonpartisan platform for civic engagement and governing, providing technology that informs and empowers people and makes government work better for everyone.

Tools/resources: Look up federal legislation (including links to the full text, as well as sponsors, of each bill) and write messages to your lawmakers. You can also follow organizations, and see letters they've written recently to Congress.

URL: www.popvox.com

RepresentWomen

About: RepresentWomen's mission is to strengthen our democracy by advancing reforms that break down barriers to ensure more women can run, win, serve, and lead.

Tools/resources: Check out their research, including the Gender Parity Index, which ranks US states when it comes to political gender parity, as well as proposed solutions to getting more women running, winning, and leading (e.g., ranked-choice voting).
URL: www.representwomen.org

Running Start

About: Running Start is committed to training a diverse group of young women to run for political office on a nonpartisan basis, offering training programs focused on educating young women about leadership, campaign strategy, and teamwork, without a partisan lens.
Tools/resources: Running Start offers training programs for high school and college women, including a congressional fellowship for college women, where fellows intern for women in Congress for a semester.
URL: www.runningstart.org

She Should Run

About: She Should Run is a nonpartisan nonprofit working to dramatically increase the number of women considering a run for public office.
Tools/resources: She Should Run provides training opportunities for women considering a run for office, including the Incubator, an online platform with a nonpartisan curriculum. Or you can use the Ask a Woman to Run tool—where you can ask a woman in your life to run for office!
URL: www.sheshouldrun.org

StateScape

About: StateScape was the first company to offer comprehensive state legislative and regulatory information online and is now a leader in county and municipal proposal monitoring.
Tools/resources: Use this site to learn more about your state legislative process, from which party controls your state legislature to state legislature session schedules to links to your state's official government websites. Also includes overviews of the local ordinance

process. In addition, there are paid features to track state-level legislatures.

URL: www.statescape.com

The 19th

About: The 19th is a nonprofit, nonpartisan newsroom reporting at the intersection of gender, politics, and policy. They aim to empower women—particularly those underserved by and underrepresented in American media—with the information, community, and tools women need to be equal participants in our democracy.

Tools/resources: Sign up for their daily newsletter for a briefing on gender, politics, and policy news. You can also pitch stories to their team or sign up for events featuring women leaders from across the country and on both sides of the aisle.

URL: www.19thnews.org

The Campaign School at Yale

About: The Campaign School at Yale University is a nonpartisan, issue-neutral leadership program, whose mission is to increase the number and influence of women in elected and appointed office in the United States and around the globe.

Tools/resources: The Campaign School at Yale offers in-person training, including a weeklong session at Yale University, for women who are interested in running for office or running a political campaign.

URL: www.tcsyale.org

The OpEd Project

About: The OpEd Project was founded to change who writes history. Working with universities, think tanks, foundations, nonprofits, corporations, and community organizations across the nation, the OpEd Project scouts and trains underrepresented experts (especially women) to take thought leadership positions in their fields (through op-eds and much more).

Tools/resources: The OpEd Project offers free resources and tips for how to write op-eds, including submission contact information at newspapers across the country. They also offer in-person and virtual workshops for individuals and companies (they are paid, but scholarship opportunities are available).
URL: www.theopedproject.org

TurboVote

About: TurboVote is an online tool that makes voting easy, helping every American vote in every election—local, state, and national.
Tools/resources: TurboVote keeps track of elections happening in your district and sends notifications about registration deadlines, what's on the ballot, voting locations, and more.
URL: www.turbovote.org

US House of Representatives

About: This is the official website for the US House of Representatives.
Tools/resources: In addition to information about members, committees, and legislative activity, you can also learn more about the legislative process and the history of the House. You can even watch live House sessions (when they're in session) and also look up your own representative.
URL: www.house.gov

US Senate

About: This is the official website for the US Senate.
Tools/resources: Similar to the official US House of Representatives site, you can use this to check out information on your senators, learn more about committees they serve on, find out about the history of the Senate, watch the Senate live webcast when they're in session, or check out the Senate calendar.
URL: www.senate.gov

Vote Run Lead

About: Vote Run Lead trains women to run for political office and win.

Tools/resources: Access the Vote Run Lead resource library—filled with online trainings on topics from building your campaign team to how to write a stump speech to how to reach voters through Instagram.

URL: www.voterunlead.org

Vote Smart

About: Vote Smart's mission is to provide free, factual, unbiased information on candidates and elected officials to all Americans.

Tools/resources: In addition to voting records and issue positions, you can look up which organizations have endorsed your elected officials on a range of issues, as well as their speeches (and official positions) on various topics, their top campaign contributors, and more.

URL: www.votesmart.org

When We All Vote

About: When We All Vote is a nonprofit, nonpartisan organization that is on a mission to increase participation in every election and close the race and age voting gap by changing the culture around voting, harnessing grassroots energy, and through strategic partnerships to reach every American.

Tools/resources: Take action to make sure you're prepared to vote—whether registering to vote, finding out the next election in your community, or getting state-specific information on voting. You also can sign up to lead a Voting Squad, which is a volunteer team that works to help register others in your community.

URL: www.whenweallvote.org

ACKNOWLEDGMENTS

This book would not have been possible if I did not first believe in my own voice, and for that, I am deeply indebted to my parents. Thank you, Mom and Dad, for your unwavering support and confidence, and for the incredible example you set for your girls. And to my sisters, Jillian and Meredith, without whom I am truly not sure who I would be: you inspire me every day with your brilliance, ambition, and grit. I love you all very much.

This book also would not have been possible without the encouragement and vision of my dear friend and agent, Kiele Raymond. You believed in this project long before I did; thank you (and the entire Thompson Literary Agency team!) for helping me believe it, too. And for helping that vision come to life, thank you to the entire BenBella team, in particular, my editor, Leah Wilson. I'm certain that working with a first-time author is no easy feat, but you made the entire process feel like a true partnership.

I also want to thank my AIT cofounders, Lauren Leader and Edda Collins Coleman. It is because of you that I've had the privilege of doing this work, and I am beyond grateful to you both for your vision, passion, and friendship. Thank you as well to the entire AITeam (past and present!): Priya Elangovan, Guadalupe Gonzalez, Colleen Gorman, Simone Leiro, Maylin Meisenheimer, and Clare Platt. Building something from the ground up takes persistence and passion—something all of you have in spades.

To my friends: I love you all so much, and I really would not have had the guts to do this without your support. I'm beyond lucky to have so many strong, brilliant women (and men!) in my life. A huge thank-you in particular to my friends who graciously read and provided feedback when this book was still a 300-plus-page Word document: Genevieve Joy and

Ameneh Bordi. Your smart, thoughtful insights got me unstuck more times than I can count (true of this book, and also in life!).

To my husband, Charlie: I'm not sure I have the words to express how thankful I am for you (and not just because you were an English major in college, although I'm thankful for that, too). Thank you for believing in me so deeply, and for keeping me sane throughout the process of writing this book. All those fresh notebooks, inky pens, replacement toners, magically refilled cups of coffee, hours of citation editing, comforting back rubs, and listening to me endlessly rant about campaign-finance reform have not gone unnoticed. I love you and am so very grateful for your partnership in all things, including pet parenthood to our dog, Banana (a constant source of ridiculous, fluffy joy).

Last (but certainly not least): Thank you to the women who inspired me to start writing, and then to keep writing—the women running for office, serving in office, and advocating and engaging every day to make their communities better. There are women leading change everywhere, and I am beyond grateful so many of them agreed to share their wisdom for this book and in these pages: State Senator Alessandra Biaggi, Rachna Choudhry, County Commissioner Angela Conley, Katie Fahey, Lieutenant Governor Peggy Flanagan, Bianca Jackson, Katie Kottenbrock, Sherry Leiwant, Eve Reyes-Aguirre, Rina Shah, Cynthia Terrell, State Representative Safiya Wazir, Tonya Williams, and Libby Wuller. Thank you for fighting for all of us. Our world is better for it.

NOTES

Introduction

1   Laura Bassett, "People Are Starting to Prioritize Politics Over Sex in Online Dating," *Huff-Post*, January 23, 2019, https://www.huffpost.com/entry/millennials-are-starting-to-prioritize-politics-over-sex-in-online-dating_n_5c48e26fe4b083c46d651034.

2   Pew Research Center, "Partisanship and Political Animosity in 2016," June 22, 2016, https://www.people-press.org/2016/06/22/partisanship-and-political-animosity-in-2016/.

Chapter 1

1   World Economic Forum, *The Global Gender Gap Report 2018*, December 18, 2018, http://reports.weforum.org/global-gender-gap-report-2018/results-and-analysis/.

2   Mary Beard, *Women & Power: A Manifesto* (New York: Liveright, 2017), 86.

3   Center for American Women and Politics, Eagleton Institute of Politics, Rutgers University, "Gender Differences in Voter Turnout," September 16, 2019, http://www.cawp.rutgers.edu/sites/default/files/resources/genderdiff.pdf?nl=morning-briefing&em_pos=large&emc=edit_nn_20160818.

4   Heather L. Ondercin and Daniel Jones-White, "Gender Jeopardy: What Is the Impact of Gender Differences in Political Knowledge on Political Participation?," *Social Science Quarterly* 92, no. 3 (2011): https://10.1111/j.1540-6237.2011.00787.x.

5   Harvard Kennedy School Institute of Politics, "Spring 2020 Harvard IOP Youth Poll," March 23, 2020, https://docs.google.com/spreadsheets/d/1jmexhlMEnxYKegYws4zgnjHKHghdwfIzR9hVwppHXJQ/edit#gid=1735255588.

6   Gender on the Ballot, "Stepping Up and Standing Out: Women's Political Participation in 2020," January 2020, https://www.genderontheballot.org/women-voters-research/.

7   C. Karpowitz and T. Mendelberg, *The Silent Sex: Gender, Deliberation, and Institutions* (Princeton, NJ: Princeton University Press, 2014), 38.

8   Organisation for Economic Co-Operation and Development, *OECD.Stat*, "Employment: Length of Maternity Leave, Parental Leave, and Paid Father-Specific Leave," https://stats.oecd.org/index.aspx?queryid=54760.

9   Elizabeth Warren, "What Is a Women's Issue? Bankruptcy, Commercial Law, and Other Gender-Neutral Topics," *Harvard Women's Law Journal* 25 (Spring 2002): https://papers.ssrn.com/sol3/papers.cfm?abstract_id=310544.

10 Jennifer Cheeseman Day and Cheridan Christnacht, "Women Hold 76% of All Health Care

Jobs, Gaining in Higher-Paying Occupations," United States Census Bureau Report, August 14, 2019, https://www.census.gov/library/stories/2019/08/your-health-care-in-womens-hands .html; National Partnership for Women & Families, "The Female Face of Family Caregiving," Fact Sheet, November 2018, https://www.nationalpartnership.org/our-work/resources/economic-justice/female-face-family-caregiving.pdf.

11   Shannan Catalano, "Intimate Partner Violence: Attributes of Victimization, 1993–2011," US Department of Justice, Bureau of Justice Statistics Special Report, November 2013, https://www.bjs.gov/content/pub/pdf/ipvav9311.pdf.

12   Ruth Bordin, *Woman and Temperance: The Quest for Power and Liberty, 1873–1900* (Philadelphia: Temple University Press, 1981).

13   Allen F. Davis, *American Heroine: The Life and Legend of Jane Addams* (Chicago: Ivan R. Dee, 2000).

14   Chimamanda Ngozi Adichie, *Dear Ijeawele, or A Feminist Manifesto in Fifteen Suggestions* (New York: Knopf, 2017), 59.

15   C. Karpowitz and T. Mendelberg, *The Silent Sex*, 22.

16   C. Zukin, S. Keeter, M. Andolina, et al., "The Civic and Political Health of the Nation" (2002), https://doi.org/10.3886/ICPSR37047.v2.

17   Krista Jenkins, "Gender and Civic Engagement: Secondary Analysis of Survey Data," CIRCLE Working Paper 41, June 2005, https://circle.tufts.edu/sites/default/files/2019-12/WP41_GenderandCivicEngagement_2005.pdf.

18   All In Together, "Many Democrats Remain Undecided but Liberal, Younger, and Non-White Voters Are Driving Action," February 24, 2020, https://aitogether.org/poll-feb-2020/.

19   Harvard Kennedy School Institute of Politics, "Spring 2019 Harvard IOP Youth Poll," April 22, 2019, https://docs.google.com/spreadsheets/d/1v76HyyKfhaamPmOeviBHCWKRmBQ3i RjI1tnLTpUXHzw/edit#gid=1571261527.

20   Marta Fraile and Irene Sánchez-Vítores, "Tracing the Gender Gap in Political Interest Over the Life Span: A Panel Analysis," *Political Psychology* 41, no. 1 (May 29, 2019): https://doi .org/10.1111/pops.12600.

21   Congressional Research Service, *Women in Congress: Statistics and Brief Overview*, January 15, 2020, https://fas.org/sgp/crs/misc/R43244.pdf.

22   Katherine Baldiga, "Gender Differences in Willingness to Guess," *Management Science* 60, no. 2 (2014): 434–48.

23   L. Bian, S.-J. Leslie, and A. Cimpian, "Gender Stereotypes About Intellectual Ability Emerge Early and Influence Children's Interests," *Science* 355, no. 6323 (January 27, 2017): 389–91.

24   Jenkins, "Gender and Civic Engagement," 10.

25   Jones, Robert P., Daniel Cox, Molly Fisch-Friedmanm, and Alex Vandermaas-Peeler, "Diversity, Division, Discrimination: The State of Young America," PRRI/MTV, 2018."

26   Vandermaas-Peeler, et al., "Diversity, Division, Discrimination."

27   Brittany Packnett, "How to Build Your Confidence and Spark It in Others," filmed April 2019 in Vancouver, Canada, TED video, 13:07, https://www.ted.com/talks/brittany_packnett_how_to_build_your_confidence_and_spark_it_in_others/transcript?language=en#t-109721.

28   David E. Campbell and Christina Wolbrecht, "See Jane Run: Women Politicians as Role Models for Adolescents," *Journal of Politics* 68, no. 2, 233–47, at 234.

29   Harvard Kennedy School IOP, "Spring 2019 Harvard IOP Youth Poll."

30   Deborah Howell, "An Op-Ed Need for Diverse Voices," *Washington Post*, May 25, 2008, https://www.washingtonpost.com/wp-dyn/content/article/2008/05/23/AR2008052302308.html.

31   Frank Bryan, *Real Democracy* (Chicago: University of Chicago Press, 2004).

32   Kristina Miler, interviewed by Peter Slen, "Constituency Representation in Congress," *Book TV's*

College Series, C-SPAN, 12:05, December 2, 2011, https://www.c-span.org/video/?303077-1/constituency-respresentation-congress.

33   Audre Lorde, "Learning from the 60s," in *Sister Outsider: Essays and Speeches by Audre Lorde* (Berkeley, CA: Crossing Press, 2007), 138.

34   AAPI Civic Engagement Fund and Groundswell Fund, "Ahead of the Majority: Foregrounding Women of Color," August 20, 2019, https://aapifund.org/wp-content/uploads/2019/08/8.20_Final_WOC_web.pdf.

35   Abby Vesoulis, "The 2018 Elections Saw Record Midterm Turnout," *Time*, November 12, 2018, https://time.com/5452258/midterm-elections-turnout/.

36   Adichie, *Dear Ijeawele*.

Chapter 2

1   Emeralde Jensen-Roberts, "How Many People Know Their Senators?," *Boston Globe* , March 29, 2015, https://www.bostonglobe.com/magazine/2015/03/28/how-many-people-know-their-senators/yfgXyHR96X7YGhesaNQbnM/story.html.

2   Pew Research Center, "Public Trust in Government: 1958–2019," April 11, 2019, https://www.people-press.org/2019/04/11/public-trust-in-government-1958-2019/.

3   Congressional Management Foundation and the Society for Human Resource Management, *Life in Congress: The Member Perspective*, joint research report, March 2013, http://www.congressfoundation.org/projects/life-in-congress/the-member-perspective.

4   CMF and SHRM, *Life in Congress*.

5   CMF and SHRM, *Life in Congress*.

6   Tonya Williams, interview with the author, October 18, 2019.

7   Williams, interview.

8   Cynthia Terrell, interview with the author, September 3, 2019.

9   Rose Minutaglio, "How Rep. Katie Porter Got the CDC to Promise Free Coronavirus Testing for All," *ELLE*, March 13, 2020, https://www.elle.com/culture/career-politics/a31468179/katie-porter-coronavirus-testing-interview/.

10   GovTrack, "Statistics and Historical Comparison," accessed September 2, 2020, https://www.govtrack.us/congress/bills/statistics.

11   Nicholas Fandos, "With Move to Remote Voting, House Alters What It Means for Congress to Meet," *New York Times*, May 15, 2020, https://www.nytimes.com/2020/05/15/us/politics/remote-voting-house-coronavirus.html.

12   U.S. Senate, "Filibuster and Cloture," accessed July 29, 2020, https://www.senate.gov/artandhistory/history/common/briefing/Filibuster_Cloture.htm.

13   U.S. Senate, "Filibuster and Cloture."

14   Wendy J. Schiller, "Filibuster and the Mission of the U.S. Senate," Brown University, December 13, 2012, https://news.brown.edu/articles/2012/12/filibuster.

15   GovTrack, "Statistics and Historical Comparison."

16   The Brookings Institution, "Chapter 6: Legislative Productivity in Congress and Workload," *Vital Statistics on Congress*, March 4, 2019, https://www.brookings.edu/wp-content/uploads/2019/03/Chpt-6.pdf.

Chapter 3

1   Clara Hendrickson, "Local Journalism in Crisis," Brookings Institution, November 12, 2019, https://www.brookings.edu/wp-content/uploads/2019/11/Local-Journalism-in-Crisis.pdf.

2   Katerina Eva Matsa and Jan Lauren Boyles, "America's Shifting Statehouse Press," Pew Research

Center, July 10, 2014, https://www.journalism.org/2014/07/10/americas-shifting-statehouse -press/.

3   Dana Goldstein, "Two States. Eight Textbooks. Two American Stories.," *New York Times*, January 12, 2020, https://www.nytimes.com/interactive/2020/01/12/us/texas-vs-california -history-textbooks.html.

4   Goldstein, "Two States. Eight Textbooks. Two American Stories."

5   Goldstein, "Two States. Eight Textbooks. Two American Stories."

6   Daniel Moritz-Rabson, "Nevada Gives 77,000 Ex-felons Right to Vote in 2020," *Newsweek*, May 30, 2019, https://www.newsweek.com/nevada-gives-77000-ex-felons-right-vote-2020 -1439774.

7   Daisuke Wakabayashi, "California Passes Sweeping Law to Protect Online Privacy," *New York Times*, June 28, 2018, https://www.nytimes.com/2018/06/28/technology/california-online -privacy-law.html.

8   Jonathan Wolfe, "New York Today: With New Family Leave Law, Savoring the Early Days," *New York Times*, January 10, 2018, https://www.nytimes.com/2018/01/10/nyregion/new-york -today-family-leave.html.

9   Leah Willingham, "N.H. Passes Law Requiring Public Schools to Provide Free Pads, Tampons in Bathrooms," *Concord Monitor*, July 17, 2019, https://www.concordmonitor.com/ Bill-requiring-schools-to-provide-feminine-hygiene-products-in-bathrooms-moves -to-governor-s-desk-27014726.

10 New State Ice Co. v. Liebmann, 285 U.S. 262 (1932).

11 Alessandra Biaggi, interview with the author, September 18, 2019.

12 Biaggi, interview.

13 Sherry Leiwant, interview with the author, October 11, 2019.

14 Leiwant, interview.

15 National Conference of State Legislatures, "State Redistricting Deadlines," accessed May 6, 2020, https://www.ncsl.org/research/redistricting/state-redistricting-deadlines637224581.aspx.

16 David J. Andersen and John Weingart, "Governors Who Became President," Rutgers University, Eagleton Institute of Politics, Center on the American Governor, accessed July 29, 2020, https:// live-ru-eip-governors.pantheonsite.io/governors-and-the-white-house/.

17 National Conference of State Legislatures, "Number of Legislators and Length of Terms in Years," accessed May 6, 2020, https://www.ncsl.org/research/about-state-legislatures/number -of-legislators-and-length-of-terms.aspx; National Conference of State Legislatures, "Legislatures at a Glance," accessed May 6, 2020, https://www.ncsl.org/research/about-state-legislatures/ legislatures-at-a-glance.aspx.

18 Center for American Women and Politics, "Women of Color in Elective Office 2019," accessed May 6, 2019, https://cawp.rutgers.edu/women-color-elective -office-2019.

19 Catalyst, "Women of Color in the United State," https://www.catalyst.org/research/women-of -color-in-the-united-states/.

20 NCSL, "Number of Legislators and Length of Terms in Years"; Ballotpedia, "Comparison of state legislative salaries," accessed May 6, 2020, https://ballotpedia.org/Comparison_of_state_ legislative_salaries; Ballotpedia, "Dates of 2019 state legislative sessions," accessed May 6, 2020, https://ballotpedia.org/Dates_of_2019_state_legislative_sessions.

21 Biaggi, interview.

22 Permanent and session staff; last census taken in 2015 (National Conference of State Legislatures, "Size of State Legislative Staff," https://ncsl.org/research/about-state-legislatures/staff -change-chart-1979-1988-1996-2003-2009.aspx).

23 National Conference of State Legislatures, "2020 Legislative Session Calendar," accessed May 7, 2020, https://www.ncsl.org/Portals/1/Documents/NCSL/2020_session_calendar1.pdf.

24 Safiya Wazir, written interview with the author, September 22, 2019.

25 Wazir, interview.

26 Biaggi, interview.

27 Biaggi, interview.

28 New Hampshire State, Legislature, Senate, *Senate Calendar, First Year of the 166th Session of the New Hampshire General Court*, No. 35, September 12, 2019, http://gencourt.state.nh.us/Senate/calendars_journals/calendars/2019/sc%2034.pdf.

29 New Hampshire State, Legislature, "A Primer on Legislative Process," http://www.gencourt.state.nh.us/misc/legprocess.html.

Chapter 4

1 Urban Institute, "State and Local Expenditures," accessed May 6, 2020, https://www.urban.org/policy-centers/cross-center-initiatives/state-and-local-finance-initiative/state-and-local-backgrounders/state-and-local-expenditures.

2 Ryan Nunn, Jana Parsons, and Jay Shambaugh, *Nine Facts About State and Local Policy*, Hamilton Project, January 2019, https://www.brookings.edu/wp-content/uploads/2019/01/StateandLocal_Facts_Web_20190128.pdf.

3 Angela Conley, interview with the author, September 30, 2019.

4 Conley, interview.

5 National League of Cities, "Local US Governments," accessed May 6, 2020, https://www.nlc.org/local-us-governments.

6 NLC, "Local US Governments."

7 National League of Cities, "Forms of Municipal Government," https://www.NLC.org/forms-of-municipal-government.

8 Suburban Stats, "Population Demographics for Marblehead, Massachusetts in 2020, 2019," accessed May 6, 2020, https://suburbanstats.org/population/massachusetts/how-many-people-live-in-marblehead.

9 New York City Mayor's Office, "Paid Safe Leave: New York City Expands Paid Leave to Domestic Violence, Sexual Assault, Stalking and Trafficking Survivors," press release, November 6, 2017, https://www1.nyc.gov/office-of-the-mayor/news/716-17/paid-safe-leave-new-york-city-expands-paid-leave-domestic-violence-sexual-assault-stalking.

10 New York City Council, "Biography of Julissa Ferreras-Copeland," accessed May 6, 2020, https://council.nyc.gov/julissa-ferreras-copeland/.

11 National Association of Towns and Townships, "Town and Township Government in the United States," https://www.toi.org/Resources/87748A89-B591-4209-AB28-4F81CA6DA1C9/NATAT%20About%20Towns%20and%20Townships.pdf.

12 NLC, "Local US Governments."

13 NLC, "Local US Governments."

14 America Counts Staff, *From Municipalities to Special Districts, Official Count of Every Type of Local Government in 2017 Census of Governments*, US Census Bureau, October 29, 2019, https://www.census.gov/content/dam/Census/library/visualizations/2019/econ/from_municipalities_to_special_districts_america_counts_october_2019.pdf.

15 America Counts Staff, *From Municipalities to Special Districts*.

16 Town of Stratham, New Hampshire, "Town Government," accessed May 6, 2020, https://www.strathamnh.gov/select-board/pages/town-government.

Chapter 5

1   U.S. Department of Education, Office for Civil Rights, "Title IX and Sex Discrimination," https://www2.ed.gov/about/offices/list/ocr/docs/tix_dis.html.

2   Princeton University, Office of Institutional Research, "All Enrolled Undergraduate and Graduate Degree Seeking Students by Academic Year and Gender," accessed May 6, 2020, https://ir.princeton.edu/sites/ir/files/resource-links/degree_seeking_students_by_academic_year_and_gender_2019.xlsx.

3   National Women's Law Center, "Title IX, The Battle for Gender Equity in Athletics in Colleges and Universities," fact sheet, June 2017, https://nwlc-ciw49tixgw5lbab.stackpathdns.com/wp-content/uploads/2015/08/Battle-for-GE-in-Colleges-and-Universities.pdf.

4   National Collegiate Athletic Association, *Gender-Equity Report, 2004–2010*, January 2012, http://www.ncaapublications.com/productdownloads/GEQS10.pdf.

5   EY, *Why Female Athletes Make Winning Entrepreneurs*, 2017, https://assets.ey.com/content/dam/ey-sites/ey-com/en_gl/topics/entrepreneurship/ey-why-female-athletes-make-winning-entrepreneurs.pdf.

6   National Federation of State High School Associations, *High School Athletics Participation History (1969–2008)*, accessed September 3, 2020, https://www.nfhs.org/media/1020206/hs_participation_survey_history_1969-2009.pdf.

7   National Federation of State High School Associations, "2018–19 High School Athletics Participation Survey," accessed September 3, 2020, https://www.nfhs.org/media/1020412/2018-19_participation_survey.pdf.

8   Moira Donegan, "USA's Formidable Women's Soccer Team Is No Accident. It's a Product of Public Policy," *The Guardian*, July 6, 201, https://www.theguardian.com/commentisfree/2019/jul/06/usa-womens-world-cup-netherlands-title-xi.

9   US Congress, House of Representatives, Committee on Education and Labor, *Sex Discrimination Regulations: Hearings Before the Subcommittee on Postsecondary Education of the Committee on Education and Labor*, 94th Cong., 1st sess., 1975.

10   Tom Goldman and Bill Chappell, "How Bernice Sandler, 'Godmother of Title IX,' Achieved Landmark Discrimination Ban," NPR, January 10, 2019, https://www.npr.org/2019/01/10/683571958/how-bernice-sandler-godmother-of-title-ix-achieved-landmark-discrimination-ban.

11   Goldman and Chappell, "How Bernice Sandler."

12   Princeton University, *Report of the Steering Committee on Undergraduate Women's Leadership*, March 2011, http://wayback.archive-it.org/5151/20171216175914/https://www.princeton.edu/reports/2011/leadership/documents/SCUWL_Report_Final.pdf.

13   Princeton University, *Report of the Steering Committee on Undergraduate Women's Leadership*.

14   Jennifer L. Lawless and Richard L. Fox, *Girls Just Wanna Not Run: The Gender Gap in Young Americans' Political Ambition*, American University, School of Public Affairs, March 2013, https://www.american.edu/spa/wpi/upload/girls-just-wanna-not-run_policy-report.pdf.

15   D. Cantor, B. Fisher, S. Chibnall, et. al., *Report on the AAU Campus Climate Survey on Sexual Assault and Sexual Misconduct*, Association of American Universities report, September 21, 2015.

16   Princeton Students for Title IX Reform, "A Call to End Sexual and Interpersonal Violence at Princeton," accessed July 29, 2020, https://princetonixnow.com/reforms.

17   Alexandria Ocasio-Cortez, Instagram story, September 9, 2019.

18   Robert D. Putnam, *Bowling Alone* (New York: Simon & Schuster, 2000).

19   New York City Council, "Council Members and Districts," accessed May 6, 2020, https://council
      .nyc.gov/districts/.
20   Ameneh Bordi, interview with the author, June 1, 2017.
21   Bordi, interview.
22   Bordi, interview.
23   Alessandra Biaggi, interview with the author, September 18, 2019.

Chapter 6

1   National Conference of State Legislatures, "Online Voter Registration," February 3, 2020, https://
      www.ncsl.org/research/elections-and-campaigns/electronic-or-online-voter-registration.aspx.
2   NCSL, "Online Voter Registration."
3   National Conference of State Legislatures, "Initiative, Referendum and Recall," September 20,
      2012, https://www.ncsl.org/research/elections-and-campaigns/initiative-referendum-and-recall
      -overview.aspx.
4   National Conference of State Legislatures, "Recall of State Officials," July 8, 2019, https://www
      .ncsl.org/research/elections-and-campaigns/recall-of-state-officials.aspx.
5   League of Women Voters of Washington, *Washington Ballot Summary: Initiative Measure No.
      976*, September 24, 2019, https://lwvwa.org/resources/Documents/BallotMeasures/2019/
      LWVWA%202019%20I-976%20Washington%20Ballot%20Summary.pdf.
6   New York City Council, "Participatory Budgeting," accessed May 6, 2020, https://council.nyc
      .gov/pb/.
7   National Conference of State Legislatures, "Voter Identification Requirements | Voter ID Laws,"
      February 24, 2020, https://www.ncsl.org/research/elections-and-campaigns/voter-id.aspx.
8   T. Rogers, D. Green, J. Ternovski, et al., "Social Pressure and Voting: A Field Experiment Con-
      ducted in a High-Salience Election," *Electoral Studies* 46 (2017): 87–100.
9   Jill Lepore, "Rock, Paper, Scissors," *New Yorker*, October 6, 2008, https://www.newyorker.com/
      magazine/2008/10/13/rock-paper-scissors.
10   Lepore, "Rock, Paper, Scissors."
11   Sofia Gross and Ashley Spillane, *Civic Responsibility: The Power of Companies to Increase Voter
      Turnout*, Harvard Kennedy School, Ash Center for Democratic Governance and Innovation,
      June 2019, https://ash.harvard.edu/files/ash/files/harvard-casestudy-report-digital_copy.pdf.
12   Gross and Spillane, *Civic Responsibility*.

Chapter 7

1   All In Together, *Community Organizing 101*, webinar, July 30, 2019, https://www.youtube.com/
      watch?v=qUh7IeYnNTk.
2   AIT, *Community Organizing 101*.
3   AIT, *Community Organizing 101*.
4   Congressional Management Foundation, *Communicating with Congress: Perceptions of Citizen
      Advocacy on Capitol Hill*, 2011, http://www.congressfoundation.org/storage/documents/CMF_
      Pubs/cwc-perceptions-of-citizen-advocacy.pdf.
5   The OpenGov Foundation, *From Voicemails to Votes*, "Section 3: Beliefs," January 29, 2017,
      https://v2v.opengovfoundation.org/beliefs-b214dce6f504.
6   CMF, *Communicating with Congress*.
7   Vanessa K. Bohns, "A Face-to-Face Request Is 34 Times More Successful Than an Email,"

Harvard Business Review, April 11, 2017, https://hbr.org/2017/04/a-face-to-face-request-is-34-times-more-successful-than-an-email.

8   Karenna Gore Schiff, *Lighting the Way: Nine Women Who Changed Modern America* (New York: Miramax Books, 2005), 144–45.

9   German Lopez, "A Former Congressional Staffer Explains How to Best Stand Up to Trump Through Congress," Vox, November 15, 2016, https://www.vox.com/policy-and-politics/2016/11/15/13641920/trump-resist-congress.

10   All In Together, *Showing Up as an Effective Advocate*, webinar, September 24, 2018, https://www.youtube.com/watch?v=nzy1TMVx00U.

11   All In Together, *Advocating for Survivors*, webinar, https://www.youtube.com/watch?v=WTNqHb2CZY0.

12   Libby Wuller, interview with the author, September 5, 2019.

13   The OpenGov Foundation, "3.3 Staff Perspectives on the Best Ways to Get Heard," *From Voicemails to Votes*, January 29, 2017, https://v2v.opengovfoundation.org/staff-perspectives-on-the-best-ways-to-get-heard-5d30c85eb9f5.

14   Peggy Flanagan, interview with the author, November 25, 2019.

15   AIT, *Showing Up as an Effective Advocate*.

16   Libby Wuller, interview with the author, September 5, 2019.

17   Wuller, interview.

18   Sherry Leiwant, interview with the author, October 11, 2019.

19   Rachna Choudhry, interview with the author, March 25, 2020.

20   AIT, *Advocating for Survivors*.

21   Kimberly Probolus, "A Women's Plea: Let's Raise Our Voices!," letter to the editor, *New York Times*, January 31, 2019, https://www.nytimes.com/2019/01/31/opinion/letters/letters-to-editor-new-york-times-women.html.

22   Editor, "Women, Please Speak Out," *New York Times*, February 13, 2020, https://www.nytimes.com/2020/02/14/opinion/letters/letters-editor-nytimes-gender.html.

23   Foreign Policy Interrupted, "How Many Women Are on the Op-Ed Page?," August 2, 2018, https://www.fpinterrupted.com/2018/08/02/how-many-women-are-on-the-op-ed-page/.

24   Jessica Durando, "March for Our Lives Could Be the Biggest Single-Day Protest in D.C.'s History," *USA Today*, March 24, 2018, https://www.usatoday.com/story/news/nation/2018/03/24/march-our-lives-could-become-biggest-single-day-protest-d-c-nations-history/455675002/.

25   Alix Langone, "These Photos Show How Big the March for Our Lives Crowds Were Across the Country," *Time*, March 25, 2018, https://time.com/5214706/march-for-our-lives-us-photos/.

26   March for Our Lives, "Our Leadership," accessed May 6, 2020, https://marchforourlives.com/leadership/.

27   Larry Buchanan, Quoctrung Bui, and Jugal K. Patel, "Black Lives Matter May Be the Largest Movement in U.S. History," *New York Times*, July 3, 2020, https://www.nytimes.com/interactive/2020/07/03/us/george-floyd-protests-crowd-size.html.

28   Laura Barrón-López, "Why the Black Lives Matter Movement Doesn't Want a Singular Leader," Politico, July 22, 2020, https://www.politico.com/news/2020/07/22/black-lives-matter-movement-leader-377369.

Chapter 8

1   Soo Rin Kim, "The Price of Winning Just Got Higher, Especially in the Senate," OpenSecrets, November 9, 2016, https://www.opensecrets.org/news/2016/11/the-price-of-winning-just-got-higher-especially-in-the-senate/.

2   New York City Campaign Finance Board, *Helen K Rosenthal Candidate Summary*, accessed May 6, 2020, https://www.nyccfb.info/VSApps/CandidateSummary.aspx?as_cand_id=1233&as_election _cycle=2013&cand_name=Rosenthal,%20Helen%20K&office=CD%2006&report=summ.

3   Libby Wuller, interview with the author, September 5, 2019.

4   Wuller, interview.

5   Center for Responsive Politics, Common Cause, and Representation2020, *Individual and PAC Giving to Women Candidates*, joint report, November 2016, https://www.commoncause.org/ wp-content/uploads/2018/03/individual-and-pac-giving-to.pdf.

6   RepresentWomen, "PACs & Donors: Agents of Change for Women's Representation," June 2020, https://www.representwomen.org/research_pacs_donors.

7   OpenSecrets, "Donor Demographics," accessed May 6, 2020, https://www.opensecrets.org /overview/donordemographics.php?cycle=2016&filter=G.

8   Elahe Izadi, "Why Women Thrive in Political Fundraising," *The Atlantic*, November 12, 2013, https://www.theatlantic.com/politics/archive/2013/11/why-women-thrive-political-fundraising /355129/.

9   National Partnership for Women & Families, "What's the Wage Gap in the States?," accessed May 6, 2020, https://www.nationalpartnership.org/our work/economic-justice/wage-gap/.

10   National Partnership for Women & Families, *Black Women and the Wage Gap*, fact sheet, March 2020, https://www.nationalpartnership.org/our-work/resources/economic-justice/ fair-pay/african-american-women-wage-gap.pdf.

11   National Partnership for Women & Families, and Unidos US, *Beyond Wages: Effects of the Latina Wage Gap*, joint report, November 2019, https://www.nationalpartnership.org/our-work/ resources/economic-justice/fair-pay/latinas-wage-gap.pdf.

12   National Partnership, "What's the Wage Gap in the States?"

13   National Conference of State Legislatures, "Campaign Contribution Limits: Overview," October 4, 2019, https://www.ncsl.org/research/elections-and-campaigns/campaign-contribution-limits -overview.aspx.

14   National Conference of State Legislatures, "Campaign Contribution Limits: Overview," October 4, 2019, https://www.ncsl.org/research/elections-and-campaigns/campaign-contribution-lim- its-overview.aspx.

15   OpenSecrets, "2020 Campaign Contribution Limits," accessed May 6, 2020, https://www.open secrets.org/overview/limits.php.

16   Wuller, interview.

17   Peggy Flanagan, interview with the author, November 25, 2019.

18   Angela Conley, interview with the author, September 30, 2019.

19   Anna North, "The Women Aiming to Unseat Rep. Peter King Had to Win a Fight Over Child Care First," Vox, November 3, 2018, https://www.vox.com/midterm-elections/2018/11/3/ 18051980/midterm-election-2018-liuba-grechen-shirley-peter-king.

20   Madison Feller, "Nabilah Islam Gave Up Her Health Insurance to Run For Congress. Now What?," *Elle*, May 18, 2020, https://www.elle.com/culture/career-politics/a32499393/nabilah -islam-congress-georgia-healthcare-pandemic/.

Chapter 9

1   K. Smith, M. Hibbing, and J. Hibbing, "Friends, Relatives, Sanity, and Health: The Costs of Politics," *PLOS ONE*, September 25, 2019, https://doi.org/10.1371/journal.pone.0221870.

2   M. Cohn and B. Frederickson, "In Search of Durable Positive Psychology Interventions:

Predictors and Consequences of Long-Term Positive Behavior Change," *Journal of Positive Psychology* 5, no. 5, October 20, 2010, https://dx.doi.org/10.1080%2F17439760.2010.508883.

3   Carol Dweck, "What Having a 'Growth Mindset' Actually Means," *Harvard Business Review*, January 13, 2016, https://hbr.org/2016/01/what-having-a-growth-mindset-actually-means.

4   Catherine Rampell, "Catherine Rampell: Women Should Embrace the B's in College to Make More Later," *Washington Post*, March 10, 2014, https://www.washingtonpost.com/opinions/catherine-rampell-women-should-embrace-the-bs-in-college-to-make-more-later/2014/03/10/1e15113a-a871-11e3-8d62-419db477a0e6_story.html.

5   Soraya Chemaly, *Rage Becomes Her* (New York: Atria Books, 2018), *xx*.

Chapter 10

1   Cynthia Terrell, interview with the author, September 3, 2019.

2   Niv M. Sultan, "Election 2016: Trump's Free Media Helped Keep Cost Down, but Fewer Donors Provided More of the Cash," OpenSecrets, April 13, 2017, https://www.opensecrets.org/news/2017/04/election-2016-trump-fewer-donors-provided-more-of-the-cash/.

3   U.S. Department of Education, *Fiscal Year 2018 Budget Summary and Background Information*, May 23, 2017, https://www2.ed.gov/about/overview/budget/budget18/summary/18summary.pdf.

4   Stephen Castle, "Britain's Campaign Finance Laws Leave Parties with Idle Money," *New York Times*, May 5, 2015, https://www.nytimes.com/2015/05/05/world/europe/britains-campaign-finance-laws-leave-parties-with-idle-money.html.

5   Citizens United v. FEC, 558 U.S. 310 (2010); Buckley v. Valeo, 424 U.S. 1 (1976).

6   John Wagner and Scott Clement, "'It's Just Messed Up': Most Think Political Divisions as Bad as Vietnam Era, New Poll Shows," *Washington Post*, October 28, 2017, https://www.washingtonpost.com/politics/its-just-messed-up-most-say-political-divisions-are-as-bad-as-in-vietnam-era-poll-shows/2017/10/27/ad304f1a-b9b6-11e7-9e58-e6288544af98_story.html.

7   Bradley Jones, "Most Americans Want to Limit Campaign Spending, Say Big Donors Have Greater Political Influence," Pew Research Center, May 8, 2018, https://www.pewresearch.org/fact-tank/2018/05/08/most-americans-want-to-limit-campaign-spending-say-big-donors-have-greater-political-influence/.

8   OpenSecrets, "What Is a PAC?," accessed May 6, 2020, https://www.opensecrets.org/pacs/pacfaq.php.

9   Women Under Forty Political Action Committee, home page, accessed May 6, 2020, https://www.wufpac.org/.

10   U.S. Federal Election Commission, "Contribution limits," accessed May 6, 2020, https://www.fec.gov/help-candidates-and-committees/candidate-taking-receipts/contribution-limits/.

11   U.S. Federal Election Commission, "Contribution limits."

12   SpeechNOW.org vs. FEC, 599 F.3d 686 (DC Circ. 2010).

13   Derek Willis, "Shedding Some Light on Dark Money Political Donors," *ProPublica*, September 12, 2018, https://www.propublica.org/nerds/shedding-some-light-on-dark-money-political-donors.

14   Sultan, "Election 2016."

15   Adam Nagourney and Jeff Zeleny, "Obama Forgoes Public Funds in First for Major Candidate," *New York Times*, June 20, 2008, https://www.nytimes.com/2008/06/20/us/politics/20obamacnd.html.

16   Justin Elliot, "Obama's Flip Flops on Money in Politics: A Brief History," *ProPublica*, January 30, 2011, https://www.propublica.org/article/obamas-flip-flops-on-money-in-politics-a-brief-history; Nagourney and Zeleny, "Obama Forgoes Public Funds in First for Major Candidate."

17 Libby Watson, "Why Did Only 1 Presidential Candidate Take Public Financing?," Sunlight Foundation, January 27, 2016, https://sunlightfoundation.com/2016/01/27/why-did-only-1 -presidential-candidate-take-public-financing/

18 Sultan, "Election 2016."

19 E.g., Alison Moodie, "Before You Read Another Health Study, Check Who's Funding the Research," *The Guardian*, December 12, 2016, https://www.theguardian.com/lifeandstyle/2016/ dec/12/studies-health-nutrition-sugar-coca-cola-marion-nestle.

20 DeNora Getachew and Hazel Dukes, "Public Financing Can Elevate Diverse Voices," Brennan Center for Justice, March 20, 2014, https://www.brennancenter.org/our-work/research-reports/ public-financing-can-elevate-diverse-voices.

21 Steven M. Levin, *Keeping It Clean: Public Financing in American Elections*, Center for Governmental Studies, 2006, http://research.policyarchive.org/4523.pdf.

22 Charlie Albanetti, "Women Legislators and Groups Join Forces to Support Fair Elections," Fair Elections for New York, March 5, 2014, https://fairelectionsny.org/posts/women-legislators -groups-join-forces-support-fair-elections/5190.

23 Cynthia Terrell, interview with the author, September 3, 2019.

24 New York City Campaign Finance Board, "Limits and Thresholds," accessed May 6, 2020, https://www.nyccfb.info/candidate-services/limits-thresholds/2021/.

25 New York City Campaign Finance Board, "Impact of Public Funds," accessed May 6, 2020, https://www.nyccfb.info/program/impact-of-public-funds/.

26 Seattle City Government, "Democracy Voucher Program: Information for Seattle Residents," accessed May 6, 2020, http://www.seattle.gov/democracyvoucher/i-am-a-seattle-resident.

27 National Conference of State Legislatures, "Public Financing of Campaigns: Overview," February 8, 2019, https://www.ncsl.org/research/elections-and-campaigns/public-financing-of -campaigns-overview.aspx.

28 Campaign Finance Institute, "Public Matching Funds in NY State, Reversing the Financial Influence of Small & Large Donors, Would Leave the Candidates 'Whole' While Costing New Yorkers only $2/year," April 1, 2013, http://www.cfinst.org/Press/PReleases/13-04-01/Updated_ CFI_Research_on_Public_Matching_Funds_Proposal_for_New_York_State.aspx.

29 Bill Allison and Mark Niquette, "Bloomberg Tops Half a Billion Dollars in Campaign Advertising," *Bloomberg*, February 24, 2020, https://www.bloomberg.com/news/articles/2020-02-24/ bloomberg-tops-half-a-billion-dollars-in-campaign-advertising.

Chapter 11

1 John Adams, *Thoughts on Government* (Philadelphia: John Dunlap, 1776), 9.

2 Drew DeSilver, "U.S. Population Keeps Growing, but House of Representatives Is Same Size as in Taft Era," Pew Research Center, May 31, 2018, https://www.pewresearch.org/fact -tank/2018/05/31/u-s-population-keeps-growing-but-house-of-representatives-is-same-size -as-in-taft-era/.

3 U.S. House of Representatives, "Determining Apportionment," accessed May 6, 2020, https://history.house.gov/Institution/Apportionment/Determining-Apportionment/.

4 DeSilver, "U.S. Population Keeps Growing."

5 DeSilver, "U.S. Population Keeps Growing."

6 Kathryn Crespin, "U.S. House Districts Are Colossal. What's the Right Size?," University of Virginia Demographics Research Group, November 15, 2017, http://statchatva.org/2017/11/15/u-s -house-districts-are-colossal-whats-the-right-size/.

7 Ricardo Hausmann, Laura D. Tyson, and Saadia Zahidi, *The Global Gender Gap Report 2006*,

World Economic Forum, November 23, 2006, http://www3.weforum.org/docs/WEF_Gender-Gap_Report_2006.pdf.

8   World Economic Forum, *Global Gender Gap Report 2020*, December 16, 2019, http://www3.weforum.org/docs/WEF_GGGR_2020.pdf.

9   Center for American Women and Politics, "Women in the U.S. Congress 2019," accessed May 6, 2020, https://www.cawp.rutgers.edu/women-us-congress-2019.

10 Center for American Women and Politics, "Women of Color in Elective Office 2019," accessed May 6, 2019, https://cawp.rutgers.edu/women-color-elective-office-2019.

11 Center for American Women and Politics, "History of Women of Color in U.S. Politics," accessed July 29, 2020, https://cawp.rutgers.edu/history-women-color-us-politics.

12 R. Rocha, C. Tolbert, and D. Bowen, "Race and Turnout: Does Descriptive Representation in State Legislatures Increase Minority Voting?," *Political Research Quarterly*, August 25, 2010, https://doi.org/10.1177/1065912910376388; K. Lowande, M. Ritchie, and E. Lauterbach, "Descriptive and Substantive Representation in Congress: Evidence from 80,000 Congressional Inquiries," *American Journal of Political Science* 63, no. 3, June 17, 2019, https://doi.org/10.1111/ajps.12443.

13 Center for American Women and Politics, "Women in State Legislatures 2020," accessed May 6, 2020, https://cawp.rutgers.edu/women-state-legislature-2020.

14 Center for American Women and Politics, "Current Numbers," accessed May 6, 2020, https://cawp.rutgers.edu/current-numbers.

15 Editorial Board, "America Needs a Bigger House," *New York Times*, November 9, 2018, https://www.nytimes.com/interactive/2018/11/09/opinion/expanded-house-representatives-size.html.

16 Editorial Board, "America Needs a Bigger House," *New York Times*.

17 Kathryn Crespin, "U.S. House Districts Are Colossal."

18 Editorial Board, "America Needs a Bigger House," *New York Times*.

19 Andrew Douglas, "Ranked Choice Voting and Civility: New Evidence from American Cities," FairVote: The Center for Voting and Democracy, April 2014, https://fairvote.app.box.com/v/rcv-new-evidence-us-cities.

20 S. John, H. Smith, E. Zack, C. Terrell, et al., *The Impact of Ranked Choice Voting on Representation: How Ranked Choice Voting Affects Women and People of Color Candidates in California*, Representation2020, August 2016, https://fairvote.app.box.com/s/vtp8x7z2n2g6vff1gndqt4m5lsloo364.

21 Tina Trenkner, "Oakland, Calif. Elects First Female, Asian-American Mayor," Governing, March 2011, https://www.governing.com/topics/politics/oakland-california-elects-first-female-asian-american-mayor.html.

22 Rob Richie, "Ranked Choice Voting's Midterm Report," FairVote, July 11, 2018, https://www.fairvote.org/ranked_choice_voting_s_midterm_report.

23 Catie Edmondson, "The Gerry Behind Gerrymandering," *Boston Globe*, June 22, 2017, https://www.bostonglobe.com/metro/2017/06/22/the-gerry-behind-gerrymandering/QUbhL72qv6TuM3Kklg6REM/story.html.

24 Katie Fahey, interview with the author, September 27, 2019.

25 Adam Liptak, "Supreme Court Bars Challenge to Partisan Gerrymandering," *New York Times*, June 27, 2019, https://www.nytimes.com/2019/06/27/us/politics/supreme-court-gerrymandering.html.

26 Associated Press, "Number of States Using Redistricting Commissions Growing," March 21, 2019, https://apnews.com/4d2e2aea7e224549af61699e51c955dd.

27 Brennan Center for Justice, "Redistricting Commissions: What Works," accessed July 29, 2020, https://www.brennancenter.org/sites/default/files/analysis/Redistricting%20Commissions%20-%20What%20Works.pdf.

28   Editorial Board, "A Congress for Every American," *New York Times*, November 10, 2018, https://www.nytimes.com/interactive/2018/11/10/opinion/house-representatives-size-multi-member.html.

Chapter 12

1   Drew DeSilver, "U.S. Trails Most Developed Countries in Voter Turnout," Pew Research Center, May 21, 2018, https://www.pewresearch.org/fact-tank/2018/05/21/u-s-voter-turnout-trails-most-developed-countries/.

2   Center for American Women and Politics, Eagleton Institute of Politics, Rutgers University, September 16, 2019, https://cawp.rutgers.edu/sites/default/files/resources/genderdiff.pdf.

3   Nicholas Rathod, "Honoring Rosa Parks: Moving from Symbolism to Action," Center for American Progress, December 1, 2005, https://www.americanprogress.org/issues/courts/news/2005/12/01/1743/honoring-rosa-parks-moving-from-symbolism-to-action/.

4   Ari Berman, *Give Us the Ballot: The Modern Struggle for Voting Rights in America* (New York: Macmillan, 2015), 17.

5   Editorial Board, "Now We Finally Know How Bad Voter Fraud Is in North Carolina," *Charlotte Observer*, April 24, 2017, https://www.charlotteobserver.com/opinion/editorials/article146486019.html.

6   Enrico Cantoni and Vincent Pons, "Strict ID Laws Don't Stop Voters: Evidence from a U.S. Nationwide Panel, 2008–2018," working paper, February 2019, https://doi.org/10.3386/w25522.

7   Dan Hopkins, "What We Know About Voter ID Laws," FiveThirtyEight, August 21, 2018, https://fivethirtyeight.com/features/what-we-know-about-voter-id-laws/.

8   MIT Election Data + Science Lab, "Voter Identification," accessed May 6, 2020, https://electionlab.mit.edu/research/voter-identification.

9   MIT Election Data + Science Lab, "Voter turnout," accessed May 6, 2020, https://electionlab.mit.edu/research/voter-turnout.

10   George Pillsbury and Julian Johannesen, *America Goes to the Polls 2016: A Report on Voter Turnout in the 2016 Election*, Nonprofit VOTE and U.S. Elections Project joint report, March 2017, pg. 11, https://www.nonprofitvote.org/documents/2017/03/america-goes-polls-2016.pdf/.

11   Katy Owens Hubler, "Improving Voter Turnout," National Conference of State Legislatures, October 2014, https://www.ncsl.org/research/elections-and-campaigns/improving-voter-turnout.aspx.

12   Hubler, "Improving Voter Turnout."

13   Sean McElwee, Brian Schaffner, and Jesse Rhodes, "Oregon Automatic Voter Registration," Demos, July 26, 2017, https://www.demos.org/sites/default/files/publications/AVR%20in%20Oregon%20FINAL.pdf.

14   National Conference of State Legislatures, "Automatic Voter Registration," April 14, 2020, https://www.ncsl.org/research/elections-and-campaigns/automatic-voter-registration.aspx.

15   Brennan Center for Justice, "Automatic Voter Registration, a Summary," July 10, 2019, https://www.brennancenter.org/our-work/research-reports/automatic-voter-registration-summary.

16   Henry S. Farber, "Increasing Voter Turnout: Is Democracy Day the Answer?," Princeton University working paper, 2009, https://ideas.repec.org/p/pri/indrel/546.html.

17   Jan Leighley and Jonathan Nagler, *Who Votes Now?: Demographics, Issues, Inequality, and Turnout in the United States* (Princeton, NJ: Princeton University Press, 2013); Jan Leighley and Jonathan Nagler, "Increase Turnout by Informing Voters about Policy Differences," *Stanford Social Innovation Review*, March 14, 2016, https://ssir.org/articles/entry/increase_turnout_by_informing_voters_about_policy_differences.

18   MIT Election Data + Science Lab, "MEDSL Explains: Voter Turnout," May 3, 2018, https://medium.com/mit-election-lab/medsl-explains-voter-turnout-caf753d03b24.

Conclusion

1   Donald Trump, Twitter post, July 14, 2019, 5:27 AM, https://twitter.com/realDonaldTrump/status/1150381395078000643.

2   Thrush, Glenn, "Stacey Abrams Draws Credit and Praise as Biden Inches Ahead in Georgia, *New York Times*, November 6, 2020, https://www.nytimes.com/2020/11/06/us/elections/stacey-abrams-draws-credit-and-praise-as-biden-inches-ahead-in-georgia.html.

3   US Census Bureau, "Haverhill City, Massachusetts," QuickFacts, accessed July 29, 2020, https://www.census.gov/quickfacts/haverhillcitymassachusetts.

4   Eitan Hersh, "College-Educated Voters Are Ruining American Politics," *The Atlantic*, January 20, 2020, https://www.theatlantic.com/ideas/archive/2020/01/political-hobbyists-are-ruining-politics/605212/.

INDEX

ABOUT THE AUTHOR

COURTNEY EMERSON is the cofounder and former chief operating officer of the All In Together Campaign (AIT), a nonpartisan nonprofit that encourages, educates, and empowers voting-age women to participate fully in America's civic and political life. Courtney graduated magna cum laude from Princeton University with a degree in politics. Originally from New Hampshire, she currently lives in the Pacific Northwest with her husband, Charlie, and their dog, Banana.